SINO-SOVIET RELATIONS
AND
ARMS CONTROL

Written Under the Auspices of the

CENTER FOR INTERNATIONAL AFFAIRS

and the

EAST ASIAN RESEARCH CENTER

Harvard University

SINO-SOVIET RELATIONS
AND
ARMS CONTROL

Edited by
MORTON H. HALPERIN

 THE M.I.T. PRESS
Massachusetts Institute of Technology
Cambridge, Massachusetts, and London, England

Contents

SINO-SOVIET RELATIONS
AND
ARMS CONTROL

1

Introduction

MORTON H. HALPERIN

No reader of the polemics in the Sino-Soviet dispute can fail to have noticed the importance of issues of nuclear war and disarmament. Among the most bitter exchanges were the statements issued by the spokesmen of the two governments following the signing of the limited test ban treaty in 1963. The Chinese have launched a broad attack on the Soviet position on disarmament issues, most notably in the Fifth Comment on the Soviet Open Letter published on November 8, 1963.

The Chinese have complained about a number of aspects of Soviet disarmament policy. Currently they accuse the Russians of seeking a nonproliferation agreement to prevent the further development of Chinese nuclear forces and as part of the attempt of the two superpowers to dominate the world. The Chinese also continue to attack the three-environment nuclear test ban treaty. Beginning in 1960, the Chinese have also denounced the Soviet position on general and complete disarmament (GCD), charging that disarmament could come only after the overthrow of Western imperialism and could not be negotiated with the Western powers. Moreover, the Chinese accuse the Soviets of subordinating their support for wars of national liberation to their desire for disarmament agreements with the West. They claim that the Soviets should

1

concentrate on support for revolutionary movements and should abandon the effort to negotiate with the West.

The Soviets have launched a full-scale counterattack on the Chinese position, attempting to meet the Chinese arguments and also making their own charges against Chinese policy. The new Soviet leadership argues that disarmament in fact aids the national liberation struggle, that far from subordinating support for wars of national liberation to efforts to negotiate disarmament, the Soviets are using disarmament as a powerful weapon in support of revolution. Moscow in turn charges that Peking is subordinating efforts to control nuclear weapons to its own desire to develop a national nuclear capability. At least until recently the Soviets asserted that the Chinese had no need for such a capability because they could be sure of Soviet protection, and they also asserted that the Chinese drive for nuclear weapons was jeopardizing the efforts to prevent further proliferation of nuclear weapons and nuclear disarmament. The Soviets charge that the Chinese do not understand the dangers of nuclear war and do not realize that nuclear weapons ignore class differences and hence create a need for disarmament even when imperialism still exists.

The references to disarmament in the polemics indicate that both the Soviet Union and Communist China believe that their objectives in engaging in public dispute with each other can be enhanced by alluding to disarmament issues. However, to understand the role of disarmament issues in the Sino-Soviet dispute, we need to go beyond an enumeration of the issues raised to a consideration of the purpose of the polemics and the interaction between the Sino-Soviet dispute and the arms control policies of the Soviet Union, China, and the United States.

Without attempting to assess the general role of polemics in the Sino-Soviet dispute, it is possible to identify three purposes of the discussion of disarmament issues.

The references to disarmament have from time to time served as a concrete way of talking about general issues of major importance in the Sino-Soviet dispute. At the core of much Sino-Soviet disagreement has been the question of how to treat the United States. The Soviets argue that because of the changing balance of forces in the world, sober leaders in the West recognize the need to come to terms with the Communist bloc. This creates the possibility for limited agreements that advance the cause of revolution. The Chinese, on the other hand, argue that agreements with the United States remain impossible and that the way to counter American actions is with militant policies rather than with efforts to negotiate. This disagreement has had a number of aspects, but one has been the dispute about GCD. In arguing that GCD is both possible and desirable, the Soviets are stating in effect that agreements with the West before the overthrow of imperialism are possible and desirable and that there are men in the West with whom such agreements can be negotiated. In denouncing GCD the Chinese are taking exception to the Soviet position. The Chinese assert that there is an inevitable contradiction between efforts to come to agreements with the West and support for wars of national liberation. Peking charges that the Soviets are subordinating support for wars of national liberation to their attempt to improve relations with the United States. Here again disarmament has been a concrete focus of the disagreement.

In addition to using disarmament issues as a specific way of talking about more general and perhaps more sensitive issues, the Soviet Union and China have used them as a way of exposing the undesirable policies of the other country in their competition for support in the third world and within the Communist bloc.

In the early 1960's, Khrushchev launched an extensive campaign designed to demonstrate that the Chinese were against peace and were willing to risk a nuclear war in pursuit of their national policies. Whatever his original intentions in proposing the negotiation of a GCD treaty and in advocating a test ban, Khrushchev ended up using both of these issues very largely as sticks with which to beat the Chinese. The Chinese refused to sign the test ban treaty and opposed efforts to negotiate GCD, making it possible for Khrushchev to argue that this demonstrated their warlike nature and their reluctance to recognize the facts of the nuclear age, and also to use this in appealing to other groups in the third world and even within the Communist bloc.

The Chinese have been somewhat on the defensive on these issues and have attempted to counter. First, they have denied the Soviet charge that they desire a nuclear war and do not understand the destructive effects of nuclear weapons. Second, they have put forward their own disarmament proposals, particularly the proposal for a ban on the first use of nuclear weapons. Finally, they have counterattacked against what they see to be the vulnerabilities in the Soviet position. The Chinese charge that Soviet negotiations with the United States are simply a manifestation of the effort of the two superpowers to come to terms with each other and hence to dominate the world.

Whatever other purposes are served by the Sino-Soviet polemics, both countries have used them to express genuine disagreements about the issues that caused the Sino-Soviet rift. There is little doubt that the Sino-Soviet polemics on disarmament have reflected real disagreements between Russia and China about appropriate policy on such issues as a nuclear test ban treaty and other limited arms control measures. These differences appear to have had an important impact on the arms control policy of the Soviet Union, in particular, but also of China and, in less direct ways, of the United States. In turn, these disagreements have affected and in some cases exacerbated and accelerated the Sino-Soviet rift.

Until very recently the subjects of arms control and the Sino-Soviet dispute tended to be examined separately by observers with very different interests and perspectives. However, the introduction of arms control issues into the Sino-Soviet dispute has made it important for students of the dispute, as well as arms control specialists, to come to grips with the subject matter of the other field.

In an effort to promote such cross-fertilization and to elucidate the impact of the Sino-Soviet dispute on prospects for arms control and disarmament, as well as to examine more generally the attitudes toward arms control issues of the Soviet Union and China, the United States Arms Control and Disarmament Agency has supported a series of summer conferences and research studies.[1] The first of these conferences was held in 1963 and led to the publication of a report written by Alexander Dallin and others on Soviet attitudes.[2] The second study, held in 1964, focused on Chinese attitudes, and also resulted in a report, *Communist China and Arms Control*.[3] A third conference sponsored by the United States Arms Control and Disarmament Agency was held at Airlie House in Virginia in the summer of 1965 to consider specific questions concerning the interrelations between the Sino-Soviet dispute and prospects for arms control and disarmament. The conference on "Sino-Soviet Relations and Arms Control," sponsored, as was the China conference, by the Center for International Affairs and the East Asian Research Center, Harvard University, and chaired by J. M. H. Lindbeck, served as the principal stimulus for a number of papers in this volume.[4]

The first three chapters deal with aspects of the impact of the Sino-Soviet dispute on the arms control policies of the Soviet Union, China, and the United States. Young's paper examines one current arms control issue, that of the possi-

1 *Fifth Annual Report of the United States Arms Control and Disarmament Agency* (89th Cong., 2d Sess., 1965), House Doc. 382, pp. 19–20.

2 Alexander Dallin and others, *The Soviet Union, Arms Control and Disarmament* (New York: School of International Affairs, Columbia University, 1964), available commercially as *The Soviet Union and Disarmament* (New York: Praeger, 1964).

3 Morton H. Halperin and Dwight H. Perkins, *Communist China and Arms Control* (Cambridge: Harvard University, 1965, and New York: Praeger, 1965).

4 The judgments expressed in the papers are those of the authors, however, and do not necessarily reflect the views of the Arms Control and Disarmament Agency or any other governmental department or agency or Harvard University. The authors of the papers owe a debt to the participants in the conference, who are listed in Appendix B. The editor is also indebted to Mrs. Ann Mostoller for performing many of the tasks for which he was responsible. The paper by Clemens was published in a slightly different form in *Orbis*. The papers by Young and Sonnenfeldt were published in *The China Quarterly*. We are grateful to the respective publishers for permission to reproduce this material.

The conference on "Sino-Soviet Relations and Arms Control" was also the stimulus for several other publications, including William E. Griffith, *Sino-Soviet Relations, 1964–1965* (Cambridge: The M.I.T. Press, 1967). A two-volume report based on the conference has been published by the Center for International Affairs and the East Asian Research Center, Harvard University (Cambridge, 1966).

bility and desirability of preventing the spread of nuclear weapons from the point of view of the Chinese. He attempts to lay out the costs and gains to the Chinese of the further spread of nuclear weapons and suggests that their policy may now be in flux. The paper takes a middle position between the view, expressed by Alice Hsieh, that the Chinese are already substantially concerned about the dangers of proliferation, in particular to Japan, and the position I have taken that the Chinese are not concerned about the further spread of nuclear weapons.[5]

Sonnenfeldt's paper examines the extent to which Soviet policy has been influenced by the Chinese factor, that is, by the likely reaction of China to Soviet arms control moves and by the use to which the Soviets could put their arms control policy in their competition with the Chinese. Stone's paper might have been called "The Chinese Factor in American Arms Control Policy" since it deals with the extent to which American policy on arms control issues should be modified or circumscribed to take account of the growing independence and power of China. Stone demonstrates, contrary to what many have asserted, that Chinese participation is not necessary for many potential arms control agreements. Perhaps reflecting the different approach and interest of arms controllers, as opposed to specialists on the Sino-Soviet dispute, Stone's paper concentrates on the future and contains a number of proposals for American policy, while Sonnenfeldt's concentrates mainly on raising questions about past Soviet behavior. Both papers indicate that the Soviet Union and the United States will not ignore China in making calculations about disarmament, although the authors suggest that the two superpowers may find broad areas in which they can come to agreement even over the opposition of the Chinese.

The following two papers by Halperin and Clemens examine the general impact of Chinese pressure on Soviet dis-

5 Alice L. Hsieh, "Foreword to the Japanese Edition of *Communist China's Strategy in the Nuclear Age:* Implications of the Chinese Nuclear Detonations" (RAND P-3152, June 1965); Morton H. Halperin, *China and Nuclear Proliferation,* Occasional Paper of the Academy for Policy Study, University of Chicago (Chicago, 1966).

armament policy with particular reference to the nuclear test ban treaty. They also consider the impact of the Soviet efforts to negotiate a test ban treaty on Sino-Soviet nuclear relations and, particularly in Clemens' paper, on the growing Sino-Soviet rift.

Sonnenfeldt's paper warns against overrating the extent to which the Chinese have influenced Soviet disarmament policy, and to some extent reflects the view that Halperin and Clemens exaggerate the impact of arms control issues on the Sino-Soviet dispute. At the same time, however, Sonnenfeldt calls for more research into these issues, and the two following papers may be seen as a response to that proposal.

Halperin's paper argues, somewhat controversially, that the Soviet efforts to negotiate a test ban were closely related with the timing and extent of Soviet nuclear assistance to China. It suggests that an important motivation for the Soviet willingness to give substantial nuclear aid, beginning in late 1957, was their desire to have Chinese support for a test ban treaty, and that the Chinese were prepared to sign such a treaty up until mid-1959 because of the aid they were getting from the Soviet Union. Other analysts tend to doubt that the Soviet interest in a test ban was an important motivation in Soviet aid to China, and some argue that Soviet aid has been much less extensive than the analysis implies.

Clemens begins essentially where the Halperin paper leaves off, focusing on the interaction of the test ban with the Sino-Soviet dispute in the period since 1959. Clemens is dealing with significantly less esoteric matters and reconstructs the relationship in a way that is unlikely to be challenged. He demonstrates that the Soviets' reluctance to aid the Chinese nuclear program, beginning in 1960, and their efforts to negotiate a test ban treaty and a nonproliferation agreement with the United States contributed to the worsening of Sino-Soviet relations. He points to the signing of the test ban in 1963 as one of the decisive factors leading to the beginning of sharp open polemics between Peking and Moscow and to a widening of the split within the international Communist movement. Clemens' analysis suggests that in the period prior to their own nuclear detonation the Chinese were vigorously opposed to a nonproliferation agreement, although, as Young points out, their view might be undergoing a change at the present time.

We do not yet have any definitive reconstruction of the events in Sino-Soviet relations in the 1950's and early 1960's that has been able to make use of the revelations from the Sino-Soviet polemics. Donald Zagoria's *The Sino-Soviet Conflict, 1956–1961*[6] remains the standard work on that period but fails to cover critical events of the years following 1961, and was written before many of the revelations in the polemics were available. In one sense the papers in Parts II and III may be seen as contributions to a new over-all history of Sino-Soviet relations. All of them suffer from the fact that they cannot simply be adding or subtracting from existing definitive history but have had, in effect, to construct their own framework of Sino-Soviet relations within which to discuss particular events. Thus, for example, the difference between Halperin and Clemens on the Chinese attitude toward the test ban in 1957 and the extent of Soviet nuclear aid to China is attributable, at least in part, to a broader disagreement about the nature of Sino-Soviet relations in 1957 and 1958. Similarly, the disagreement about the extent of Sino-Soviet cooperation during the 1958 Quemoy crisis, reflected in Sonnenfeldt's, Mackintosh's, and Hinton's dissent from the contention by Halperin and Tsou that there was no major disagreement between the two countries, rests in part on differing evaluations of the contemporary nature of Sino-Soviet relations.

The papers in Part III all deal, from different perspectives, with the question of Sino-Soviet relations during a possible Chinese-American crisis. The first three trace this problem historically through the period of the Sino-Soviet dispute and then seek to provide a current assessment. The fourth paper considers in detail their still obscure relations during the 1958 Quemoy crisis. All of the papers emphasize the great difficulty in obtaining reliable information about the governments' calculations on this question and also stress the un-

[6] Princeton: Princeton University Press, 1962 (paperback edition: Atheneum, 1964).

certainty with which governments themselves have had to gauge the degree of possible Soviet involvement in a Chinese-American confrontation. Hinton's paper, written from the perspective of Peking, and Mackintosh's paper, viewing the situation from the vantage point of Moscow, conclude that potential Soviet support for China was much less than the American government, judging by Quester's paper, presumed it to be. At least, until very recently, the United States was assuming that Soviet support would be available for China in the event of virtually any Chinese-American military clash. Hinton and Mackintosh both emphasize that such support was problematical at best. At the present time both the Russians and the Chinese seem to be assuming that Russian intervention would come only when perceived as necessary for the narrow Russian national interest and would almost certainly be confined to defense of North China and Manchuria, and possibly to an effort to maintain some kind of friendly regime at least in part of China. Hinton suggests that the extent of Soviet intervention would depend in part on whether the American action was provoked by China. Mackintosh, on the other hand, seems to imply that Soviet aid would be calculated in terms of a narrow national interest regardless of the presence or not of Chinese provocation.

The papers reveal that efforts to communicate about this issue have been beset with difficulties and uncertainties. For example, Hinton notes that Dulles' massive retaliation speech was taken by the Chinese to indicate an American attempt to make a separate threat against China on the assumption that Russia would not be involved. Quester shows that, on the contrary, the massive retaliation speech was made in the context of an assumption that Russia and China would necessarily stand together in the event of an American attack.

Although the American government has become increasingly skeptical about the possibility of Russian involvement in a Chinese-American clash, it still seems to be assuming a greater probability of involvement, and a greater involvement, than either Hinton or Mackintosh would suggest is likely.

Currently in Vietnam, and very likely in a number of other instances in the future, the U.S., Chinese, and Soviet govern-

ments will have to calculate the prospects and possibilities
for Soviet intervention in the event of a Chinese-American
clash. These papers not only elucidate the way in which these
calculations have influenced past history but also provide a
better basis for prediction. Moreover, the prospects and possibilities for arms control arrangements between the United
States and the Soviet Union depend in part on the belief
that China is a separate enemy that can and must be dealt
with apart from the kinds of military arrangements evolving
between the United States and the Soviet Union.

This symposium, then, is designed as a contribution to an
understanding of the nature of the three-way security-arms
control relationship between the United States, the Soviet
Union, and Communist China. The papers all seek to illum-
inate the security problems facing the United States in the
context of the Sino-Soviet dispute and the prospects for arms
control and disarmament as they are affected by the conflict
in the Communist world.

PART I

ARMS CONTROL

2

Chinese Views on the Spread of Nuclear Weapons

ORAN R. YOUNG

Introduction

This paper focuses on the development of attitudes and policies in China concerning the spread of nuclear weapons. The Soviet position on the proliferation question is set forth in a preliminary section to provide a standard for comparison and contrast, but the bulk of the paper concerns the development of Chinese policy. It is of particular interest to note that policy in this area has changed significantly over time as various important events have occurred and there are noticeable variations within the more general Chinese position on proliferation concerning, for example, the diffusion of nuclear weapons to socialist states as opposed to non-socialist ones.

There is one substantial asymmetry between China and the Soviet Union regarding the spread of nuclear weapons that deserves mention at the outset. From the point of view of the Soviet Union, China is basically an Nth country and a potentially very powerful one at that. As a consequence, the general Soviet position on the spread of nuclear weapons has been strongly influenced by the development of the Chinese nuclear program and by the increasing cleavages in Sino-Soviet relations in recent years. For the Chinese, however, the question of nuclear diffusion refers only to the possible spread of nuclear weapons beyond the group of five powers that presently possess at least some nuclear capability. And although there are several additional powers in the international arena with nuclear potentials that might eventually pose problems for China, none constitutes the immediate challenge of China herself as far as the Soviets are concerned.

The Soviet Stand on Proliferation

The Soviet view of nuclear proliferation has shown a decided tendency over time to move toward a stronger condemnation of the further spread of nuclear weapons. This development coincides, above all, with a rather rapidly increasing Soviet awareness of the dangers and destructiveness of nuclear warfare that has been evident since at least the late fifties.[1] This is not to say that the need to take active steps to halt nuclear proliferation has even now assumed a top position on the Soviet scale of priorities; there is evidence to suggest that a number of other items stand above it. But the issue has become a very real one for the Soviets.

The developing stand on proliferation has progressed through several distinguishable phases, of which three seem to stand out clearly. Phase one covers the period from the mid-1950's, when the so-called Nth country problem first became a real issue, to June 1959, when tension arose over the Sino-Soviet agreement of 1957 concerning the transfer of nuclear technology and sample materials from the Soviet Union to China. The dominant feature of this phase is a growing ambivalence on the part of the Soviet Union toward the whole question of proliferation coupled with a tendency to conceptualize the question of proliferation primarily in terms of the Sino-Soviet relationship. Perhaps the single dominant development of the period encompasses the signing of an agreement with the Chinese, in October 1957, on nuclear tech-

---

1 See, in general, Raymond Garthoff, *Soviet Strategy in the Nuclear Age* (New York: Praeger, 2nd ed. 1962); and Thomas Wolfe, *Soviet Strategy at the Crossroads* (Cambridge: Harvard University Press, 1964).

nology and the final, unilateral downgrading of this agreement.[2] The upshot of the agreement was a *de facto* decision to help China, at least, to acquire nuclear weapons no matter what the Soviets may have felt about proliferation in the abstract and no matter what they may have stated in a declaratory fashion.

However, the Soviets were far from all-out or even open support of nuclear proliferation during this period. To begin with, they never argued, in any verbal or doctrinal way, that the spread of nuclear weapons to China or to any other country was desirable. And the actual nuclear aid given to the Chinese, although far from insignificant, was very much circumscribed and limited. There was apparently never any willingness to transfer finished weapons to China, and, in fact, the aid that was given was substantially limited to technical assistance and technological information.[3] Moreover, so far as is known, China is the only country that has ever received nuclear assistance of direct weapons application from the Soviet Union.

Soviet declaratory and negotiating positions in the 1958–1959 period also began to show signs of a developing interest in efforts to prevent the further diffusion of nuclear weapons. At least from mid-1958, the Soviets began to argue the case against a Chinese nuclear program. At various times since early 1958, and perhaps even since 1957, the Soviet Union has advanced or supported proposals for nuclear-free zones that imply a real interest in circumscribing the spread of nuclear weapons. And at times such proposals have even been pushed over the evident displeasure of the Chinese. This

2 Neither the existence nor the abrogation of this treaty was known with certainty in the West for a long time. The details were first made clear by the Chinese in their statement of August 15, 1963. See William E. Griffith, *The Sino-Soviet Rift* (Cambridge: The M.I.T. Press, 1964), p. 351. There had of course been speculation before 1963 that the Soviets had aided the Chinese nuclear program. On this point consult Alice Hsieh, *Communist China's Strategy in the Nuclear Era* (Englewood Cliffs, N.J.: Prentice-Hall, 1962).

3 There is some controversy over the importance of this aid to the Chinese program resulting in the October 16, 1964, detonation. Consult Alice Hsieh, *The Sino-Soviet Nuclear Dialogue: 1963* (RAND P-2852, January 1964), pp. 31–38; and Morton H. Halperin, *China and the Bomb* (New York: Praeger, 1965), especially pp. 78–82.

period also saw a decided upswing in the possibilities of a test ban treaty, a measure that the Soviets almost certainly associated with the whole question of nuclear proliferation.

Phase two in the development of the Soviet stand on nuclear proliferation covers the period from June 1959 to the Soviet decision to accept the partial test ban treaty during June and July 1963. During this period, the Soviets clearly became more worried about the negative consequences of proliferation: the destabilizing military effects and the changes in relative political power and influence. In this connection, they showed a definite interest in the movement against proliferation in the General Assembly of the United Nations,[4] and their proposal of March 15, 1962, to the first session of the Eighteen Nation Disarmament Conference contained a provision aimed at regulating the spread of nuclear weapons.[5]

Moreover, the Soviets began actively to oppose the Chinese program for the acquisition of nuclear weapons and their attitude on the spread of nuclear weapons to still further countries. But throughout this period there was an interesting hesitancy in the Soviet opposition to proliferation as well as a number of indications that the Soviets were even a little embarrassed at the prospects of pushing a policy of nonproliferation too strongly. In particular, they showed very great sensitivity to charges that they were selling out the Communist movement and selfishly attempting to arrange with the United States an agreement to rule the world. As a result, the Soviets' clear interest in slowing the spread of nuclear weapons remained very circumscribed in the realm of action policy at least until the decision on the test ban treaty.

The third phase in the development of the Soviet position on proliferation was born out of the severe splits within the Soviet bloc over the test ban treaty of 1963, and continues into the present period. This has been a period of strong

4 Cf. especially the affirmative Soviet vote on the "Swedish resolution" at the sixteenth session in 1961: *Yearbook of the United Nations, 1961* (New York: Columbia University Press, 1962), pp. 17–18.

5 The relevant section is article 16 of the March 15, 1962, draft treaty. See *Documents on Disarmament 1962* (Washington, D. C.: U.S. Government Printing Office, 1963), p. 113.

and sustained Soviet advocacy of nonproliferation, although it would probably still be inaccurate to ascribe an extremely high position to this policy plank in the Soviet system of priorities. In general, this sustained position on the proliferation issue has developed against a backdrop of sharpening emphasis on the desirability of avoiding nuclear warfare, increasing belief in the limited utility of strategic nuclear weapons, growing indications of the existence of effective military parity between the Soviet Union and the United States,[6] and unfolding *détente* between the superpowers on at least a limited range of issues.

During this phase the Soviets have become more concrete about the proliferation problem. They now tend to view nuclear proliferation principally in terms of the dangers attendant on the spread of weapons to China, West Germany, and, occasionally, Japan.[7] In this context, and especially with reference to China, the Soviet decision to go ahead with the test ban treaty in the summer of 1963 represents a decisive turning point. Although the test ban is very far from being a generally effective nonproliferation agreement, it represents the first formal step on the part of the members of the "nuclear club" to prohibit the spread of nuclear weapons. And it is now clear that the Soviets, just as the Americans, found in the nonproliferation implications of the treaty a principal motive for agreeing to it and implementing it.

In the Soviet case, moreover, the decision to negotiate the test ban agreement was a major turning point in the Sino-Soviet dialogue. Casting aside the hesitancy already mentioned, the Soviet Union, at this time, took a clear-cut stand against the Chinese from which it would prove difficult to turn back. And in so doing, it is clear that the Soviets were well aware of the general reaction they would get from the Chinese[8] and of the enormous impact their action would

[6] On this and the preceding points consult Wolfe, *op. cit.*

[7] Hsieh, *The Sino-Soviet Nuclear Dialogue: 1963, op. cit.*, p. 21; and Alexander Dallin and others, *The Soviet Union, Arms Control, and Disarmament* (New York: Columbia University Press, 1964).

[8] The 1963 polemics show that the Chinese indicated clearly before the summer of 1963 what their general reaction would be.

have on Sino-Soviet relations.[9] This more or less conscious step, therefore, seems to signify, among other things, a Soviet decision to break irrevocably with the Chinese on the issue of nuclear proliferation. As a result, one would expect the Soviets to be more interested in further steps to limit the spread of nuclear weapons in the aftermath of the test ban agreement. Having burned their bridges on this issue, the Soviets have more reason than ever to push for nonproliferation. If they do not do so, they stand in danger of getting the worst of both worlds since they have already lost the fight to keep the Chinese from acquiring a nuclear capability; moreover a failure to push for new measures to restrict proliferation will mean that additional Nth countries are by no means precluded from acquiring nuclear weapons.

As far as the Federal Republic of Germany is concerned, the Soviet worries about nuclear diffusion have come to the surface primarily in the context of the American multilateral force (MLF) proposal, which the Soviets have opposed violently since its inception.[10] The Soviets, who sometimes appear to be irrationally afraid of a potentially resurgent German military threat, denounce the MLF primarily on the grounds that it represents a first step toward the nuclear arming of Germany. Despite Chinese allegations to the contrary in the 1963 polemics,[11] there is every reason to suppose that the Soviets are very strongly against the MLF and that they see this as one of the principal channels along which the dangers of nuclear proliferation may progress.[12]

In recent months there have been several interesting indications of the problems that the Soviets have in making policy on the question of nuclear diffusion. In the aftermath of each of the Chinese nuclear detonations, the Soviets have immediately reaffirmed their commitment to and support of the

[9] Morton H. Halperin and Dwight Perkins, *Communist China and Arms Control* (New York: Praeger, 1965), pp. 168–169.

[10] For a recent discussion of the Soviet reaction to the MLF proposal see Zbigniew Brzezinski, "Moscow and the MLF: Hostility and Ambivalence," *Foreign Affairs*, Vol. 43, No. 1 (October 1964), pp. 126–134.

[11] See, for example, the Chinese government statement of August 15, 1963 (Griffith, *op. cit.*, pp. 347–348).

[12] Dallin and others, *op. cit.*, p. 141.

policy of nonproliferation, and this has been done on at least one occasion through the pages of *Pravda*.[13] On the other hand, the Soviets have not seen fit to launch any violent attacks on the Chinese for their detonations, and the reaction following the second detonation on May 14, 1965, was especially quiet. Toward the end of 1964 several Australian analysts began to talk about the possibility of a Soviet-Indonesian nuclear arrangement, at least for the emplacement of a Soviet nuclear base in Indonesia.[14] The suggested Soviet motive was an effort to oppose the Chinese for support of the nonaligned countries of Southeast Asia. The Australians themselves, however, were unable to cite any evidence to support this suggestion, and it is impossible to find any indications of such a move emanating from the Soviet Union. Even more recently the Soviets apparently showed a tendency to play at politics with the proliferation issue at the 1965 session of the U.N. Disarmament Commission.[15] Evidently this action did not stem from a lack of worry over the disadvantages of proliferation, about which the Soviets still give every indication of being seriously concerned. On the contrary, the hesitancy at the 1965 meetings has been ascribed to Soviet sensitivity to severe Chinese criticisms of their "selling out" to the capitalists and to a felt need on the part of the Soviets to demonstrate that they are still pushing the cause of world communism. If this is in fact the case, it would appear as another manifestation of the priorities problem. Sustained support for a policy of nonproliferation is no guarantee that problems with even higher priority will not intervene between a general desire for nonproliferation and concrete steps to implement it.[16]

[13] On the October 16, 1964 detonation see *Asian Recorder*, Vol. X, No. 50 (December 9–15, 1964), p. 6186 (citing *Pravda*). On the May 14, 1965 case see *The New York Times*, May 15, 1965, p. 2.

[14] *Proceedings of the Seminar on Nuclear Dispersal in Asia and the Indo-Pacific Region, September 5–6, 1964* (Canberra, Australia: The Australian National University, Defense Studies Project), pp. 3–5.

[15] This and the following points concerning the meetings of the U.N. Disarmament Commission are based on a verbal communication from Sir Harold Beeley, principal British disarmament negotiator, at the Center for International Affairs, Harvard University, May 17, 1965.

[16] The Soviets' initiative in July 1965 in reopening the Eighteen Nation

The Chinese Record on Proliferation

The Chinese have made declaratory statements about proliferation on a number of occasions in recent years. The extent to which such stated positions represent straightforward revelations of a sincere viewpoint, however, is an important question, even if one that presents difficulties for analysis. In this instance, the fact that there are substantial divergences between the manifest Chinese attitudes in the period following their nuclear detonation on October 16, 1964, and those elaborated in the predetonation period must be taken as an important factor in interpreting the underlying motives.

The Predetonation Period

The Chinese did not have anything much to say on the issue of proliferation before the beginning of the sixties. In earlier years they had acquiesced in a position that subordinated them, in nuclear matters at least, to the protective covering of the Soviet Union and had refrained from saying anything concerning the possession of nuclear weapons by states other than the bloc leader.[17] When they did break their silence,

Disarmament Conference in Geneva and their subsequent tabling of a draft treaty on nonproliferation may well have signified, among other things, that they were less sensitive in the summer to the various Chinese criticisms than they were in the spring. The fact that the U.N. Disarmament Commission was apparently chosen as an arena for disarmament discussions in early 1965 primarily for its value as a political forum emphasizes this view.

The Soviet position on proliferation is probably also somewhat affected by the conflict between the "modernists" and the "traditionalists" within the Soviet decision-making system. The policy of nonproliferation is almost certainly emphasized far more by the modernists than by the traditionalists who may well have reservations. Although Khrushchev was a leader of the modernists on such issues, the general Soviet orientation does not appear to have shifted markedly since the change in leadership of October 1964. On the general differences between modernists and traditionalists see Dallin and others, *op. cit.*, pp. 50–51.

17 One important exception to this generalization, which adumbrates the later position of the Chinese, appeared as early as 1951. At that time they argued that "only the fact that other countries, in the first place the Soviet Union, possess the atomic weapon can bring America to believe that there is not the slightest advantage in atomic militarism." *Jen-min Jih-pao*, October 7, 1951, *Survey of the China Mainland Press (SCMP)*, No. 190 (October 7–9, 1951), pp. 1–2.

however, the Chinese began to develop a strongly stated and doctrinally buttressed position in favor of the spread of nuclear capabilities to socialist states other than the Soviet Union and possibly to nonsocialist states as well. From this time until the 1964 detonation, Chinese thinking on the question of proliferation showed sustained support for the spread of nuclear weapons coupled with an increasing sophistication in the presentation of arguments in favor of this stand.

In reconstructing the Chinese view on this question, it is of considerable importance to distinguish between their attitude toward the socialist countries and toward nonsocialist countries. In the case of the socialist states, the Chinese showed no hesitation in arguing quite clearly and insistently that nuclear proliferation would have clear-cut, positive consequences. Here they argued the importance of making a class analysis. As the Chinese themselves put it on August 15, 1963:

> With regard to preventing nuclear proliferation, the Chinese Government has always maintained that the arguments of the U.S. imperialists must not be echoed, but that a class analysis must be made. Whether or not nuclear weapons help peace depends on who possesses them. It is detrimental to peace if they are in the hands of imperialist countries; it helps peace if they are in the hands of socialist countries. It must not be said indiscriminately that the danger of nuclear war increases along with the increase in the number of nuclear powers.[18]

Taking this stand as their starting point, the Chinese proceeded to elaborate several more specific reasons why it would be desirable for additional socialist countries to possess nuclear weapons.

Perhaps the most salient factor from the Chinese point of view was the argument that national nuclear capabilities are necessary for the defense of socialist countries. There are two distinguishable prongs to this line of reasoning. One prong encompasses a kind of generalized view that socialist countries are primarily responsible for their own defense coupled with a belief that the very possession of nuclear weapons will somehow increase over-all defensive strength. "In fighting im-

---

[18] Chinese government statement, August 15, 1963 (Griffith, *op. cit.*, p. 347).

perialist aggression and defending its security every socialist country has to rely in the first place on its own defense capability, and then — and only then — on assistance from fraternal countries and the people of the world."[19] The Moscow statement of 1960 was evoked in support of this doctrine,[20] and the proposition that socialist countries possess nuclear weapons solely for purposes of defense came to the fore repeatedly.[21]

The other prong to this argument deals more specifically with the notion of deterrence. On one side, the Chinese argued that nuclear weapons in the hands of a number of socialist countries will increase the credibility of the over-all socialist deterrent, both by increasing the probability, in the eyes of the United States, of retaliation in response to any aggressive or provocative initiative and by reducing the opportunities for peripheral initiatives by the United States that could be kept below the threshold level required to catalyze direct Soviet retaliation.[22] On the other side, the Chinese pointed out that the development of rough strategic parity between the two superpowers increases the danger to them of defending their allies, and they suggested that it was not difficult to imagine situations in which Soviet military strength would not be used to protect one or more members of the socialist camp. These arguments were clearly intended as a defense of the Chinese nuclear program, but the Chinese extended them explicitly to all socialist countries. One of the most striking things about these attitudes is their marked similarity to some of the central propositions voiced in the NATO alliance in recent years by Britain and France.[23]

A somewhat related Chinese argument of the predetonation period dealt with the danger of blackmail by the United States

19 *Ibid.* (Griffith, *op. cit.,* pp. 346–347).

20 *Ibid.* (Griffith, *op. cit.,* p. 347).

21 For a typical example see the fifth Chinese comment on the Soviet open letter of July 14, 1963, November 18, 1963 (Griffith, *op. cit.,* p. 486).

22 See, for example, speech by Liao Cheng-chih, August 1, 1963, "People of the World Unite, for the Complete, Thorough, Total and Resolute Prohibition and Destruction of Nuclear Weapons" (Peking: Foreign Languages Press, 1963), pp. 69–70.

23 Halperin, *op. cit.,* pp. 45–46.

against the socialist countries. The problem here was not to deter an outright attack but rather to reduce the ability of the enemy to get its way by making various kinds of nuclear threats and military demonstrations. In this connection, the Chinese were evidently willing to argue that even a relatively small nuclear capability in the hands of the various socialist countries would go a long way toward vitiating such blackmail tactics emanating from the United States. As the Chinese themselves stated the case:

> It is very clear that nuclear weapons in the hands of socialist countries are important guarantees to defeat the imperialist policy of nuclear blackmail. . . . This is entirely different in nature from the possession of nuclear weapons by the imperialists. . . .[24]

They of course indicated an awareness of the desirability of acquiring nuclear superiority in order to achieve this goal.[25] But their sense of realism concerning the impossibility of achieving nuclear superiority did not alter their view that even a small nuclear capability in the possession of individual socialist countries would be a good counter to imperialist blackmail.

The Chinese also made several more general statements in favor of the spread of nuclear weapons to socialist countries during the predetonation period. From time to time they maintained that the diffusion of nuclear weapons in this fashion would increase the over-all strength of the socialist camp in some definite but undefined manner.

> So long as the imperialists refuse to ban nuclear weapons, the greater the number of socialist countries possessing them, the better the guarantee of world peace. A fierce class struggle is now going on in the world. In this struggle, the greater the strength of our side, the better. Does it make sense to say the less the better?[26]

The logical implication of this argument is that nuclear

---

[24] Jen Ku-ping, "The Tito Group — An Army Corps of U.S. Imperialism in its Grand Strategy of Counter-Revolution," New China News Agency (NCNA), Peking, September 21, 1962, *SCMP*, No. 2826, September 26, 1962, pp. 34–35.

[25] *Ibid.*, pp. 34–35.

[26] Chinese government statement, August 15, 1963 (Griffith, *op. cit.*, p. 347).

weapons should be distributed to as many members of the socialist camp as possible. Finally, there was the argument that the spread of nuclear weapons to a large number of socialist countries would increase the prospects for world-wide nuclear disarmament.[27] This view crops up also in the context of Chinese attitudes toward proliferation to nonsocialist countries, and will be discussed in a little more detail at that point.

While the Chinese attitude on the question of nuclear proliferation to socialist countries is clear, there are some ambiguities in their position on the spread of nuclear weapons to nonsocialist countries. A further distinction is necessary at this point between those nonsocialist states that are nonaligned and neutralist and those that fall into the category of capitalist and imperialist states. The Chinese, during this period, tended to label the nonaligned states as "other peace-loving countries" and to approve of the spread of nuclear weapons to them, although not as adamantly as in the case of socialist countries. In particular, they extended the two prongs of the argument on defense and deterrence to the "other peace-loving countries" with a fair degree of frequency.[28] Other arguments were less applicable to these states and therefore simply not mentioned. In addition, the Chinese did not argue the case for proliferation to these states separately from the discussion of the spread of nuclear weapons to socialist countries. When they did make a distinction, they tended simply to augment their basic arguments by speaking of "socialist and other peace-loving states" in the same breath.

The Chinese have never advanced any doctrine explicitly favoring the proliferation of nuclear weapons to additional capitalist or imperialist states. During 1963 they showed sympathy with the French stand in favor of a national nuclear deterrent.[29] But this sympathy was extended to France as an individual state rather than as a capitalist country, and this

---

[27] *Jen-min Jih-pao*, editorial, August 9, 1962, *SCMP*, No. 2799, August 15, 1962, p. 22.

[28] See, for example, Liao Cheng-chih, *op. cit.*, pp. 69–70, and *Jen-min Jih-pao*, editorial, December 22, 1961, *SCMP*, No. 2648, December 1961, p. 38.

[29] Halperin, *op. cit.*, pp. 50–51.

whole episode is so deeply involved in the polemical Sino-Soviet dialogue of the period that it cannot be taken as a true indication of Chinese attitudes on the more general proliferation problem. At the time, the French position on nuclear weapons in the NATO alliance bore a striking resemblance to the Chinese position vis-à-vis the Soviet Union, and the evidence suggests that Chinese sympathy, expressed in the spring of 1963, was a veiled argument in favor of a Chinese nuclear capability rather than a plug for proliferation in general. Moreover, on several occasions during this period the Chinese came out specifically against the spread of nuclear weapons to additional imperialist states. In the 1963 polemics they went so far as to accuse the Soviets of selling out to the West on the issue of nuclear arms for West Germany while they themselves continued to carry on the fight against such a development.[30] The Chinese doctrine to the effect that the possession of nuclear weapons by imperialist states is detrimental to peace has already been quoted.

What the Chinese did do during this period, however, was to elaborate several arguments in favor of nuclear proliferation without making any distinction as to the recipients of the weapons involved.[31] It may therefore be argued that by implication they suggested a willingness to condone the spread of nuclear weapons to all countries. In particular, the Chinese argued on several occasions that the spread of nuclear weapons to as many countries as possible would definitely increase the prospects for the prohibition and destruction of nuclear weapons on a world-wide basis.[32] Evidently there were two points to this argument. On the one hand, there was the belief that a really extensive spread of nuclear weapons would drastically increase the inclination of leading states to

[30] For an example consult Chinese government statement of August 15, 1963 (Griffith, *op. cit.*, pp. 347–348).

[31] It should also be pointed out that these arguments were made somewhat less frequently and less insistently than the arguments favoring proliferation to additional socialist countries.

[32] Wilton Cole's interview with Marshal Chen Yi, October 5, 1961, and an article by General Liu Ya-lou in 1958 cited by Alice Hsieh, "Communist China and Nuclear Force," in R. N. Rosecrance, ed., *The Dispersion of Nuclear Weapons* (New York: Columbia University Press, 1964), p. 159n.

take the resultant dangers seriously and therefore catalyze actions to do something about them. On the other hand, the Chinese have always maintained that one of the keys to nuclear disarmament is to break the monopoly of the so-called "nuclear club" and in so doing to vitiate the tendency of a small number of powers to retain nuclear weapons while denying them to others.

A second Chinese argument for general proliferation is implied in the Chinese attitude toward the statistics of nuclear spread:

> Did the danger of nuclear war become greater or less when the number of nuclear powers increased from one to two? We say it became less, not greater.[33]

And although this is an obvious reference to the acquisition of nuclear weapons by the Soviet Union, the implication is very strong that the Chinese are here pushing a certain notion of safety in numbers rather than simply supporting the achievements of the peace-loving Soviet Union.[34] Furthermore, the Chinese have never shown any indication of being worried by the statistical argument about the dangers of nuclear proliferation, which is extremely common in the West and becoming more evident in the Soviet Union. On the contrary, virtually all of their arguments on proliferation seem to suggest a lack of concern over such dangers.

The Chinese position on proliferation did not show any significant changes as a result of the negotiation of the partial test ban treaty in 1963. During the period prior to the 1964 detonation, their views gradually became more intense and were expressed more frequently. And it is true that Chinese vehemence on this issue reached a high point during the 1963 polemics following the Soviet acceptance of the test ban treaty. Perhaps the most extended Chinese treatment of the proliferation issue on record occurs in the August 15, 1963, statement

[33] Chinese government statement, August 15, 1963 (Griffith, *op. cit.*, p. 347).

[34] The point here is that it is bad for the distribution of nuclear weapons in the international arena to be unbalanced and asymmetrical since this would encourage aggressive or disruptive actions on the part of powers with superior nuclear capabilities.

of the Chinese government. Nevertheless, the Chinese had not only made clear their favorable attitude toward proliferation in the period prior to the test ban controversy; they had also stated, at least briefly, virtually all of the major themes that they were to develop in building a case for the spread of nuclear weapons both to socialist states and more generally.

What is the explanation of the relatively clear-cut and well-defined Chinese position in favor of nuclear proliferation in this period? It is quite possible that these views were genuine and sincere in the sense that they represented straightforward Chinese calculations of the most desirable policy alternative. It is true that the Chinese manifested very few signs of the typical Western fears concerning the dangers and destabilizing consequences of the spread of nuclear weapons. And they may have felt that the spread of nuclear weapons would lead to very significant gains for their policy goals in both military and political terms. The ideological cast of many of the specific arguments in favor of proliferation agrees essentially with this interpretation since most analysts believe that the Chinese show a very pronounced tendency to equate interest calculations for China's foreign policy with those called for by the demands of maintaining and spreading world communism.[35]

A second line of explanation suggests that the Chinese advocacy of nuclear proliferation during the predetonation period should be looked upon primarily as a tactic in the attempt to justify their nuclear program both to the Soviet Union and to the nonaligned and neutralist countries of the world. It would certainly have appeared somewhat ingenuous to argue that China somehow had a need for nuclear weapons but that other countries did not. In this sense, the argument in favor of more general proliferation may very well have played a role in legitimizing the Chinese program. Two brief comments are in order on this point. One is that the evidence from various Chinese statements, and especially from the Sino-Soviet polemics of 1963, suggests rather conclusively that this was at least a contributing element in the Chinese position on nuclear diffusion in general. The other, however, is that it is

35 See, for example, Halperin and Perkins, *op. cit.*, Chapter 1, and especially p. 1.

very difficult for a group of leaders to argue a position with the consistency, detail, and duration of the Chinese stand in favor of proliferation without coming to believe, at least to some extent, in the substance of the position itself.

Yet another basic line of explanation centers on the proposition that the Chinese position can be accounted for by a desire to curry favor with various countries, especially in the context of the Sino-Soviet rift, coupled with the existence of major areas of ignorance and lack of understanding concerning the dangers and problems that would follow the spread of nuclear weapons. Whatever the validity of the first half of this argument, however, the explanation tends to fall because of the inaccuracy of the second part of the proposition concerning ignorance and lack of understanding. Several analysts have argued fairly conclusively that the Chinese have, in fact, understood the significance and the implications of nuclear warfare for some time.[36] And, above all, the detail and sophistication of the Chinese arguments in favor of proliferation make the suggestion of ignorance very doubtful. There is some controversy concerning the specific level of sophistication of the Chinese analysis, but there is little doubt that the level is respectable, and there are those who suggest that the Chinese arguments may, in fact, be highly sophisticated.

The Early Postdetonation Period

The single most outstanding change in the Chinese position on nuclear proliferation in the period between the detonation on October 16 and the second one on May 14, 1965, was a pronounced tendency to de-emphasize the whole question of proliferation and to bypass it in the course of discussions on related topics. It was not that the Chinese had suddenly begun to advance arguments against the further spread of nuclear weapons; they had not. The significant thing was their marked

---

[36] See, for example, the work of Alice Hsieh who, though she agrees that Chinese ignorance on various aspects of nuclear warfare may have been a relevant consideration in the fifties, concludes that this has not been the case since at least the late fifties: Hsieh, in Rosecrance, ed., *op. cit.,* pp. 163–169. The same conclusion is suggested by Alice Hsieh's book, *Communist China's Strategy in the Nuclear Era, op. cit.*

silence on a subject on which they were formerly prepared to argue in detail. The only clear-cut Chinese statements in this period that can be interpreted as reaffirmations of a favorable view on proliferation appeared very shortly after the detonation itself. The first of these, in fact, is in the statement of the Chinese government released on the very day of the first detonation. This statement includes a section which maintains that

> . . . the more the U.S. imperialists and their partners hold onto their nuclear monopoly, the more is there danger of a nuclear war breaking out.
>
> They have it and you don't and so they are very haughty. But once those who oppose them also have it, they would no longer be so haughty, their policy of nuclear blackmail and nuclear threat would no longer be so effective, and the possibility for a complete prohibition and thorough destruction of nuclear weapons would increase.[37]

The policy of favoring proliferation is not clearly stated here, but it is implied that the spread of nuclear weapons would have positive consequences. The argument involved seems to bear a relationship to the earlier view that proliferation would increase the prospects for nuclear disarmament even though the statement clearly leaves the impression of opposition to the spread of nuclear weapons to additional members of the Western alliance.

Then in a *Jen-min Jih-pao* editorial of October 22, 1964, the Chinese went even further in indicating support for the spread of nuclear weapons, although even here they were far less explicit than they had been in the earlier period. The relevant portions of this editorial are given:

> The policy of nuclear blackmail of U.S. imperialism is founded on nuclear monopoly. When a further breach is made in U.S. nuclear monopoly, its policy of nuclear blackmail will be of no avail.[38]

> The hope of preventing nuclear war and prohibiting nuclear weapons does not in the least lie in consolidating U.S. nuclear

---

[37] Statement of the government of China, October 16, 1964, *Peking Review*, Vol. VII, No. 42 (October 16, 1964).

[38] *Jen-min Jih-pao*, editorial, October 22, 1964, *SCMP*, No. 3325, October 27, 1964, p. 22.

monopoly but in breaking it. And the more thoroughly it is broken, the greater will be the possibility of completely prohibiting and thoroughly destroying nuclear weapons. Such is the dialectics of the development of things.[39]

There are several points worth noting in this statement. The Chinese here seem to bc indicating a rather definite opposition to the spread of nuclear weapons to any country allied with the United States. The phrase, "the more thoroughly it is broken," however, is certainly a rather ambiguous one. Did the Chinese really want to advocate (a) a more extensive development of their own nuclear program, or (b) the spread of nuclear weapons to other countries? And if the latter interpretation is correct, did the Chinese now favor proliferation only to socialist countries, to "socialist and other peace-loving" countries, or to any states that qualify as opponents of the United States? In short, it seems reasonably likely that the ambiguities of this statement were deliberate.

As now becomes apparent, the differences between these early postdetonation statements[40] and the predetonation position go considerably beyond the question of frequency, although the almost total absence of indications of a favorable attitude toward proliferation in the first five months of 1965 should also be mentioned. The October 1964 statements give the impression of a certain real confusion in the distinctions between proliferation to socialist, nonaligned, and capitalist countries that were clear in the predetonation period. Moreover, the arguments are presented with far less clarity and with a pronounced absence of detail. The very early postdetonation statements give the impression of vague and general declarations, as opposed to the fairly elaborate arguments of the preceding years. Finally, both of the statements just cited make an explicit link between proliferation and the prospects for nuclear disarmament, a theme that was present but far from

---

[39] *Ibid.*, p. 25.

[40] There was a very small number of additional cases in which the Chinese mentioned proliferation by implication rather than directly. For example, the statement of November 22, 1964, mentions the right of non-nuclear countries to develop nuclear weapons twice although it says nothing about proliferation per se or the positive consequences of it: *Peking Review*, Vol. VII, No. 48 (November 27, 1964), pp. 12–14.

central before. In the months following the first detonation, proliferation seemed to take on an instrumental relationship to the achievement of disarmament, with the implication that more countries must acquire nuclear weapons before any will give them up. As the Chinese themselves put it, "Such is the dialectics of the development of things."

A number of other developments in Chinese politico-military attitudes appear to shed light on these early postdetonation shifts with regard to proliferation. To begin at the level of broad-scale impressions, the Chinese have gone to some lengths to create an aura of great reasonableness since the detonation of October 1964. In the realm of military considerations, they have made no move to suggest that the acquisition of a minimal nuclear capability has given them any new military prowess or prerogatives. On the contrary, they have played down the utility of nuclear weapons and maintained a discreet silence concerning any possible changes in the balance of military power in the Far East. At the same time, the Chinese have stepped up their declaratory campaign for the complete prohibition and destruction of nuclear weapons by all countries and for taking the first steps toward a world without nuclear capabilities. On the political side, they have generally been even more cautious in recent months than they were in the period immediately preceding the 1964 detonation. They have certainly not given up their support for wars of national liberation, especially in Southeast Asia, and they have come down fairly hard on the positive consequences of breaking the Soviet-American nuclear monopoly, but they have gone to some lengths to demonstrate their trustworthiness and to avoid giving the United States any rationale for taking military initiatives detrimental to Chinese interests.

Several factors appear to play a significant role in this general restraint in Chinese foreign policy. There is a good deal of evidence to support the view that the Chinese, in the period since the 1964 detonation, have been genuinely afraid of an American attack either on the mainland generally or specifically against their nuclear installations. Whether or not this fear is well founded is debatable, but Chinese perception of the danger seems highly likely. In addition, the Chinese are

being careful to mend their fences with the Latin Americans
and the Afro-Asians in the wake of an action that was basically
rather unpopular. In this connection, they are emphasizing
their trustworthiness and good intentions as well as allowing
a period of time for any ill effects of a political nature to blow
over. Finally, it seems clear that the Chinese are acutely aware
that they still have a considerable distance to go before achieving a nuclear capability that is really significant in military
terms. For this reason it seems highly desirable to avoid any
steps that might lead to the restriction or destruction of their
incipient nuclear capability and at the same time to reap the
various political gains that accrue from the very fact of having
broken into the nuclear column.

The Chinese set forth a series of more specific policy positions in the early postdetonation period that, taken together,
add to the impression of a shift away from their strong positive
emphasis on proliferation. To begin with, in expressing grati-
tude for the favorable responses in some quarters to their
nuclear detonation, the Chinese showed an inclination to cast
a protective umbrella over certain other countries and suggested that various other states should view the Chinese
nuclear capabilities as their own. Liu Shao-chi stated in a
speech on October 30, 1964, for example: that

> All oppressed nations and peoples and all peace-loving countries
> and people have felt elated over the successful explosion of
> China's first atom bomb [sic], as they hold the view that they, too,
> have nuclear weapons.[41]

At the same time, the Chinese explicitly reiterated their earlier
doctrine that the bomb is a paper tiger and that people, rather
than weapons, will ultimately determine the course of politico-
military struggles. As the *People's Daily* said on December 31,
1964, "We have always held that the atom bomb is a paper
tiger. That was the way we felt about it when we did not have
nuclear weapons. And this is the way we feel about it now that
we have them."[42] Man created nuclear weapons, and, accord-

---

[41] Liu Shao-chi, speech, Peking Domestic Service in Mandarin, 14:00
GMT, October 30, 1964.

[42] *People's Daily*, December 31, 1964; Peking NCNA International Service in English, 03:09 GMT, December 31, 1964.

ing to the Chinese, man will eliminate the weapons rather than himself. While these attitudes certainly did not preclude a policy in favor of proliferation, they did correlate well with the stepped-up Chinese campaign for a concrete program of nuclear disarmament and they seemed to indicate that the Chinese did not attach undue importance to some of their earlier arguments concerning the military benefits of proliferation.

Somewhat related to these developments of the early post-detonation period is the diligence with which the Chinese have expanded on the doctrine that their nuclear weapons are solely for the purposes of defense and would be used only on the utmost provocation and with the greatest circumspection. They have repeatedly and solemnly declared "that China will never at any time and under any circumstances be the first to use nuclear weapons,"[43] and they have invited the other nuclear powers to join with them in a "no first use" agreement. Furthermore, they continue to adhere to their predetonation doctrine that nuclear weapons are of little or no use to socialist states in the prosecution of wars of national liberation[44] — the most important and promising category of wars from the Chinese point of view. And they have flatly rejected any suggestion that they should take steps to become regular participants in the so-called "nuclear club." As the Chinese themselves put it, "We will not join such a club even if an invitation is sent us together with a sedan chair."[45] These last points do not indicate an explicit Chinese disenchantment with the policy of nuclear proliferation. Such a policy, especially in regard to socialist countries, would not necessarily be incompatible with these developments. But they do indicate that the Chinese are very far from viewing the acquisition of nuclear weapons as a cure for all ills and that they are

[43] Statement of the government of China, October 16, 1964, *Peking Review*, Vol. VII, *op. cit.*, p. ii. This position has since been repeated on a number of occasions.

[44] For the original statement of this view see the fifth Chinese comment on the Soviet open letter of July 14, 1963, November 18, 1963 (Griffith, *op. cit.*, pp. 486–487). The Chinese have implied since the 1964 detonation that they see no reason to change this view.

[45] Chinese government statement, November 22, 1964, as cited in Halperin and Perkins, *op. cit.*, p. 178.

generally more oriented toward a situation in which no one has nuclear weapons than toward one in which virtually everyone has them.

Before dealing with the developments of the early postdetonation period, a few additional words are in order concerning the question left open at the end of the preceding section on the predetonation period. Developments immediately following the 1964 detonation seem generally to support the view that the strongly proproliferation position of the Chinese in the earlier period was, above all, a tactical and instrumental stand in the push for their own nuclear capability. Their position on nuclear diffusion has tended to waver in the face of the success of their program to acquire a nuclear capability. The sharp drop in Chinese support for proliferation immediately following the detonation certainly argues against a serious and sustained commitment to a proproliferation policy at least at any significantly high priority level. But these conclusions should not be overstated. The Chinese statements of October 16 and 22, 1964, remain a part of the record and cannot simply be ignored. Moreover, the same conclusions do not demonstrate that the Chinese have no interest in the further proliferation of nuclear weapons. It is certainly plausible that such views were so unpopular during this period that they were suppressed, that the Chinese were holding back until they had a greater technological capacity to aid nuclear programs in other countries, or that the Chinese had not yet fully conceptualized some of their potential interests in nuclear proliferation.

There are again several principal channels of explanation with regard to the developments of the very early postdetonation period. One can argue that the Chinese were following an expected pattern for states that break the nuclear barrier when they called for a halt to nuclear proliferation after crossing the barrier themselves and when they indicated that other states do not need a nuclear capability because they can consider China's as their own. Unlike other lines of explanation, however, this one appears to be seriously deficient. For one thing, it suggests that China will soon become interested in becoming a regular member of the so-called "nuclear club," a development that now seems very unlikely in the near future. Furthermore, this view does not account adequately for the general Chinese approach to the efficacy of nuclear weapons. But above all, it does not square at all with more recent developments in Chinese policy.

A second view suggests that the Chinese were not really serious about the drift of their arguments that tended to de-emphasize the positive results of proliferation and to play up the fundamental significance of nonnuclear confrontation. The notion here is that the Chinese understood that their position on proliferation was internationally unpopular, that they were genuinely worried about the possibilities of an American attack, and that they felt a strong need to mend their fences with the nonaligned and neutralist countries of the world. The early postdetonation period of caution and circumspection becomes, in this context, a hiatus calculated to last only until the Chinese have a greater technical capacity to aid the spread of nuclear weapons and circumstances seem more appropriate for the resumption of earlier policies. Although certain elements of this interpretation are undoubtedly valid, it seems to attribute an almost implausibly high level of political sophistication to the Chinese in confusing and covering their real intentions in order to explain the various developments adequately. But there is no doubt that this view is generally consistent with at least some interpretations of Chinese political behavior.

Yet another view of the early postdetonation developments focuses on the notion that the Chinese themselves were very uncertain about the proper course of action and were inclined to feel their way around for a little after breaking through the nuclear barrier. Broad disarmament proposals always seem to be politically safe, and they appeared desirable to pacify those who may have been disquieted by the development of the Chinese nuclear program. Furthermore, such an orientation may have provided the best framework to capitalize on their nuclear development since it allowed them to reap various political benefits even while their nuclear capability remained militarily insignificant. At the same time, the disarmament proposals and a generally cautious outlook allowed the Chinese to retain a flexible position on the proliferation question. While they were no longer mentioning proliferation positively, they did not denounce it and they made several ambiguous statements that gave them the ability to turn either way in the future without great embarrassment. This is a generally attractive interpretation. And although it certainly does not account for all of the postdetonation developments, it does not have any obvious and vitiating deficiencies.

A final line of explanation is somewhat more complicated and may constitute a more adequate representation of Chinese perspectives on a complex of politico-military issues, among which proliferation is a secondary consideration. This view suggests that the traditional variables are insufficient to explain the postdetonation developments. The Chinese are known to be very politically oriented, and it is highly likely that, at least for the present, they are analyzing their success in the nuclear field in terms of political payoffs. In this connection, the important considerations may well be prestige, leadership of the third world, and political uses of the development of a nuclear capability in relations with the Soviet Union and the United States. There is a real probability that the Chinese were thinking in terms of becoming the acknowledged leaders of a third force in the world,[46] in clear-cut opposition to the Western alliance but also free from dependence on the Soviet Union. The leader of such a bloc could hardly be a nonnuclear power. This would therefore account for the Chinese effort to push their nuclear program as rapidly as possible, one major area in which they have not apparently become more cautious or circumspect in the wake of the 1964 detonation.[47] On the other hand, a "no first use" doctrine makes sense in this context since the Chinese have a clear-cut interest in reaping the political benefits of being a nuclear power while

[46] An interesting indication of Chinese thinking along these lines is to be found in Edgar Snow's report of his recent interview with Mao Tse-tung. Edgar Snow, "Interview With Mao," *New Republic,* Vol. 152, No. 9 (February 27, 1965), p. 20. See also "China's Effort in Africa," *The Interpreter* (March 1965), pp. 11–16.

[47] The rapid push of the Chinese on their nuclear program and the detonation of a second nuclear device on May 14, 1965, provide perhaps the best available indications of this orientation.

minimizing the danger of being caught in a situation in which one of the superpowers used its nuclear weapons directly against China's interests or threatened to do so. At the same time, a very mixed attitude toward nuclear diffusion would also make sense in this context. There would still be political benefits in appearing to favor nuclear proliferation from the point of view of stirring up trouble and of undermining the positions of the superpowers in various areas of the world. But the Chinese clearly would be against proliferation to other Western countries, and the spread of nuclear weapons to many additional members of the "third world" would probably have negative consequences for China's image as the definite and acknowledged leader of a new political bloc. There is evidence to support the validity of certain elements of this explanation, particularly in regard to the highly political orientation of the Chinese and their desire to become an influential political force over a broad geographical area. And the uniquely Chinese focus of this explanation makes it attractive. Nevertheless, in the absence of detailed information on the Chinese decision-making process, this explanation, like the other alternatives, remains essentially speculative.

The Second Detonation and After

During the summer of 1965, the Chinese began to show signs in their declaratory policy of resuming some of their earlier positions in favor of nuclear proliferation. This first appears in May 1965, and the correlation with the second Chinese nuclear detonation is notable. In a government statement of June 27, for example, the Chinese again took up the point:

> When only they [the United States and associates] have nuclear weapons and others do not they can do whatever they like, but when not only they have nuclear weapons and their opponents also possess nuclear weapons, then they cannot remain so awe-inspiring, and their policies of nuclear threat and menace will not do. Also this increases the possibility of the complete banning and complete destruction of nuclear weapons, which can also further guarantee world peace.[48]

[48] Peking, in Hindi to India, June 27, 1965.

This formulation is remarkably similar to that of the Chinese statement of October 16, 1964, at the time of their first detonation.

Chou En-lai's message to the Tokyo Anti-Bomb Conference in July suggested that efforts to halt nuclear proliferation would amount to acceptance of the American nuclear monopoly together with an abdication of the right of self-defense on the part of other countries.[49] And the *People's Daily* argued on August 11:

> Before U.S. imperialism is forced to agree to destroy its nuclear weapons and guarantee not to use or produce them any more, the development of nuclear weapons by peace-loving countries will help prevent U.S. imperialism from launching a nuclear war and be beneficial to the defense of world peace.[50]

Chen Yi's press conference on September 29 is particularly interesting in this context because it demonstrates several of the angles of the new Chinese shift on the proliferation issue. Chen Yi told the correspondents that

> Any country with a fair basis in industry and agriculture in science and technology will be able to manufacture atom bombs, with or without China's assistance. China hopes that Afro-Asian countries will be able to make atom bombs themselves, and it would be better for a greater number of countries to come into possession of atom bombs.
>
> In our view, the role of atom bombs should not be overstressed. The United States has been brandishing the atom bomb for atomic blackmail over the past twenty years, but it has failed. The just struggle of Afro-Asian countries against imperialism and colonialism is the best atom bomb.[51]

This highly politicized statement suggests that the Chinese think they can gain some advantages from the proliferation issue by verbally encouraging various countries to move toward nuclear weapons. At the same time, China may be worried about the dangers to itself in actually giving nuclear assistance, and the continued insistence on downgrading the

---

[49] Peking NCNA International Service in English, July 27, 1965.

[50] Peking NCNA International Service in English, August 11, 1965.

[51] Chen Yi, "China is Determined to Make All Necessary Sacrifices for the Defeat of U.S. Imperialism," *Peking Review*, Vol. VIII, No. 41 (October 8, 1965), pp. 8–9.

over-all importance of nuclear weapons indicates that the Chinese are fully aware that their own nuclear capabilities are still inadequate for any serious military application.

There are several interesting aspects of this new shift of Chinese policy relating to nuclear proliferation. To begin with, the beginning of the shift correlates with the second Chinese nuclear detonation. It may be that this detonation increased the confidence of the Chinese in their own ability to develop a significant nuclear capability to a point where they are less fearful of American or Soviet responses and can give more serious consideration to the possibilities of encouraging, or threatening to encourage, other countries to start nuclear programs.

The Chinese silence of the early postdetonation period has now been broken. But some of the other distinctions between the predetonation period and the early postdetonation period are still relevant. The absence of the detail and sophistication of the 1963 statements is still notable. And above all, during the summer of 1965 the Chinese continued to link their favorable attitude toward further nuclear proliferation explicitly with the question of nuclear disarmament. This continued insistence on the proposition that a further spread of nuclear weapons will serve the interests of world peace by breaking the nuclear monopoly of the superpowers and increasing the prospects for over-all nuclear disarmament has replaced the more detailed arguments of earlier periods and marks the present Chinese position on nuclear proliferation as a highly politicized one.

Several further elements of this latest shift in Chinese policy remain to be noted. Virtually all of the recent Chinese statements argue the case for the spread of weapons very specifically in terms of the need to build up defenses against American imperialism. While the long-run argument now emphasizes increasing the prospects for nuclear disarmament, the Chinese have begun to stress the short-term goal of countering American "atomic blackmail." A Chinese policy of this kind may, in reality, be counterproductive in these terms.[52] But it may

52 The point is that a Chinese declaratory policy of this kind might increase the inclination of the United States to take military steps against

be a manifestation of Chinese worries about recent trends in the Vietnam war. And the resultant de-emphasis on Soviet nuclear collusion with the United States correlates with the absence of a strong Soviet reaction to the two Chinese nuclear detonations.

Finally, it is important to note that, along with some new indications of a positive view of nuclear diffusion, the Chinese have also made several statements hinting that they are really more interested in gaining third world support for an expanded Chinese nuclear capability than in encouraging the development of a lot of token nuclear programs.[53] They apparently view the decisive breaking of the American "nuclear monopoly" as a prerequisite for either nuclear parity or nuclear disarmament. But this monopoly can be broken by diffusion of some nuclear weapons to many states or by substantial increases in the Chinese nuclear capabilities. Recent statements seem to imply that the Chinese would really prefer the latter course of developments but that at such an early stage they are willing to explore both possibilities.

The Implications of Chinese Disarmament Proposals

In recent years the Chinese have propounded several major disarmament proposals, which at face value have major implications for the Chinese stand on the question of nuclear proliferation. They have consistently maintained that comprehensive disarmament is presently irrelevant since

. . . universal and complete disarmament can be realized only after imperialism, capitalism and all systems of exploitation have been eliminated. To make propaganda about the possibility of realizing "a world without weapons, without armed forces and without wars" through universal and complete disarmament while imperialism still exists, is to deceive the people of the world and is detrimental to the struggle for world peace.[54]

China without increasing the Chinese ability to put up a serious defense against such a move.

[53] See, for example, the speech by Liu Ning-i, CPR Delegate to the Tokyo Conference (July 28), Peking NCNA International Service in English, July 28, 1965, and the speech by Liu Ning-i (July 31), Peking NCNA International Service in English, August 1, 1965.

[54] Chinese government statement, September 1, 1963 (Griffith, *op. cit.*, p. 386).

The Chinese nevertheless profess to believe "that the complete and thorough prohibition of nuclear weapons can be achieved while imperialism still exists, just as poison gas was prohibited."[55] Exactly why nuclear disarmament alone is possible has never been made clear, but they have held on to this doctrine with remarkable tenacity through both the predetonation and the postdetonation periods.

Although the Chinese began to speak favorably of nuclear disarmament some years ago, the first systematic elaboration of their disarmament program occurred in the government statement of July 31, 1963, on the partial test ban treaty. In this statement it was proposed that "all countries in the world, both nuclear and non-nuclear, solemnly declare that they will prohibit and destroy nuclear weapons completely, thoroughly, totally and resolutely."[56] Countries were to fulfill their undertakings under this agreement step by step, with the following four steps being initiated first:[57] (1) the dismantling of all military bases and nuclear weapons on foreign soil, (2) the establishment of nuclear-free zones for Asia and the Pacific region, Central Europe, Africa, and Latin America, (3) agreement to "refrain from exporting and importing in any form nuclear weapons and technical data for their manufacture," and (4) agreement to "cease all nuclear tests, including underground nuclear tests." The Chinese called for a summit conference of all the countries of the world to discuss the question of nuclear disarmament generally and to draw up a detailed plan for carrying out the four first steps of this program.

The July 1963 statement remained the official Chinese disarmament program throughout the rest of the predetonation period. Since the detonation of October 16, 1964, the Chinese have remained adamant in their demand for a thorough destruction and prohibition of nuclear weapons without any other disarmament measures. At the same time, there has been a definite increase in emphasis on disarmament since the detonation, and the volume of commentary on this question has risen noticeably. Peking now seems to be involved in an effort

---

[55] *Ibid.* (Griffith, *op. cit.*, p. 386).
[56] Chinese government statement on the test ban treaty, July 31, 1963 (Griffith, *op. cit.*, p. 328).
[57] *Ibid.* (Griffith, *op. cit.*, pp. 328–329).

to make political capital by paying great attention to the desires and reactions of various nonaligned and neutralist states concerning nuclear disarmament.[58]

The Chinese statement on arms control of November 22, 1964, the latest comprehensive Chinese statement on this subject, however, shows some specific changes from the July 1963 program. While the over-all framework remains the same, in emphasizing complete nuclear disarmament and calling for a world-wide summit conference, the only step that the Chinese now endorse wholeheartedly is an agreement among the nuclear powers never to be the first to use nuclear weapons under any circumstances.[59] Specifically, their proposal now seems to call for voluntary acceptance and implementation of the "no first use" doctrine. In the November statement, the Chinese de-emphasized their earlier proposal for a complete ban on nuclear tests since such an arrangement would work only to the advantage of states with superior nuclear capabilities unless it were coupled with definite steps to destroy and prohibit nuclear weapons.[60] Moreover, the same statement pointed out certain limitations on the usefulness of nuclear-free zones to the Chinese. Unless the creation of such zones were accompanied by the acceptance of a workable "no first use" agreement, the result would be only to restrict the actions of the present nonnuclear powers while leaving the nuclear powers free to advance their nuclear programs.[61] The Chinese, it appears, are still in favor of nuclear-free zones but only as a follow-up to a credible and workable "no first use" agreement among the nuclear powers. These particular reservations are of special interest since less than a month before, on October 29, 1964, the Chinese had reiterated their previous support for a nuclear-free zone in the Far East without attaching these strings.[62]

58 For example, many replies to Chou En-lai's letter of October 17, 1964, were printed in the *People's Daily* and reprinted in English in the *Peking Review*.

59 Chinese government statement, November 22, 1964, as cited in Halperin and Perkins, *op. cit.*, p. 175.

60 *Ibid.* (Halperin and Perkins, *op. cit.*, p. 174).

61 *Ibid.* (Halperin and Perkins, *op. cit.*, pp. 175–176).

62 Joint statement by the Chinese and a delegation of Japanese Socialists, October 29, 1964, NCNA in English, Peking, October 29, 1964, *SCMP*, No. 3330, November 3, 1964, p. 33.

The central idea of these disarmament proposals is diametrically opposed to the spread of nuclear weapons. The complete prohibition and destruction of nuclear weapons is virtually impossible to square with a stand in favor of proliferation. Moreover, the Chinese suggestions amount essentially to proposals for nonproliferation agreements. And while they raised some doubts in the November 1964 statement, the Chinese certainly indicated that they were still in favor of nuclear-free zones as sequels to a "no first use" agreement. There would appear to be only two ways of explaining these positions on nuclear disarmament without precluding a policy in favor of the spread of nuclear weapons. One is that the Chinese sincerely believe that nuclear weapons must spread further in order to make nuclear disarmament a real possibility and that they are willing to stake their whole disarmament program on this proposition. The other is that the Chinese see absolutely no chance of their disarmament proposals being accepted, with the result that their disarmament position is virtually irrelevant for political and military calculations on such problems as nuclear proliferation. Such an orientation could result either from a complete lack of sincerity on the part of the Chinese in making disarmament proposals or from a confident judgment that the other nuclear powers will never come close to accepting their proposals. In either event, the Chinese proposals for nuclear disarmament would not preclude a policy favoring the spread of nuclear weapons.

Whatever the real motives behind the Chinese disarmament proposals, the evidence presently lends very strong support to the conclusion that the Chinese are using the disarmament issue primarily for political purposes. China is acting in this respect very much as though it is dead set on acquiring a significant nuclear capacity but realizes the political importance of appearing to be generally favorable toward disarmament. At this point, its approach appears to be highly analogous to that of the Soviet Union in the late forties when the latter was emphasizing sweeping but nonoperational "ban the bomb" proposals in disarmament negotiations.[63] In addition,

63 See also Morton H. Halperin, *Chinese Nuclear Strategy: The Early*

the Chinese are apparently becoming more and more suspicious of the whole subject of disarmament and arms control as a direct function of increasing indications of Soviet-American collaboration in this area. As one recent study puts it, "Arms control and disarmament have come, for the Chinese, to be equated with an effort by the United States and the Soviet Union to establish a duopoly of power in the world."[64]

There are several more specific explanations of this Chinese orientation toward disarmament. Morton Halperin and Dwight Perkins have set forth what is probably the most detailed view.[65] They maintain that the Chinese are absolutely set on developing a significant nuclear capability and that actually they do not want agreement on nuclear disarmament, especially at this point in time. China is clearly an anti *status quo* power and is against the stabilizing impact of a serious disarmament program. Although they certainly fear the prospects of Soviet-American duopoly and want to take steps to counter it, the Chinese lack any direct incentive of military security to favor disarmament and they would very likely repudiate their own proposals for nuclear disarmament in the event that their bluff were called. The Chinese program of nuclear disarmament is therefore entirely political. In particular, the Chinese are anxious to use this program (1) to recoup losses of friendship in various quarters resulting from their unpopular position on the test ban and from their own nuclear detonation in 1964, and (2) to cement friendly relations in various Afro-Asian and Latin American nations. Halperin and Perkins have also drawn the analogy between the present Chinese position on disarmament and the Soviet position in earlier years, and they place great emphasis on the Chinese determination to become a modern superpower as a factor in demonstrating that the Chinese are not seriously interested in nuclear disarmament.

Perhaps the simplest explanation of the Chinese disarmament proposals is that offered by the Soviet Union. The

Post-Detonation Period, Adelphi Papers, No. 18 (London: Institute for Strategic Studies, May 1965).

64 Halperin and Perkins, *op. cit.*, pp. 132.

65 *Ibid.*, pp. 133 ff.

Soviets made themselves very clear on this point in the exchanges following the negotiation of the test ban treaty in 1963. On August 3, 1963, they replied to the Chinese proposals of July 31 with the announcement that

> . . . the gist of the statement of the PRC government does not at all lie in the radical programme which lists proposals long since submitted by others, but in the fact that in the particular case they are trying to use this programme to cover up a refusal by the PRC to sign a treaty banning nuclear weapons tests.[66]

And the Soviet condemnation of September 21, 1963, is even more sweeping. At this point, they went so far as to proclaim that

> . . . the Chinese leaders do not have any program for disarmament; they are not waging and do not want to wage a struggle for this great aim and if they do sometimes talk about disarmament, they do so only to cover up their real intentions.[67]

These remarks are, of course, highly polemical and they probably do not represent any extended analysis on the part of the Soviets. They do, nevertheless, indicate that American analysts are not alone in denying the sincerity of the Chinese disarmament program.

A third explanation is couched more in terms of the "joker theory" of disarmament exchanges.[68] The point here is that Chinese insistence on separating nuclear disarmament from other forms of disarmament is deliberate: the Chinese probably believe that their position would be considerably enhanced in a world in which nuclear power is effectively canceled. The reduction or complete prohibition of nuclear weapons would certainly reduce present and potential threats to the Chinese interior and would also reduce the Chinese fear of Soviet-American collusion aimed at ruling the world. Under this interpretation, therefore, the Chinese may well be sincere in advancing disarmament proposals in the sense that they would like to see them accepted, but by the same token they

---

[66] Soviet government statement, August 3, 1963 (Griffith, *op. cit.*, p. 336).

[67] Soviet government statement, September 21, 1963 (Griffith, *op. cit.*, p. 432).

[68] For an explanation of this theory consult John Spanier and Joseph Nogee, *The Politics of Disarmament* (New York: Praeger, 1962), especially Chapter 2.

must be fully aware of the fact that such proposals are virtually bound to be rejected by the superpowers. This leads to the same conclusion reached under the other explanations. The Chinese presumably calculate that the probability of their nuclear disarmament proposals being accepted is virtually zero, and their reasons for advancing them at all are based primarily on the political-propaganda advantages to be reaped.

In summary, the Chinese disarmament program appears neither to preclude nor to demand a favorable Chinese outlook on the question of nuclear proliferation. Each explanation leads to the conclusion that the Chinese assume that there is no real chance of their proposals for nuclear disarmament being accepted and that they are to be explained in terms of various political motivations. For this reason, the Chinese declaratory position on disarmament probably does not have much influence one way or the other on the Chinese view of nuclear proliferation.

Chinese Interests in Proliferation

At the present time, Chinese policy on the question of nuclear proliferation is at best ambiguous. Whatever may be the real explanation of the predetonation position, the shifts since the October 1964 detonation are difficult to interpret. All this, however, certainly does not mean that the Chinese do not have substantial interests in the spread of nuclear weapons in certain situations or in aiding nuclear programs in particular countries: the Chinese have not given any indications that they are interested in a general *non*proliferation policy.

Over-all Considerations

While it is clear that more detailed considerations of Chinese interests in nuclear spread must be broken down by country, there are also some more general factors that undoubtedly form the basis of the Chinese orientation. Here it seems necessary to make a distinction between long-term and short-term calculations of Chinese interests in proliferation, especially since the balance of relevant considerations does not seem to come out the same in both cases. Long-term analysis would cover the period ten to twenty years into the future and would necessarily deal with the effects of "accomplished proliferation."[69] In terms of over-all considerations, it is difficult to escape the conclusion that China is basically against the prospect of accomplished proliferation leading to the possession of a militarily significant nuclear capability by a number of additional countries.

There are perhaps two possible factors that might result in a long-term, positive Chinese interest in nuclear diffusion. If China remains a violent enemy of the *status quo*, wants to revolutionize international relationships entirely, and is willing to take any steps that will tend to undermine the present pattern of international relations, a long-term interest in serious nuclear proliferation might be logical. This position, however, would tend to imply a lack of awareness of or disregard of the destructive potential of nuclear warfare that the Chinese certainly do not demonstrate at present. A second possible long-term interest in proliferation is an alternative rather than a complement to the first argument. If the Chinese really believe that breaking the Soviet-American nuclear monopoly by spreading nuclear weapons to more and more countries will increase the prospects for nuclear disarmament, they might very well favor the spread of nuclear weapons. But there are several important problems in this argument. First, it implies that the Chinese genuinely desire nuclear disarmament with some real priority.[70] Second, since the detonation, the Chinese have modified this argument in their own proclamations so that it now applies only to socialist countries and not to capitalist ones.[71] And furthermore, the argument that proliferation will aid nuclear disarmament runs almost directly counter to the outlook of most countries on the effects of accomplished proliferation.

[69] "Accomplished proliferation" refers to a situation in which additional countries have actually acquired nuclear capabilities, as opposed to a situation in which they are only taking steps in this direction.

[70] In particular, it is hardly reasonable to suppose that the Chinese could maintain this view along with that implied in the first argument stated.

[71] This at least is the implication of the *Jen-min Jih-pao* editorial of October 22, 1964, already cited, *SCMP*, No. 3325, October 27, 1964, p. 22.

The negative arguments seem considerably more substantial. Above all, significant proliferation, especially in Asia, would raise major security problems for the Chinese, probably involve them in various arms race activities, and almost certainly lead to heavy economic costs. Moreover, the long-term political results would be rather negative. The hope for political hegemony in Asia, which is generally considered an important objective of Chinese foreign policy,[72] would be very seriously jeopardized, if not destroyed, if several Asian states acquired a significant nuclear capability. The Japanese case is the most outstanding in this connection, but several others are clearly relevant. Chinese leadership of an Afro-Asian bloc, stemming from the Chinese "intermediate zones" theory,[73] would clearly suffer in the event that additional members of the bloc became serious nuclear powers. If such a bloc develops, Chinese leadership will certainly depend, at least in part, on China's position as the core state and as the only significant nuclear power. In addition, over the long term China will almost certainly be influenced to some extent by the considerations of stability and relative influence that tend to make nuclear powers move more and more toward conservatism on the nuclear diffusion issue once they themselves go nuclear, regardless of their ideology and positive foreign policy objectives.[74] China seems determined to become a modern superpower, but this would be a difficult goal to reach in a world characterized by the proliferation of significant nuclear capabilities to a number of additional countries. Finally, it might result in a reputation for irresponsibility and recklessness, and the Chinese, with their political ambitions, are far from immune to calculations of this kind.

The balance of long-term considerations therefore seems to be against a Chinese policy favoring nuclear proliferation.

72 Hsieh, in Rosecrance, ed., *op. cit.*, p. 160; and Halperin, *China and the Bomb, op. cit.*, pp. 44–45.

73 One statement of the extended version of the "intermediate zone" theory, one of the more recent developments in Chinese doctrine, appears in "Mao Interview," *Pravda*, September 2, 1964, and Moscow Domestic Service in Russian, 13:00 GMT, September 6, 1964.

74 Richard Rosecrance, "International Stability and Nuclear Diffusion," in Rosecrance, ed., *op. cit.*, p. 307.

Nevertheless, considerably shorter-term considerations typically exercise as much or more influence in the foreign policy decision-making processes of states. The demands of the present and the pressures to act on immediate requirements almost inevitably lead to a substantial downgrading of the influence of long-term calculations on actual policy. In this connection, it is always possible to argue in favor of looking at short-term considerations on the grounds that longer-term problems are likely either to take care of themselves or to change before they become fully relevant. In the context of the Chinese position on proliferation, the short-term outlook differs substantially from the longer-term situation. The fact that the time frame is the immediate future makes it possible to think in terms of steps and actions with implications only for nuclear spread rather than for accomplished proliferation. This means that arguments based on the possession of significant nuclear capabilities by various additional countries can be shunted aside in favor of more immediate calculations. The arguments in favor of Chinese support for nuclear proliferation then seem much stronger.

In this short-term context, the arguments favoring proliferation are primarily political. Above all, the Chinese may be able to utilize a favorable view of proliferation in wooing certain states of the third world into their own political orbit or at least away from alignment with the United States or the Soviet Union. Here the Chinese may find that they have a substantial comparative advantage in certain modest programs of nuclear aid to selected countries. The Soviet Union and the United States are presently unwilling to give any nuclear aid of military application, and they are not likely to change their policies in this area in the foreseeable future. For this reason, even very circumscribed moves by the Chinese to supply nuclear aid may give them major political advantages in certain countries.

Next, the anti *status quo* orientation of the Chinese may lead them to place a positive value on the potential of nuclear diffusion for stirring up nationalisms and even for mustering the forces of the South against those of the North in the international arena. It is quite possible that the Chinese feel they could make political gains from the upheavals that would follow almost inevitably without specifying the nature of these gains ahead of time. Similarly, they might see positive payoffs in a favorable orientation toward proliferation because it might bolster the spirit of oppressed nations and activate or strengthen various national liberation movements, an objective to which the Chinese apparently attach very high priority. Less plausible but still conceivable, the Chinese might favor proliferation on the somewhat irrational grounds of racism. Although the notion of spreading nuclear weapons to non-white peoples might appeal to a racist outlook, available evidence suggests that any Chinese racism that does exist would be unlikely to express itself along these lines.[75] Furthermore, noticeable movements in the direction of nuclear diffusion might very well tend to devalue and undermine American alliances and defense commitments in the non-European areas of the world. In this connection, it might be possible for the Chinese to make some political gains without having to deliver very much in terms of concrete actions.

It is also possible that the Chinese may be able to trade nuclear assistance for worth-while technological data and resources in the possession of other countries. The Soviets apparently made some gains along these lines when they were giving nuclear aid to the Chinese. They seem to have acquired some unprocessed uranium, and they may well have reaped some benefits from research by a number of top Chinese scientists at the Dubna installation outside Moscow. There is evidence that the French, too, are getting useful technological returns from their nuclear cooperation with the Israelis. At the present time, it is not clear what the Chinese could receive from the likely candidates for their nuclear aid that would be technologically or scientifically valuable. There is, however, the possibility that technological returns may become more relevant in the future. Finally, some observers suggest that the Chinese would obtain real satisfaction from a program under which scientists from various states came to China to learn about nuclear physics. The notion of China as a seat of learning has a long tradition among the Chinese, and it raises

[75] Halperin and Perkins, *op. cit.*, p. 10.

images that are gratifying to those in China (and they are apparently numerous) who are still oriented toward a view of China as the "middle kingdom."

The short-term picture, therefore, looks much more favorable for the Chinese. There are, however, important short-term disadvantages to a policy favoring the spread of nuclear weapons that should not be forgotten. Several of the most important of them center around American reactions to any Chinese move toward proliferation. Such a move might very well increase the dangers of American military attacks on the Chinese mainland in general, or at least on her nuclear installations. There is evidence that this possibility was discussed at some length by the American government at the time of the first Chinese nuclear detonation and that one of the important negative factors at that time was the lack of a real provocation to justify attacks.[76] Here anything but the most modest Chinese actions in favor of the spread of nuclear weapons might come dangerously within range of providing a provocation for American action. The actual likelihood of American action is debatable, but it is clear that the Chinese perceive the prospects as significant and are worried. Furthermore, Chinese support for nuclear proliferation might result in an increase in American political actions designed to counter Chinese moves. Possibilities would include a more active program against the establishment of Chinese influence in African and Latin American countries or an increase in the tendency of the United States to intervene actively in the politics of the Far East and of Southeast Asia. Finally, any Chinese steps with significant implications for nuclear spread might lead to American military responses other than attacks on the Chinese nuclear installations. If nothing else, there might be a lessening of the constraints on the United States to avoid damaging China or involving China in various Southeast Asian military confrontations. While such reactions might not be prohibitive

[76] For indications of U.S. thinking on this subject see Ray Cromley, "Drastic Moves Against China Are Discussed," *Washington News,* November 13, 1964; Ray Cromley, "Peking Poses the Great Imponderable," *Washington News,* November 17, 1964; and Stewart Alsop, "The One Great Question," *Saturday Evening Post,* November 14, 1964.

for a Chinese policy in favor of proliferation they would certainly weigh negatively.

There are other negative short-term considerations of major importance. Any outspoken support for nuclear proliferation might begin to scare the countries of the third world. Some of them might become anti-Chinese or at least fail to lean toward China. Moreover, at the present time serious support for nuclear proliferation would be bound to evoke negative reactions on the part of world opinion.

On balance, the short-term picture on a proliferation policy looks better than the long-term one, but the outcome is still ambiguous. The Chinese do not seem to worry about the straightforward statistical argument against proliferation. This may tip the balance in favor of such a policy for the Chinese where the Americans and the Soviets would almost certainly go the other way on the basis of their general fear of the destabilizing results. Nevertheless, the exact outcome of Chinese calculations will depend on the way in which they perceive the various issues involved and on the relative weights that they attach to them. But, about all, these over-all considerations are likely to be extensively modified by more specific factors relating to specific countries that are candidates for a nuclear capability.

Before shifting to specific cases, however, it is important to add a few comments on the various possible types of support for nuclear proliferation. In fact, there are a number of possible forms ranging from declaratory advocacy, or partial advocacy, all the way to an outright policy of handing over operational nuclear capabilities to other states. As yet, the Chinese have shown absolutely no inclination to take steps that would lead to the rapid acquisition of nuclear capabilities by other states, and the preceding analysis indicates that their interests would be strongly against such a course. What the Chinese have done, however, is to combine a very ambiguous declaratory policy on the spread of nuclear weapons with several very tentative ventures into action policy that fall near the minimum end of the spectrum.[77] In short, the Chinese have so far been extremely cautious in this area.

[77] The Chen Yi interview of September 28, 1965, indicates that the

An important set of middle-range actions with substantial implications for the spread of nuclear weapons covers the various concepts of nuclear sharing. The Chinese have never yet demonstrated any interest, however, in utilizing the various forms of nuclear sharing under any circumstances. This may be only because they have not previously had the technological capability to do so, but their experiences to date indicate that there are additional problems in this area. In 1958 the Soviets evidently made a sharing proposal that for various reasons was met by a violently negative reaction on the part of the Chinese.[78] This experience seems to have left the Chinese with a suspicious outlook on the whole concept of nuclear sharing. The Chinese have posed as violent critics of the American multilateral force (MLF) proposals for nuclear sharing.[79] Their negative reactions in this case include two distinguishable strands. They sometimes argue that the MLF proposals are really an American plot to retain control of nuclear weapons in the Western alliance under the guise of sharing. At other times they maintain that nuclear sharing is the first step in a plan to give nuclear weapons to the West Germans. Unlike the Soviets, however, the Chinese appear to set more store by the first of these arguments in attacking the MLF. The political context of their experiences makes the Chinese disinterest in such programs understandable. But it seems likely that in terms of the proliferation issue, some forms of sharing might become increasingly attractive to them as

Chinese are presently taking a very cautious view even at this minimum end of the spectrum. Chen Yi differentiated aid in furthering the peaceful uses of atomic energy from assistance in the manufacture of atom bombs, and he suggested that China would take a more favorable view of the former than of the latter. It is, of course, possible to take a variety of militarily significant steps under cover of this distinction between peaceful and military applications of nuclear technology. But the statement by Chen Yi at least indicates that the Chinese were feeling rather cautious about this issue as of September 1965. See Chen Yi, *op. cit.*, p. 8.

[78] On this point see the first Chinese comment on the Soviet open letter of July 14, 1963, September 6, 1963 (Griffith, *op. cit.*, p. 339).

[79] For the various strands of the Chinese attitude toward the MLF consult Yang Chun-fong, "A Nuclear Force Without a Name," *Peking Review*, Vol. 6, No. 24 (June 14, 1963), pp. 9–13, and "Nuclear Proliferation: Bonn's Finger on the Trigger?" *Peking Review*, Vol. 7, No. 43 (October 23, 1964), pp. 20–21.

their technological capabilities increase in the nuclear field. Whether the Chinese will soon begin to demonstrate a shift from a recipient to an initiator mentality in this regard, however, remains to be seen.

The indications of Chinese caution in this area may simply indicate a healthy appreciation of the negative considerations to be taken into account. More likely, on the other hand, is the possibility that the Chinese are becoming cognizant of the arguments against proliferation but still hope to make some short-term political capital without endangering their long-term interests. In this connection, the Chinese may well take certain steps that have positive implications for nuclear diffusion even while being ultimately against the effects of accomplished proliferation. They may feel pushed by the possibilities for short-term political gains, and they may calculate that if things go well in the short term they can recapture the drive toward proliferation at a later date before substantial harm is done to their long-term interests.

Asia

The most important potential nuclear powers, from the Chinese point of view, are the various states of Asia, and in particular India, Indonesia, Japan, and Australia. At the outset, a distinction is necessary between Indonesia and the other candidates since Indonesia is the only one that does not have the scientific and technological capability to produce nuclear weapons on its own in the near future. These states ring China geographically and they could become a major threat to Chinese security in the future. They do not all carry the same potential military threat but, in general, military considerations are much more relevant here than in the case of countries in other parts of the world; furthermore, nuclear capabilities in the Asian countries would pose particularly important problems for Chinese political objectives. This is especially significant in the case of Chinese hopes for political dominance and hegemony in Asia. The long-term Chinese interest against nuclear proliferation in this area therefore seems clear. The interesting problem is whether it is possible for China to encourage proliferation in certain areas in such a way as to gain short-term benefits without seriously jeopardizing its long-term interests.

India. At the present time there is no doubt that India is China's most important rival for political influence in Asia, if not in the third world as a whole. China, therefore, seems to have clear reasons for being against an accomplished Indian nuclear program. And this conclusion is underlined by the fact that India quite clearly has the technological and scientific capabilities to produce at least a small nuclear capability in a short space of time.[80] Moreover, there is virtually no chance in the foreseeable future of China actually aiding an Indian program. In fact, a declaration of Chinese support for an Indian program would be looked upon with suspicion by the Indians.

There are, on the other hand, several general factors that should tend to reduce Chinese opposition to an Indian nuclear capability. Geographical asymmetries in the area are such that China has far less to fear from an Indian nuclear capability than India does from Chinese nuclear weapons. For this reason, the Chinese may feel that the security implications of an Indian nuclear program are manageable. In addition, there are indications that the Chinese simply do not believe that the Indians will show the drive to produce a serious nuclear capability even if they make moves in the direction of becoming a nuclear power. From this perspective, an Indian nuclear program might not be taken very seriously by the Chinese even in the longer term.[81] Moreover, there are several significant short-term considerations that might lead

[80] Thomas Brady, "Pressure Grows for India A-Bomb," *The New York Times,* October 27, 1964, p. 5. This is one of a number of news dispatches on a speech by Nomi Bhabha, Chairman of the Indian Atomic Energy Commission, in which he cited figures on India's nuclear program.

[81] From the Chinese point of view, one possible long-term disadvantage of an Indian nuclear program concerns Japan rather than India itself. It is conceivable that an Indian decision to go nuclear would push Japan significantly in the direction of opting for its own nuclear program. Although such a development presently seems doubtful for political reasons, the great Chinese fear of military resurgence in Japan might make even a small probability of a Japanese nuclear program seem important to the Chinese.

China to look with favor on Indian movements toward a
nuclear program and to avoid detering them. Although China
very likely cannot actually aid India in this context, it may
very well be able to create a favorable political atmosphere.

To begin with, any movement toward the acquisition of
nuclear weapons might actually reduce India's political influence, especially in the third world where it is built very
much on neutralism, an orientation toward peace, and a moral
and ethical position in terms of which nuclear weapons would
be abhorrent. The Chinese might be delighted to see a decline in Indian influence. At the same time, an Indian nuclear
program might put a strain on the Indian economy, thereby
aiding China, which already has a large military budget, in
the economic race between the two. A substantial nuclear
program would be expensive in itself. But the economic
problems would be particularly great if the program led to
major American opposition, problems with the American
aid program, and, as a consequence, an exacerbation of the
Indian foreign exchange problems. In military terms, an Indian program to acquire nuclear weapons would almost certainly reduce her chances of evoking American or Soviet aid
and guarantees of defense in the future.

There are also several more explicitly political factors. It
seems likely that any Indian initiative would lead the Pakis-
tanis to conclude that they too must acquire nuclear weapons.
From the Chinese point of view, an arms race on the sub-
continent might sufficiently absorb the attention of the protagonists to leave the Chinese a freer hand in acquiring political influence in other parts of the third world. And the
Chinese might feel that they were in a position to gain from
any disruption or chaos that would follow the nuclear arming
of India and Pakistan. Moreover, there is a very real chance
that the initiation of an Indian nuclear program would bring
down the government, cause serious political splits in the
country, and lead to near chaos in many areas. The discussion
of nuclear weapons in India following the Chinese detonation
of 1964, circumscribed as it was, demonstrated clearly their
divisive potential. In short, the Chinese may feel that the
likely payoffs to such developments would be substantially

positive in themselves and that in the long run the Indian program would never become very serious.

Indonesia. Prior to September 30, 1965, Indonesia had been veering definitely toward the Chinese political orbit.[82] Signs of mutual friendliness and indications of Indonesian willingness to make various deals with the Chinese had been capped in January 1965 by the Subandrio mission to China.[83] A joint communiqué stressed a variety of common interests, and there is evidence, not in the communiqué itself, that "China also offered to extend technical and scientific aid to Indonesia, an important part of which would consist of the training of Indonesian specialists at Chinese nuclear installations."[84] There is no evidence that this offer had been implemented prior to October of 1965 but it does constitute an important indication of Chinese willingness to consider at least modest steps that, among other things, have positive implications for nuclear proliferation.[85]

There were several considerations which affected the Chinese outlook on aid to an Indonesian nuclear program. The Indonesians might have been able to offer a valuable military *quid pro quo* since they have long-range bombers that are considerably more sophisticated than those of the Chinese.[86] The Indonesians almost certainly would not have turned over any number of bombers to the Chinese but they might have offered a prototype that the Chinese could copy, just

[82] See, for example, Tad Szulc's commentary on Chen Yi's November 1964 visit to Djakarta, "Sukarno Build-Up Linked to Peking," *The New York Times,* January 8, 1965, pp. 1–2.

[83] The joint communiqué from this visit appears in *Peking Review,* Vol. VIII, No. 6 (February 5, 1965), pp. 6–8. For an analysis of the communiqué see Research Department of Radio Free Europe, "Chinese-Indonesian Joint Communiqué," *Communist Area,* January 30, 1965.

[84] Research Department of Radio Free Europe, *op. cit.,* p. 4. See also Szulc, *op. cit.,* for another statement concerning this offer.

[85] For an unsubstantiated report that China was planning to "supply Indonesia with enough enriched uranium to permit her to explode a nuclear device" see E. R. Zilbert, "The Chinese Nuclear Explosion, N-Nation Nuclear Development and Civil Defense" (RAND, P-3074, April 1965), p. 22.

[86] The Indonesians presently have thirty Tu-16 (Badger) bombers of Soviet construction while the most advanced Chinese bomber is the greatly inferior Tu-4. See Institute of Strategic Studies, *The Military Balance, 1964–1965* (London, 1964).

as the Soviets copied the American B-29 years ago. Moreover, the Chinese had a real interest in encouraging the development of Indonesia's revolutionary potential. Indonesia might have been persuaded (coercion would also be possible) to carry out acts from time to time in the Asian arena that would work to the advantage of the Chinese.

Overshadowing all other considerations, however, seems to have been a desire to bring the Indonesians into the Chinese political orbit. This desire almost undoubtedly extended beyond wooing the country away from an inclination toward the Soviet Union and countering any possible Soviet-Indonesian deals.[87] There are indications that the Chinese hoped to bring Indonesia into a very close political relationship, perhaps even approximating that of a *de facto* satellite relationship. There had already been initial success, and it is highly likely that any Chinese nuclear aid for Indonesia would have been used to further this political relationship. Moreover, nuclear assistance might have proved to be a useful technique for winning over the Indonesian army, which was and is the most powerful source of anti-communism in the country.[88] In this connection, the Chinese may not have been very exercised about the long-term prospects of an Indonesian nuclear capability. In the event that political developments turned out well, the Indonesian nuclear program could have been terminated or suitably regulated well before it became a potential menace. There are absolutely no indications that the Chinese had any intention of setting Indonesia up as a nuclear power by giving her the bomb. And the Chinese may well have estimated that the dangers of a very modest program of nuclear assistance to Indonesia were worth risking in the light of the major positive payoffs that might have resulted. They may have hoped that nuclear aid would

---

[87] The possibility of Soviet-Indonesian deals has been brought up by the Australians. See *Proceedings of the Seminar on Nuclear Dispersal in Asia and the Indo-Pacific Region, op. cit.,* especially pp. 3–5.

[88] For another interesting Chinese attempt to influence the Indonesian army see the reports that the Indonesians were considering a proposal made by Chou En-lai to merge their volunteer and regular armed forces. *Washington Post,* June 1, 1965, p. 2, citing a UPI dispatch of May 31 from Djakarta.

permit the kind of moves to eliminate Chinese influence that the military has implemented since October 1965.

Japan. The Chinese have repeatedly and vehemently made clear their opposition to the Japanese acquisition of nuclear weapons or to any Japanese movement toward a nuclear capability so long as that country retains its close ties with the United States.[89] In recent months the Chinese have launched an extended and, at times bitter, attack on the government of Eisaku Sato in Japan.[90] Central themes in this attack are (1) that there is a real or threatened revival of militarism in Japan, (2) that Japan may become an American nuclear base or be picked as an object of American nuclear proliferation, and (3) that the Japanese are now taking a reactionary and retrogressive course in their relations with Communist China. The joint Japanese-American communiqué issued in Washington in January 1965 was the signal for especially violent attacks. And in general the Chinese have been rather assiduous in seeking to persuade Japan that it can maximize its political influence as a leader of the nonnuclear states and in attempting to play on its fears of nuclear weapons in any form.[91]

There are apparently several sources of this strong negative Chinese position in the Japanese case. Above all, it is almost undoubtedly true that Japan's economic, technological, and scientific development is such that it could outmatch China in the nuclear field if it initiated a serious nuclear program. And this is particularly significant since a Japanese nuclear capability could become a very serious threat to China. The Chinese mainland would be endangered more by a Japanese

[89] For an example see the article of Commentator in *Renmin Ribao,* February 19, 1965, reprinted in *Peking Review,* Vol. VIII, No. 9 (February 26, 1965), p. 17.

[90] For an example see the article by Commentator in *Renmin Ribao, op. cit.,* pp. 15–17.

[91] Interestingly, the Chinese have recently announced that the Kurile, Ryukyu, and Bonin Islands should be returned to Japan. This is almost undoubtedly a move to stem any Japanese inclination toward *revanchism* and resurgent militarism, although it also has implications for the Chinese dialogues with the Soviet Union and the United States. See "Chen Yi Questioned on CPR-Japan Relationship," *Tokyo Sankei,* and Peking, in Japanese to Japan, 09:00 GMT, January 19, 1965.

nuclear capability than by an equal capability in the hands
of any other Asian state. In particular, the heart of the industrial complex as well as a number of urban centers would be
open to a Japanese attack utilizing no more than short-range
delivery systems.[92] Added to this is the fact that historically
and traditionally Japan is the quarter from which China has
been attacked. This may not be a strictly rational consideration but there is no doubt whatsoever that it exercises a real
influence on the Chinese. In fact, this fear is more realistic and
less surprising than the comparable Soviet fear of a resurgent
Germany.[93] Despite the evidence of the postwar years the
Chinese even today show very definite signs of mistrusting
Japanese political intentions and objectives.

At this time, it is highly likely that the Japanese would
reject any Chinese encouragement or support in the nuclear
field even in the unlikely event that it were offered. Even
though both short-term and long-term Chinese interests generally point toward opposition, there are perhaps two reasons
for a conceivable Chinese interest in a Japanese nuclear program. Such a program might lead to a political split between
the United States and Japan,[94] and then the United States
might lose its bases in Japan and the latter would no longer
be a forward bastion of the United States in the Far East.
The probabilities of this occurring, however, seem very small
in the near future and the risks to China in gambling on such
a development seem very great. A Sino-Japanese agreement
on a *détente* and some kind of joint nuclear program are
equally unlikely. Such a development would require a prior
Japanese split with the United States, and it would also re-

92 There is now reliable information that the Japanese have made
much progress in the development of rockets, ostensibly for purposes of
orbiting satellites, that would be more than adequate to deliver nuclear
bombs against large portions of China.

93 The Japanese gross national product (GNP), for example, is far
larger than China's, while there is no comparison between the GNP of
Germany and the far larger one of the Soviet Union.

94 The Chinese have repeatedly stated their desire that Japan should
"free itself from American control" as a prelude to improved Sino-Japanese relations. For a recent example see *Tokyo Mainichi* (in Japanese),
January 18, 1965, morning edition, and Peking, in Japanese to Japan,
09:00 GMT, January 19, 1965 (translation of details of Utsunomya's interview with Chen Yi).

quire a radical upheaval in domestic Japanese politics since it is unlikely that the Japanese Socialists, the second major force in Japanese politics, would be much more willing to enter into such an agreement than the ruling Liberals.

Australia. There has been an almost total absence of statements on Australian military developments by the Chinese. This is particularly interesting in view of extensive Australian fears and discussions concerning China.

The Chinese would have every reason to oppose any Australian movement toward the acquisition of a nuclear force in the foreseeable future. This would be especially true if the Australians were to seek some kind of a nuclear sharing arrangement with the United States, a possibility that the Australians themselves have recently spoken of.[95] Australia is a full-fledged capitalist country and the acquisition of nuclear weapons by it would be as dangerous and destructive in the view of the Chinese as they now seem to claim it would be for any capitalist country. Chinese security interests would be involved, and an Australian nuclear program would only inhibit Chinese political moves in Southeast Asian areas such as the Maphilindo region. The negative quality of the contacts between the two countries in recent years only adds to the general reasons to oppose an Australian nuclear development. Even in the unlikely event that Australia could be separated from her alliance with the United States and New Zealand and brought into the framework of an "intermediate zone," China would have no desire to see Australia acquire a significant nuclear capability, since this would threaten Chinese dominance of the zone. This possibility does bring up, however, what is perhaps China's only short-term interest in an Australian nuclear program. If Australia should split with its allies as a result of an independent nuclear program, China might stand to benefit in a general way, although even here specific gains are hard to see at least in the near future. This line of development is presently so remote that the only reasonable conclusion is that China would oppose any nuclear

---

[95] On this point see A. L. Burns, "Measures Against Nuclear Dispersal in the Indo-Pacific Area," *Proceedings of the Seminar on Nuclear Dispersal in Asia and the Indo-Pacific Region, op. cit.,* pp. 89–93.

program for Australia, if this possibility is considered at all
by the Chinese leadership.

Other Areas

In certain non-Asian areas of the world China's interests
in modest programs of encouragement and support for nuclear
diffusion may make such a policy look rather desirable. In
general, the Asian countries have the greatest saliency in
China's foreign policy calculations, with the result that considerations of proliferation in other areas of the world come
through in a somewhat fainter form. But it is worth noting
that the long-term disadvantages, especially, appear to be less
emphatic in the non-Asian cases. Security and power considerations are attenuated simply by the geography of the situation. While long-range delivery capabilities may also prolifer-
ate in the future, potential threats from the Middle East,
Africa, or Latin America undoubtedly do not weigh very
heavily on Chinese thinking. And in most cases China is in
the position of an outsider seeking to woo the non-Asian
countries rather than protecting already-established relationships. In this connection, the need for political bait may appear substantial.

The most outstanding considerations in these areas are,
therefore, short term and political. And here the objective of
extending political influence beyond Asia becomes an important factor in the calculations on the proliferation issue. In
short, the shorter-term considerations are likely to become
more dominant in the non-Asian context. Even here, however,
any Chinese support for proliferation that does develop is
likely to remain very modest in its proportions because the
relationships with the countries involved are tentative rather
than close, many of the countries are simply unprepared to
handle a significant nuclear program, and there are a number
of short-term negative considerations.

The Middle East. The most outstanding candidate for
Chinese interest in the spread of nuclear weapons in the Middle East is Egypt. In fact, Egypt has been involved in several
of the very cautious and circumscribed actions that China

has undertaken in recent months. An agreement on scientific and technical cooperation between the two countries was signed in Cairo in January 1965.[96] In itself, such an agreement has few implications for proliferation, but in this case the agreement was followed in April by an announcement in the informed Egyptian newspaper, *Al Ahram,* that Egyptian scientists were to be sent to China to receive training at China's nuclear installations.[97] Whether or not this plan has yet been implemented is not known, but this does indicate that China is at least willing to hold out the possibility of nuclear aid where this seems to suit its purposes. Moreover, during the spring of 1965 the Chinese spoke several times of the possibility of a visit by President Nasser[98] in an obvious attempt to win political friendship in Egypt.

There may be several short-term gains for the Chinese from offering nuclear aid to Egypt. Above all, Egypt may very well be a test case for the notion that political capital can be made by offering various countries aid that they cannot get from the United States or the Soviet Union. And there is no doubt that the Chinese are interested in bringing the Egyptians over to their side in the political war with the superpowers. In addition, considerations of Afro-Asian solidarity and the establishment of a meaningful "intermediate zone" are probably relevant. On the other hand, the Chinese have reason for caution in handing out nuclear aid to Egypt: the Egyptians continue to deal actively with the West and with the Soviet bloc and they have played an active role, together with the Indians, in disarmament negotiations, especially at the Eighteen Nation Disarmament Conference.

The other major candidate for the acquisition of nuclear weapons in the Middle East is Israel. The Chinese, however, condemn Israel as little more than an imperialist minion directed primarily by forces in the United States. As they themselves recently put it:

[96] NCNA, Cairo, January 13, 1965, *SCMP,* No. 3380, January 19, 1965, p. 30.

[97] See *The New York Times,* April 9, 1965, p. 2, citing an AP dispatch from Cairo of April 8, 1965.

[98] For a reference to the proposed Nasser visit see "Red China: An Insistent Presence," *Newsweek,* March 15, 1965.

Israel is a tool of aggression created by U.S. imperialism and a dagger pointed at the heart of the Arab world. It is a special detachment for creating tension in the region and threatening the peace and security of the Arab people.[99]

Moreover, the Chinese have lined up strongly with the Arabs on Middle Eastern issues, especially on the Palestine question. And they have announced that they will continue to have nothing to do with Israel in the future.[100] Far from having an interest in the spread of nuclear weapons to Israel, the Chinese might be further encouraged to give a certain amount of nuclear aid to Egypt.

Africa and Latin America. The relevant considerations in these areas are almost entirely political. Most of the countries involved do not have the capacity to support a serious nuclear program and might very well reject nuclear aid if it were offered. At the same time, however, this very fact suggests that token nuclear aid could be extended to certain countries in order to reap various political gains without serious long-term disadvantages, since a little nuclear aid is unlikely to have any real impact either for security or in terms of encouraging rivalry for leadership of the third world.[101] The positive considerations would lie in such factors as the campaign to detach countries from Soviet or American influence, the comparative advantages of the notion of aid, and hopes for the eventual development of Chinese political strength as a leader of the third world. It is also possible that the Chinese may consciously approve of any action that has a real potential for stirring up conflict and confusion in the third world on the grounds that the anti *status quo* power is the one most likely to gain in such a situation.

At the same time, there would probably be real dangers for the Chinese in undertaking any moves toward nuclearizing Africa or Latin America. Such moves might bring a harvest

---

[99] Commentator, "China Backs Arab People's Just Struggle," *Renmin Ribao,* translation in *Peking Review,* Vol. VIII, No. 12 (March 19, 1965), p. 11; see also "Premier Chou Answers Questions of Middle East News Agency," *Peking Review,* Vol. VIII, No. 15 (April 9, 1965), pp. 8–10.

[100] *Peking Review,* Vol. VIII, No. 12, *op. cit.,* pp. 11–12.

[101] It is possible that something of this kind has already been broached in certain African countries.

of ill will down upon the Chinese. Sentiment against nuclear weapons is very strong in both of the continents, and a state attempting to intrude on the nuclear issue would be dealing with a very delicate and politically sensitive matter. Finally, nuclear assistance programs in these areas might catalyze a strengthening of American political operations in the same areas, to the long-run disadvantage of China.

Europe. In Europe the most significant country is West Germany. There are several points of hardheaded interest that, in theory at least, might lead the Chinese to favor German acquisition of nuclear weapons. Such a development could very well revive the Soviet Union's interest in the cold war, thus preventing her from becoming ideologically soft and willing to sell out the interests of world communism to the capitalist states. And while the Soviets were regaining a more acceptable approach to the progress of world communism, they might also turn their attention primarily to Europe leaving the Chinese a free, but not unsupported, hand[102] in Asia. Moreover, movement toward a German nuclear capability might either stir up conflicts among the European powers or lead to significant splits in the Western alliance that the Chinese might consider desirable.

Despite this, the Chinese have, in fact, come down repeatedly and explicitly against the spread of nuclear weapons to the West Germans. During the 1963 polemics, the Chinese went so far as to accuse the Soviets of selling out on the German issue, leaving China to uphold the correct position of opposition to German *revanchism.* In more recent times, the Chinese have explicitly indicated their support for the German Democratic Republic[103] and repeated their opposition to the nuclear arming of the West German revenge seekers in the strongest terms.[104] In this connection, the Chi-

---

[102] A more militant Soviet Union would probably bolster its nuclear guarantee to China although it might not have much time to take a very active part in Asian politics.

[103] See, for example, *Renmin Ribao,* editorial, April 9, 1965, reprinted in *Peking Review,* Vol. VIII, No. 16 (April 16, 1965), pp. 19–20.

[104] For an example consult the article by Commentator, *Renmin Ribao,* July 5, 1964, reprinted in *Peking Review,* Vol. VII, No. 43 (October 23, 1964).

nese have opposed the American MLF proposals right from the start.[105] Moreover, in recent months they have been increasingly negative toward the prospects of any additional capitalist country acquiring nuclear weapons. This bears some resemblance to their outlook on Japan — in terms of such factors as fear and ideological inflexibility.

China and the Control of Arms

As an alternative to the spread of nuclear weapons, China may become interested in negotiating a nonproliferation agreement either with the United States alone or with both of the superpowers.[106] China has important long-term interests that argue against the development of accomplished proliferation. As set forth in the preceding section, there are both direct security and political interests that fall into this category and that might increase Chinese support for a nonproliferation agreement. A more specific long-term interest in this area relates to Japan. It is already clear that the Chinese are very much worried about the possibility of a resurgent Japan with serious nuclear capabilities, and they might well be tempted to prevent this through the development of a nonproliferation agreement.

There are a number of more short-term and tactical interests that would probably be served by the negotiation of such an agreement. It would almost certainly constitute acceptance of China's status as a bona fide great power in world politics. And in general there would be a number of positive prestige benefits that would accrue to the Chinese from being treated as an equal by the United States or by both superpowers. Moreover, it would give the Chinese leave to continue their own nuclear program while setting up barriers to the development of significant nuclear capabilities by additional states. In this connection, the genuine fears of an American attack on their nuclear installations would also be allayed. Finally,

---

[105] See Chou En-lai's report to the third session of the National People's Congress in December 1964, NCNA, Peking, *SCMP*, No. 3370, January 1, 1965, p. 16.

[106] For a discussion of this possibility see Halperin and Perkins, *op. cit.*, p. 74.

the Chinese would certainly utilize their participation in a nonproliferation agreement to forward a reputation for reasonableness and responsibility. All these factors add up to a fairly substantial interest in negotiations to halt the spread of nuclear weapons. The payoffs seem especially positive if Chinese national interests are emphasized above the more ideological ones of world communism.

All this is not to argue, of course, that there are no powerful interests militating against a decision to enter into negotiations on a nonproliferation agreement. In fact, the present balance of interests on this question probably assigns preponderant weight to the negative consequences. To begin with, the Chinese have a number of short-term and essentially political interests that would be sufficiently served by certain limited support for national nuclear programs to make the longer-term negative possibilities worth the risk. The advantages of a nonproliferation agreement would have to outweigh those to be gained in its absence. And the fact that some of the most important advantages of such an agreement would be primarily long-term ones makes their influence on Chinese decision-making doubtful. Moreover, China with its more ideological, long-term concern for political hegemony and the spread of communism may well favor a policy that keeps the international arena stirred up and oppose actions such as a nonproliferation agreement aimed at producing a stabilizing influence on international politics. Implied here is a general proposition that the promotion of disruption and chaos is generally advantageous for the revolutionary power. Related to these points is the fact that an agreement against the spread of nuclear weapons would also tend to reduce Chinese flexibility and to create difficulties for using the proliferation issue to best advantage on a pragmatic and *ad hoc* basis.

There are also a number of more specific and immediate disadvantages that might persuade the Chinese not to enter into negotiations for a nonproliferation agreement. It is quite possible, for instance, that the Chinese may be very wary of doing any concrete business with the United States on the grounds that such a posture would reduce the credibility of their assertion that the United States is the arch imperialist and therefore the principal enemy. In addition, the Chinese would probably be very hesitant to enter an agreement that gave the United States the impression that it could get what it wanted from China without making any significant concessions. In terms of intrabloc relations, an agreement might very well appear dubious on the grounds that it would contradict and probably weaken the Chinese position vis-à-vis the Soviet Union on such matters as the struggle with international imperialism, the policy of peaceful coexistence, and the proper course to be pursued in forwarding world communism. Finally, there might well be a danger that acceptance of such an agreement would jeopardize China's potential leadership in the third world and in a third political bloc, since it might well be taken as a sign that China was accepting regular membership in the "nuclear club" and beginning to side with the other nuclear powers on the allocation and distribution of influence in the international arena.

There are some additional factors that would have an important bearing on the Chinese attitude toward an agreement on the spread of nuclear weapons. The first of these concerns the question of commitment. Regardless of concrete interests, it is possible that the Chinese have got themselves so committed to a policy of noncooperation with the United States until there has been some "normalization" of relations[107] between the two countries that they could not seriously consider entering into a nonproliferation agreement. Such a stance might be based on a combination of factors concerning (a) prestige and "face," (b) the inculcation of an anti-American bias into the mesh of bureaucratic relationships, and (c) ideological constraints and scruples related to dealing with the "enemy." The history of past Sino-American relations certainly suggests that these factors have operated with some real force on a number of occasions. On the other hand, the Chinese political system is organized in a manner that should facilitate flexibility on such issues and a rapid change of policy

---

107 "Normalization" of relations in this connection would refer to a settlement of the recognition issue and therefore of the Taiwan problem as well.

following a decision at the highest level. The two countries have, in fact, managed to conduct negotiations from time to time in arenas such as the Warsaw meetings. And there is some evidence to suggest that the Chinese might even now be willing to reach a "no first use" agreement with the United States providing the latter would accept stipulations such as voluntary implementation.

A second factor concerns the form of the proposed agreement and, in particular, the differences between a Sino-American agreement and a more nearly world-wide arrangement negotiated by, say, the United States, the Soviet Union, Britain, and China. For some time now analysts have been saying that an agreement including China, Russia, and America is impossible because any meaningful great power agreement would have to be based on the existence of either the East-West cleavage or the Sino-Soviet rift. This might make a Sino-American agreement more likely than one involving the Soviet Union as well. More recently, however, the possibility of an arrangement involving all three powers has arisen in several discussions of the issue. In particular, a calculation that tended to de-emphasize ideological motivations might turn up real advantages of a tripartite arrangement over a bilateral one. From China's point of view, it might be argued that the broader agreement would go further toward inducting China into the upper echelons of the great powers in the world and that if it were to agree to any nonproliferation agreement, it would want one that could be extended most easily to a number of additional states.

A final factor can be stated in terms of side payments. The Chinese might very well feel that they ought to gain some extra concessions from the United States as a price for entering into an agreement against the spread of nuclear weapons. This possibility would be based on the existence of several asymmetries. The United States might be more anxious to achieve such an agreement than China. But above all, the Chinese would have an interest in exacting a price for compromising their reputation as a revolutionary and violently anti *status quo* power. Concessions on the Taiwan issue would probably be most desirable for China but politically impossible for the United States. Alternatives might involve the offshore islands, American intervention in Southeast Asian situations such as Vietnam, the existence of various American military bases and installations in Asia, or the hold that the United States has on certain aspects of Japanese foreign policy.

Conclusion

It is not yet clear how Chinese interests in nuclear proliferation will develop in the future. Several comments on the zigzags in Chinese declaratory policy, which were discussed earlier, may, however, be in order at this point. There are good reasons to suppose that the Chinese do not have a substantial positive interest in proliferation for its own sake. In this light, the predetonation attitude toward nuclear diffusion begins to look more and more like a tactical and instrumental one. On the other hand, the Chinese now seem to have a number of political interests that can be forwarded by a judicious and cautious policy of manipulation. This is especially so if the main weight of their decisions falls on the balancing of short-term considerations. In this connection, the Chinese may well undertake various steps with positive implications for the spread of nuclear weapons without being at all in favor of accomplished proliferation over the longer term. Certain moves since the 1964 detonation may stem from uncertainty and the absence of a clear policy in this area at present. But the explanation offered in an earlier section that the proliferation issue is essentially an instrumental factor in the larger and primarily political context of Chinese foreign policy interests in Asia and the third world is the most useful one in explaining the developing Chinese approach to nuclear diffusion.

While the Chinese are now somewhat ambivalent about their old position, their attitudes are still a far cry from those of the Soviet Union. The Soviets give every evidence of generalizing their negative view of proliferation to all cases and they appear to be acquiring the typical American fears of the statistical dangers of proliferation. The Chinese, on the other hand, are willing to utilize the issue for political purposes. They are less worried about the potential dangers of proliferation than the Soviets and they appear to be more confident of their own ability to achieve political gains with the issue without losing control.

3

Arms Control: Can China Be Ignored?

JEREMY J. STONE

Introduction

In October 1964, the People's Republic of China exploded a nuclear weapon. This focused reluctant attention on questions of arms control that many had been content simply to ignore — conceding only that they would arise in time. Would it be possible to reach comprehensive agreement with the Soviets in the face of Chinese opposition? Would it be impossible to prevent the spread of nuclear weapons after a Chinese explosion? Would Sino-American conflict, or the threat of it, destroy informal agreements already reached? And what would be the effect of admitting China to formal disarmament talks? This paper discusses each of these questions in turn.

China and Superpower Treaties

When the world perceived the first Chinese detonation, it was persuaded that China's participation was now especially necessary for the achievement of arms control — arms control thought of as substantial reductions or general disarmament. But these agreements are unlikely to be achieved for a variety of other reasons; the Chinese posture is only a particularly simple way of establishing agreement on this fact — an accepted shorthand. Moreover, this shorthand is very likely misunderstood by most who use it. China does not, strictly speaking, pose important technical or strategic problems to such a major power treaty as a freeze of levels and characteristics of weapons.[1]

China as a Strategic Constraint

At no foreseeable time would China's forces become so strong that they could neutralize a U.S. retaliatory blow through active defense or pre-emptive attack.[2]

For example, it would require many hundreds of Chinese missiles, all of very long range, before a substantial number of the 1,000 U.S. Minuteman missiles would be threatened. And even were it possible to attack these forces effectively,

1 The United States, in early 1964, suggested that the major powers and their allies should explore the possibility of a "verified freeze" of numbers and characteristics of weapons. The notion seems to have been something like this: at an agreed and predetermined date, each major power would have continued to buy strategic missiles and aircraft only to the extent necessary to replace stocks — missiles worn out or used up — and would let the other monitor the production of replacements. Replacements would be either of the same "type" or of "similar exterior appearance," or would be controlled by some other formula that compromised the desire to constrain improvement with a hesitation to permit the inspection of interiors of missiles. The freeze would have prevented the deployment of antiballistic missile systems on the grounds that these systems would otherwise make it impossible to maintain constraints on offensive weapons.

2 By June 1965, the U.S. strategic missile force was composed of 54 Titan II missiles (Range 14,000 miles), about 33 Polaris submarines with 16 missiles each (Range 1,700 to 2,850 miles) and 750 Minuteman I missiles (Range 6,300 miles). Although the Polaris fleet will grow to 41 submarines by the end of 1966, only a few are to be based in the Pacific; the majority are assigned to cover Soviet targets and are based in the Atlantic and adjoining areas. Because Minuteman I evidently does not cover Chinese targets, there is a strong interest in extending the range of U.S. land-based missiles. The planned addition of 200 Minuteman II, and their subsequent substitution for 750 Minuteman I as these wear out, will "substantially" increase their range, according to the Department of Defense. Assuming that "substantially" means more than about 30 per cent, the problem of range will be resolved as this model is installed over the coming years. Until it is resolved, a relatively greater interest in maintaining strategic bombers can be expected. The existing bomber fleet numbers 14 heavy-bomber wings (45 planes each) of B-52's, 2 medium-bomber wings (45 planes each) of B-58's, and assorted replacements and training craft.

there is no way in which China could threaten even a few, much less all, Polaris submarines — their simultaneous destruction is quite impossible even for the Soviets. Finally, it will be many years before the Chinese can build an effective ballistic missile defense even around single sites.

In any case, it would take so long for our forces to be threatened by those of China that the on-going benefits of a treaty with the Soviets could be enjoyed for substantial periods of time; the problems of a Chinese force could be treated, when and if they arise, through the application of an abrogation clause. Put another way, no clear strategic threat to our security would arise from China if we *unilaterally* ceased to improve our forces for many years. Since there would presumably be some advantages — all things being equal — to securing a comparable halt from the Soviets, the case for a freeze on major power forces would be, in principle, largely unimpaired by the Chinese force. Speaking generally, a freeze involves much greater problems in coping with a volatile technology or with the threat posed by Soviet forces than it does with China. It is the former that places the most severe constraints on the probable lifetime of the freeze and on its design.

As the Chinese target system grows, we shall find that we wish to be able to target increasing numbers of missiles upon intermediate-range missile sites, submarine launching pens, and so on. This could probably be done in a variety of ways even under a freeze, if the will to do so existed. Thus, we might squeeze out of improvements in missile efficiency (reliability, yield, retargetability) the extra missiles required for the Chinese; that is, we might learn that we required fewer missiles to be assured of the previously specified degree of destructive ability against some Soviet target. Alternatively, we might reduce slightly the class of Soviet targets or the assurance of their destruction that the force now provides. This would not pose any serious problems — except those of inertia and bureaucracy.

It is also important to recognize the time span to which these considerations are relevant. The Chinese target system may not grow substantially for ten or fifteen years. By that

time, we may have given up completely on the targeting of
Soviet forces and reverted to a posture in which we neither
threaten, nor intend to make, large-scale attacks on Soviet
strategic forces in case of war. This change in our posture
would free many hundreds of missiles for other purposes.

Much of the same reasoning can be applied to substantial
reductions. As far as our fear of strategic attacks from China
is concerned, very little is required for deterrence. The extent
of the reductions possible would, of course, depend upon
what one thought necessary to deter the Chinese; if the destruction of one Chinese city were politically and strategically
satisfactory, a handful of submarines might be the only force
that one needed to retain. If much greater destruction were
thought necessary, for one reason or another, greater numbers
of submarines and perhaps some land-based missiles or bombers would be useful. But, unless one believes that China would
be willing to lose very substantial fractions of its population
and industry, the United States could admit first or second-
stage reductions (that is, 30–60 per cent reductions across
the board). Indeed, a reduction that cut numbers of U.S. and
Soviet forces by 30 per cent would probably decrease the efficiency of the forces by no more than the typical increase in
efficiency each few years through improvements and modifications. Of course, for such plans as general disarmament we
should require Chinese participation, but these agreements
are not only politically unrealistic but conceptually clouded
as well. In general, it is again the major power balance, and
the problems of technology, that put the relevant technical
constraints on our ability to negotiate a treaty.

While China does not threaten the technical feasibility of
a comprehensive superpower treaty it would discourage ratification and could tempt a withdrawal of those treaties that
it could not discourage. This is mainly because we might want
to defend against Chinese missiles — though vulnerable to
Soviet ones — and because we might want to maintain the
threat to strike Chinese missiles or bases — though unable to
threaten those of the Soviets. Thus, China could be left out,
if we wanted to leave her out. But we probably would not
want to. The problem is not whether we can ignore a grow-

ing Chinese strategic "threat" but whether we wish to leave our hands free to deny China the ability to deter us.

China as a Strategic Provocation

The reasons for our temptation to maintain a strategic ascendency over China are fairly clear. We fear a continuing clash of U.S. and Chinese commitments and interests in Asia. We wonder if a Chinese strategic force would enbolden the Chinese to press their claims by releasing them from the residual fear of U.S. attack. And we are tempted to maintain the capacity to threaten to exploit our strategic advantages in order to compensate for our obvious disadvantages in any Asian conflicts.

In addition, the United States can probably defend itself relatively well against Chinese threats. The temptation to do so through the procurement of suitable strategic defensive weapons is a strong and important influence on arms procurement, not only — as some will argue — because such defenses might come in handy if a losing battle in Southeast Asia seemed to call for threatening China but also because we are motivated to do what can be done. Paradoxically, it is because China is a *minor* strategic threat that it may have a *major* impact on our willingness to spend money to defend against it. In short, a tough political posture combined with a weak strategic force can be explosively provocative in their impact on U.S. arms policies. And this is how China looks to us.

Even under the most restrictive freezes that the United States could want, and the Soviets accept, many changes in the defensive systems of both sides would be permitted. Antisubmarine warfare (ASW) capabilities would not be controlled in any foreseeable U.S.-Soviet agreement simply because these activities do not lend themselves to control; for this reason, some U.S. responses to a growing Chinese submarine fleet would be possible even under an agreement. Nor would bomber defenses be constrained in any plausible treaty. As a result the major obstacle to ignoring China in a freeze proposal arises neither from the temptation to defend against Chinese bombers nor from the urge to prepare to destroy

Chinese submarines at sea. The central problem concerns the temptation to protect against future Chinese missiles with active defenses. Some background concerning ballistic missile defense is therefore appropriate.

For five years or so the Defense Department in the United States has been deferring the procurement of antiballistic missile systems for a variety of reasons. At the beginning the systems would not work; then they were not effective against offensive improvements that could easily be installed by the Soviets; at times they required more tests; and at times newer systems were likely to be much better.

Most of these objections, perhaps all of them, were weakening when the Chinese exploded their first nuclear weapon. Dr. Harold Brown, then Director of Defense Research and Engineering, had testified that Nike-X was about the best system we might expect to have for ten years; its need for tests seemed to be measured in months, not years, and estimates of its effectiveness did not reflect the pessimistic tone of past years. At this critical juncture the case for building a defense got an immense boost from the Chinese explosion, which dramatically brought home the prospect of future threats; indeed it suggested a family of new threats from new nuclear powers, though China may well be the only member of this family for a few decades.

These were threats that might be met. Our progress in building missile defenses had been enormous; it was a countervailing progress in offensive weapon technology and expectations of further progress that had made active defense a dubious proposition. The Chinese threat was made to order for active defenses not quite up to a major Soviet attack.

This is not the place to describe the significance of ballistic missile defenses in the contest between superpower strategic weapons. Suffice it to say that many believe that an at least temporary lull in strategic weapon procurement was possible if, but only if, both sides could restrain themselves from effective efforts to achieve protection against nuclear war. In the absence of such restraint, we or they or both would find ourselves compelled, in part by our reliance on deterrence, in part by the long lead times required by major power weapons, and in part by the uncertainty of the future, to step up weapon procurement in certain areas.

These problems were recognized by the U.S. freeze proposal in those provisions that called for a freeze on missile defenses. It was generally accepted by most defense analysts that a freeze on offensive weapons *only* was not feasible. When the pressures for a defense against Chinese missiles emerged, the question was reopened.[3] We felt greater interest in a freeze that permitted ballistic missile defenses to be installed. And, because the U.S. defense contemplated was generally expected to be "inadequate" to defend against Soviet missiles, it was generally thought desirable to reconsider such reasoning as had presupposed *major* defensive efforts. Perhaps we and the Soviets could overlook the construction of minor defenses; or perhaps after all the deterrent capacity of each would far exceed its requirements even after the other had made large defensive expenditures.

The extent to which we and the Soviets could acquiesce in lower, or apparently lower, capacities for deterrence is not, in the first instance, determined by strategic considerations. It is really a question of domestic and international political factors and of bureaucratic tendencies. Because the Soviet defensive system is more likely to be directed against ourselves than the Chinese, because we would like our capacity to penetrate such defenses to be well beyond political controversy or international doubt, because we believe that we can make it so, and because we have become adjusted to this political luxury, we are very unlikely to restrain our offensive response to Soviet defense systems — much less to certify, in a treaty, that we would make continuing efforts to do so. It should be added that the Soviet willingness to restrain its procurement of offensive weapons — also reflected in the treaty — would be a relatively minor consideration in our reasoning. Our concern has always been to assure ourselves first that our

[3] William Beecher reported in *The Wall Street Journal* of July 26, that the odds for a U.S. start in fiscal 1967 were 60–40, that there were shreds of evidence that the Soviets were starting to deploy a system in northeastern Russia, and that the United States had some new notions on the feasibility of a truly nationwide defense, at least against Chinese missiles.

deterrent capabilities were adequate to both our political and strategic needs; only after these fears have been allayed, and sometimes not even then, have we concerned ourselves with protection against the effects of war — with fallout shelters, air defense systems, and so on.

It is argued with some force, however, that the *Soviets* would be more willing than we to agree to a freeze if the treaty permitted the deployment of missile defenses; their relative interest in defenses has been greater than our own.

It should be added that the distinction between minor and major efforts to build a ballistic missile defense can be easily exaggerated. Any defense that we might buy would certainly — considering the cost-effective Defense Department — be built in such a way as to permit improvements. And these improvements would have a relatively high likelihood of being made, after the initial breakthrough to procurement had been effected. In any case, the Soviets might not have any clear indications of how far we intended to go upon which to base any restraint that might be incorporated in their responses.

Furthermore, technology willing, a minor defense this year may be better than last year's major defense. And in its impact on the computations and concerns of those who would maintain the ability to penetrate the defense, it may appear formidable if it is effective only against a disrupted and disorganized attack. We often tend to measure the efficiency of our defenses in terms of their capacity to protect against an initial onslaught; but others may consider them from the point of view of ensuring a retaliatory capability. Their concern can easily precede our satisfaction.

Nor will it be easy to control deployed ballistic missile defenses by treaty. There are no obvious aspects of the system that can easily be monitored and that signal clearly and unequivocally the nature of the system installed. It may be possible to imagine an agreement in which defensive batteries are limited to a few selected cities. But aside from numbers of batteries, it is not obvious what to control. And if these batteries could protect wide areas — in an area defense rather than a point defense — a relatively small number might be associated with either the minor or the major defense. In general, there is nothing so verifiable and so easy to assess in its implications as no defense at all. It requires several years and large expenditures to bridge the gap from "no defense" to deployed batteries. Certainly, no comparable firebreak exists once defenses are deployed.

Thus even a minor system, either because it was effective enough; because it could not be controlled by treaty; because it was mistaken for a better one, or could become better; because it broke down the resistance in both superpowers to pursue defenses; or because it raised a new political issue and some fears concerning Soviet systems, could have a far-reaching and unfortunate impact on the shape of the arms race and on the prospects for formal treaties.[4]

China as a Willful Disrupter of Superpower Formal Treaties

It is not only China's posture and growing nuclear force that are provocative; China can follow a course designed to disrupt superpower agreements and their presuppositions. This is nowhere more evident than in the influence that the Chinese have upon Soviet willingness to come to terms with us. Generally speaking, Sino-Soviet relations, the demands of the international Communist movement, and the explosive combination of Soviet ideology, Chinese subversion, and U.S. commitments in Southeast Asia, can keep U.S.-Soviet relations unfit for arms control for decades. If the Soviets are sensitive to Chinese criticism or if they subordinate arms control and *détente* to influence in Hanoi and solidarity at home, China will reap the credit for obstruction.

---

[4] It is interesting to note, however, that if one can assume that ballistic missile defenses would have been procured in any case — perhaps because they became very effective or simply because one or both sides could not restrain themselves — then the Chinese explosions might have a dampening effect on the arms race. As a made-to-order excuse for U.S. defenses, and possibly for Soviet ones as well, China would take some of the political and psychological "curse" off active defense. Far from being an attempt to undermine the deterrent of the other side, the active defenses could be designed for a lesser and different purpose.

The vulnerability of arms control treaties to Chinese resistance is enhanced by our unshakable tendency to magnify and exaggerate China's capabilities. Because China is large in size, because her (long-run) destiny is that of a great power, because we tend to take people and countries at their own evaluation, and because China's evaluation of herself is high, we shall probably never find it possible to estimate objectively the period during which Chinese objections to arms control can really be ignored. And our fears of Chinese aims in no way encourage us to underestimate China's powers.

Demonstrations of China's growing power supplied to a ready audience are relatively indirect ways for China to make arms control more difficult. If important agreements seemed likely, if the problem for China ceased to be one of undermining or discouraging expectations but became one either of "preventive" action or of last-minute disruption of on-going negotiations, China might be expected to take more direct action. In the political sphere, the agreements might be analyzed shrewdly. It will not be easy for us to design agreements that cannot be portrayed effectively as Western deceptions put forward for a gullible Soviet audience; indeed, much of our literature would provide ammunition for such attacks, and the Soviets probably know it.

Action that was riskier, and more deliberately Machiavellian, could destroy U.S. willingness to engage in a U.S.-Soviet treaty by deliberately fanning fears and exciting attempts to protect against the Chinese. Threats to China's neighbor, as in Sikkim, attacks on the off-shore islands, and mobilization of forces might do just that. A popular antiarms control argument has been: "you can't disarm and arm at the same time." Certainly, if China willed it, this line would someday be applied to "disarming with the Soviets," while "arming against the Chinese."

While these possibilities exist for quiet or dramatic Chinese obstructionism, they may also provide their own answers on a growing resistance in the superpowers to playing the Chinese game. This might be reflected in an increasing tendency to form an anti-Chinese coalition, in a greater perceived need for arms control, or in a greater tenacity and stubbornness in the search for superpower goals. If we owed the test ban to the open emergence of the Sino-Soviet split, what might not be possible if Chinese abuse led to a Soviet downgrading of the diplomatic status of their Chinese embassy or if there was a showdown in North Vietnam in which the Soviet influence was rebuffed and the Soviet interest in that conflict correspondingly reduced. That the Chinese have certain avenues for disruption does not mean that inadvertently they might not catalyze a great deal more arms control than they could immediately preclude or prevent.

China as a Threat to Nonproliferation Agreements

In the long run, the shape of even the superpower arms race is sure to be influenced by the course of proliferation, and the arms environment of the rest of the world is, of course, deeply dependent upon it. In turn, the acquisition and continuing procurement of nuclear weapons by China is probably the most important factor in proliferation considerations. Only China is liable to catalyze *several* arms races and to cause as widely separated countries as Japan, Australia, India, the United States, and the Soviet Union to seek new offensive or defensive systems. China has not been ignored in this regard, will not be, and cannot be.

We recognize the effect of past Chinese detonations in encouraging new nuclear powers. But these acts are only the beginning of a long series of Chinese experiments with nuclear weapons and delivery systems. If China responded to serious efforts toward a nonproliferation agreement with nuclear detonations and dramatic missile firings, her point would be missed by no one.

In the proliferation area, still more direct action might arise from Chinese willingness or apparent willingness to share weapon technology with others. If the Chinese hold out hopes to the Egyptians of selling them weapons, if they offer to share control over nuclear weapons, or even if they seem to be sharing their technology, a nonproliferation treaty close to ratification might still be prevented.

At the moment it is not clear, though it soon will be,

whether the Chinese nuclear explosion will be able to claim the credit for a rapid succession of nuclear detonations in surrounding countries and, perhaps in turn, throughout the world. The initial ripple of fears and pressures has spread; it has reduced the barriers to nuclear ownership, but perhaps not decisively. If not, much may depend upon the course of technology and later decisions made by the Chinese.

Not least among the factors of interest to China's neighbors will be its attitude toward its nuclear weapons — how it talks of, deploys, and actually uses them. So far China has been as circumspect as one might wish; its unilateral and unqualified assertion that it would not use nuclear weapons first is the strongest such statement made by any nuclear power. But China might not, if it felt otherwise inclined, acquiesce in what has become a world-wide campaign to discredit the use of fission or fusion reactions. For this it need not attack an Indian mountain pass, destroy a wandering submarine, shoot down a reconnaissance airplane or satellite with a nuclear weapon, or in some other way repudiate its pledge against first use. It might simply use nuclear devices rather freely in peaceful activities of interest. It might, in this way, artfully undermine the world-wide resistance to nuclear weapons and the resentment over its achievement of nuclear status. This would, moreover, undermine the test ban and all other comparable agreements that restrict above-ground peaceful uses. But all of this could undermine, as well, U.S. inhibitions against the first use of nuclear weapons; this is probably the major Chinese deterrent to such action at this time.[5]

Encouraging the use of nuclear weapons is not the only way in which Chinese proliferation efforts could backfire. Many latent fears of a world without arms control may be encouraged. If Chinese actions or words seem to deny the theory that caution cannot be separated from nuclear status, if China seems likely to give nuclear assistance to powers that are even less trustworthy than itself, if it refuses to go along with arms control, indeed, if it simply produces unknown and inscrutable leaders that conjure up a picture of the need for arms control, we may be the beneficiaries. It is, for example, not unrelated

5 A suggestion made by Morton H. Halperin.

to the Chinese bomb that, as the *The New York Times* recently reported, a high level report has chosen to seek a nonproliferation treaty rather than a multilateral force. The threat produces its response and, in the absence of details, it is not easy to be sure where the net effect will be.

China and the Destruction of Tacit Understandings

Perhaps most important, the Chinese threaten the presuppositions of many informal agreements. At present, especially, they threaten the existence of an on-going, and promising, U.S.-Soviet dialogue. Whether their ability to do this stems from a struggle over influence in Vietnam or from their ability to inflame internal Soviet dialogues is less important. If the Soviets are afraid to talk, and if their talks are unlikely to lead to understandings that are easily implemented, we shall have lost our ability to repair the ravages of Chinese actions and, in general, to make other progress.

Second in importance, and only second because the question of U.S.-Soviet dialogue largely includes it, are the questions of informal agreements involving proliferation. To the extent that U.S. and Soviet reluctance to assist *N*th countries arises from an agreement to trade restraint for restraint, China may catalyze not only U.S. but also, in turn, *Soviet* willingness to change its policies. If our actions in Asia influence our position on proliferation in Europe, if the Soviet position on Eastern European nuclear weapons depends upon our position on Western Europe, or, especially, if we and the Soviets are capable of competing with offers of nuclear weapons in the Middle or Far East, we are surely risking the loss of an important and existing informal agreement to avoid nuclear spread.

More generally, we and the Soviets now have a mutual interest in keeping Africa and Latin America free of nuclear weapons. While we see no present prospects that this convergence of interest could be threatened with an African or Latin American bid for nuclear power, the Chinese could undermine our hopes for an early establishment of the appropriate nuclear free zones. There is, first of all, the influence of a new nuclear power from which aid might come, encouraging those who might wish to become "renegades" in the eyes of a Western-Soviet coalition against nuclear spread. And what if Chinese submarines were to be given the right to land at certain African ports and what if they, like us, refused to say whether or not they had nuclear weapons on board? This sort of thing can be troublesome.

One popular and well-advertised U.S.-Soviet agreement concerns the right of countries to use the upper atmosphere and outer space for satellites. It may be that this understanding does not accord with Chinese preferences and that the Chinese achieve relatively early the ability with which to disrupt or threaten it. It may become relatively easy, as defensive measures go, to destroy reconnaissance satellites. If the Chinese are disinclined to let themselves be observed without harassment, if they dislike the notion of being ignored when the U.S.-Soviet agreement is worked out, if they hold legalistic, idiosyncratic, and bold opinions on their "rights" to the airspace above their heads, they may well wish to assert themselves and will be hard to ignore. At least they could, in this way, win the right to assent graciously to peaceful overflights, to harass unannounced flights, and to be informed of activities and negotiations concerning outer space. These are large gains.

It is not only in the air but also in the ocean that China might assert or provoke bolder claims than are customary. For example, a growing Chinese submarine or surface fleet might require or desire a little more elbowroom against the possibility of hostile eyes, quiet blockades, or quarantines. For our part, the threat posed by Chinese submarines might provoke quiet or open claims to very large defensive areas — much like those of World War II in which we monitored the activities of potentially hostile vehicles.

These possibilities can interact with one another but also with Soviet submarines, especially those that might now, or later, be stationed off our coasts. If we chased these away, would the Soviets act similarly in areas under their control? If we destroyed submarines, would we set back the course of informal oceanic U.S.-Soviet understandings by many years? And what if the Chinese destroyed a submarine? We cannot ignore Chinese actions or our own response to them.

This leads to a discussion of the problems of arms control in war. It is possible to argue that a certain number of agreements are already either established or well on their way to being established; by and large, these are imperiled, but rather more by the existence of China than by her willful action.

First, and possibly most important, is the tendency of the nuclear powers to support a policy of no first use of nuclear weapons or at least to express a general reluctance to act otherwise. While China entered this debate with a strong and quite unequivocal assertion of its willingness to abide by the rule, it may nevertheless trigger events that will destroy the understanding. It was, for example, widely reported that the United States had issued a warning to Peking, through a private channel, of its willingness to use nuclear weapons over Vietnam if necessary. Whether or not this warning was passed in this form, it was certainly the subject of provocative background briefings in Washington and, during the last campaign, the subject of much discussion by Senator Goldwater. This sort of thing in no way helps to maintain the world-wide revulsion against nuclear weapons or to preserve the expectations of governments that nuclear weapons will not be used; and both of these effects are important.

In any case, the possible contingencies in which nuclear weapons might be useful to us in Asia have probably undermined permanently the chance for our accession to a no first use agreement.

Considering the unresolved problems in Asia, the next most significant arms-control-in-war agreement may involve sanctuaries. Again China is putting strains on notions that were usefully increasing in strength. On July 11 Secretary of State Rusk announced:

> It is important that they [the North Vietnamese] discover that they are not going to be permitted to send tens of thousands of men into the south to attack South Vietnam and still live in safety and comfort at home. The idea of the sanctuary is dead in this situation and that's something that *all of the others* who may be supporting Hanoi must take fully into account. (Italics added.)

Furthermore, background statements suggested that Red China had been told it could not expect immunity from reprisal if it joined an attack and that it, in turn, had made known its comprehension of the U.S. position. This, as well as the bombing of North Vietnam, is making it more difficult — for good or ill — to limit the scope of future conflict in Asia; it may also be making the notion of sanctuary more difficult to apply to U.S.-Soviet conflicts in Europe as well. This informal agreement is tied up in notions of legality and in the concept of "sanctuary" itself. If it is because we support these notions in a wide range of circumstances that they have a compelling force, then our blatant denial of their utility in one or more important circumstances may impair this.

As the Chinese strategic force grows, it will begin to *enforce* the notion of sanctuary by threatening reprisals against violation. In turn, this will raise the idea of "kinds" of reprisals and hence the notion of controlled war. As in past years with the Soviets, we shall find ourselves supporting "no-cities" concepts that the Chinese will deny. While there is ample motivation for a "no-cities" doctrine in terms of the lives that might be saved in an exploding conflict, the fact remains that this doctrine is more favorable to the stronger power than to the weaker; without being able to threaten U.S. cities, China might pose little threat at all. If Chinese statements reflect earlier Soviet objections, and if the ballistic missile defenses that we purchase for the Chinese threat complicate, psychologically, our interest in agreement on the inviolability of cities, we may fail to perceive any Chinese awareness of our offer. This means that while we ourselves might take care to put many options in our war plans and to plan for controlled general war, the Soviets and the Chinese might not think it worth the money and, as important, might make no contribution, however subtle, to the expectations upon which control might depend.

The Chinese have unusual abilities to threaten the disruption of U.S.-Soviet war calculations. Their political posture permits them to threaten to respond to attacks upon the Soviets with reprisals of their own. If they were so generous as to make this offer — perhaps to embarrass the Soviets into a firmer reciprocal guarantee — our expectations for control might be correspondingly diminished. The prospect of a Chinese attack during a U.S.-Soviet war would be, at the least, a complication to prewar thinking. For that matter, if the Chinese build submarines, their capacity to offer world-wide support of Communist aims with nuclear firepower could even complicate expectations of keeping war limited in Europe. Thus, were the Soviets to lean toward support of such notions as limited war, the Chinese might argue for a suitable *unlimited* rebuff to NATO aggression. Pehaps the main point is that the Chinese may restrict severely the extent to which the Soviets can acquiesce in, or learn to anticipate, limits on war.

Somewhat surprisingly, it may be that the Chinese will support and encourage notions of limited strategic attacks while denying the less sophisticated, controlled general war. Chinese willingness to calculate limited attacks, evidenced in their odd-day attacks on Quemoy; their inability to respond rationally with an all-out attack; the number and proximity of proxies for the United States that would be suitable for limited responses; and the likelihood that attacks upon China would themselves be similarly limited in scope, all encourage the possibility. It may therefore be logical to expect the Chinese still to talk in terms of proportionate rebuffs and tit-for-tat reprisals. In this case, they might go further than the Soviets have in contemplating, and hence generating, different ways to raise tension and increase violence.

In the long run, the most pervasive effect that China may have upon the strategic weapons arms race could arise from a reputation for a combination of inscrutability and a willingness to calculate. If what they may be expected to believe, and to be capable of doing or of failing to do, is an important ingredient in the reciprocal construction of informal understanding, then the Chinese will generate an altogether different image than the Soviets. This will play its role for good or ill in any and every conflict.

Arms Control as a Chinese Weapon

Finally, something should be said in recognition of the fact that China is likely to *use* arms control as well as to disrupt it.

Thus, China may have a price for agreement. It put itself in the position of a last reluctant obstacle. It may become the spearhead of a force that will not now but might later, on suitable terms, adhere to agreements. Certainly a group of nations will arise for whom China is the excuse — the rationale — for their own failure to ratify a proliferation agreement. To this extent China will be able to demand that arms control agreements be redrafted, that she be seated in appropriate councils, even the United Nations itself, and that we acknowledge the importance of her eventual acquiescence to the agreement. These are important considerations. If China were seated in the Eighteen Nation Disarmament Conference, it would be even more difficult to design agreements around her and even more "obvious" — whether true or not — that Chinese participation was essential. If China seeks to be heard in order to enhance her importance, and if that importance is parlayed into a virtual veto over any meaningful arms control, then we shall indeed have problems.

China's use of arms control is not likely to be limited to a search for status. China has already offered, unilaterally, not to use nuclear weapons first; through this act, it presumably seeks to make a Western use of nuclear weapons against it more difficult. But no first use does not exhaust the list of similar attempts to manipulate arms control proposals. Foreign bases in the Pacific may replace foreign bases in Europe as the subject of interminable arms control negotiations. Chinese support for a nuclear-free zone in the Pacific may parallel Polish proposals for Europe. And if the Chinese are clever and thoughtful in their formulation of the proposals, neither proposing the impossible nor the meaningless, they may generate a certain amount of support.

Prognosis and Summary

As far as major power treaties are concerned, present and future problems with China could be managed if the will were there to manage them. If the United States and the Soviet Union feared the current actions of each other more than they wished to maintain certain types of nuclear superiority over the Chinese, it would be possible to design treaties that ignored China for a very long time. That this will be done is, however, unlikely. The prospects, short- and long-term, for comprehensive arms control agreements have never been good enough to impede, substantially, the pressures to achieve those military capabilities for which there is a modest case — and in psychological terms, if no other, China presents a good deal more than a modest case. China will therefore probably trigger a new round of expenditures on active defenses that might — but only might — have been avoided had the Chinese detonation never occurred. Thus its impact on the superpowers' arms competition is likely to be a catalytic one: one that encourages expenditures disproportionate to its threat. These expenditures will be produced through exaggerated responses and through the reciprocal perception in each superpower of the other's reactions and of the political and strategic threats that these pose.

U.S.-Soviet agreements that are not comprehensive will suffer mainly from Soviet sensitivity to Chinese attack. For the Soviets, and the Chinese, arms control agreements will be political indications signaling a coordinated opposition of Western and Soviet governments to China. From China's point of view, a U.S.-Soviet arms control agreement is a primitive but still significant form of military alliance against her — a military alliance not only because it refers to things military but also because it presupposes a common interest in military actions and, by the same token, a common willingness to defend these interests. Thus, any major U.S.-Soviet arms control treaty would raise in Chinese minds the question of how far either or both superpowers might go to enforce arms limitations (or other requirements) upon the Chinese — with the acquiescence or support of the other. To this extent, a U.S.-Soviet treaty could, in fact, be expected to have a sobering effect on Chinese foreign policy; is it impossible that the Soviets might seek it for this reason?

The best hopes for arms control in the face of Chinese resistance probably stem from this possibility. If a U.S.-Soviet coalition begins to form, the interests of the majority will be to strengthen it, and these interests will feed on the hostility of the isolated party. While this influence of China on U.S.-Soviet relations is not restricted to arms control, arms control does play a salient and unique role. Of all the areas in which the Soviets could first justify an interest in agreement with the West, arms control is probably the best. It is not only because the *mutual* interests in arms control are so dramatic and so well advertised; it is not only that we have been making continued efforts in that field or even that several areas of arms control are increasingly ripe for agreement; it is perhaps most important that arms control is an agreement that is justified between adversaries. If any agreements seemed, in principle at least, to provide a small target for Chinese attack and an easy Soviet transition, it might be those that talk about, and hence reflect, the opposition between the superpowers.

There is another reason why, in the long run, U.S.-Soviet arms control agreements may be the initial and unintended result of Chinese intransigence. It may be that both the United States and the Soviet Union will perceive a common interest in a military isolation, if not containment, of China. Even the Soviet Union may feel more secure if it perceives the prospects for quietly threatening joint U.S.-Soviet action against China. This action may be only diplomatic; the threats might reside only in the way in which U.S.-Soviet relations had been shaped to help carry them out. And the Soviet motivation might only be to undermine Chinese eagerness to press its border claims or simply pique at Chinese anti-Soviet statements. But if so, there may be a good case and a strong market for relatively minor agreements that ignore China and are meant to do so, perhaps even pointedly.

It is a particularly difficult period in which to assess the impact of future Chinese weapon developments and statements on the prospect for nonproliferation agreements. While these actions, in principle, add little to the problems of proliferation that were not posed by the first Chinese bomb, they do present heightened political problems. In part because it is extremely difficult to imagine a country giving up its nuclear status, and in part because it requires only one administration in a country to give it such a status, one can speculate that a gradually increasing number of countries around the Chinese periphery will "go nuclear" and that these will eventually include Japan, India, and Pakistan. But even in this case, there will be a continuing problem of "ignoring" China for countries that have to decide how much they should rely upon the United States. Whichever way proliferation goes, China will play a continuing role in its course.

More generally, the course of arms control considerations cannot be assessed without projecting the course of future political relations; this is difficult indeed. If weapon systems have deployment lives of only five to ten years, changes in political alignment have shown that they are no longer lasting. Thus we may find that the missile defense developed to defend against the Soviets may be installed to defend against the Chinese, and the understandings reached with the Soviet Union may be of central and unexpected use to us in coping with China. By the same token, five or ten years from now, we may find an altogether different political orientation in which our weapons and understandings are reorientated in ways of which their designers never dreamed.

While these considerations reflect how short the "long run" may really be, they also reflect the futility of concerning oneself too strongly with it. If sensible arms control can be achieved now, if its advantages exceed its disadvantages, we should engage in it. If China can be ignored now, perhaps we shall be able to do no less later; perhaps it will not need to be ignored or wish to be; and, for all we know, it may be Soviet actions or our own that are provoking the most problems for arms control at some future date. For the present, China has made nothing impossible except her own adherence to a nonnuclear status in a nonproliferation agreement. She has made a great deal more difficult and she may be destroying, or be destined to destroy, some of what has already been achieved. But, for the most part, her impact on arms control is what we let it be, what we make it.

4

The Chinese Factor in Soviet Disarmament Policy

HELMUT SONNENFELDT

The chief purpose of this discussion is to suggest areas of inquiry that might shed additional light on the way in which China may have influenced Soviet disarmament policy in recent years. This is not intended simply as an excursion into history but as an effort to elucidate one of the factors contributing to Soviet decisions in this field.

It should be remarked right away that one must be careful not to exaggerate the Chinese factor in Soviet disarmament policy. There are obviously many others that play their part as well: domestic political considerations, relations with the East European countries, relations with less developed countries, relations with the West, including Soviet assessment of the strategic "correlation of forces," and sometimes perhaps even disarmament considerations per se. In recent years there may have been a tendency to look too much to the Chinese factor in seeking explanations for Soviet behavior in the disarmament field, partly because the drama of the evolving Sino-Soviet split was so fascinating that all else seemed to pale in significance, and partly because "China" sometimes seemed a convenient explanation for Soviet moves that were otherwise baffling. Regrettably, as the following remarks will indicate, I am not sure that we can assess precisely what impact the Chinese factor has had at various times and how it has weighed relatively with other pertinent influences on Soviet behavior.

In considering Soviet disarmament policy I propose, rather arbitrarily, to break it down into four categories: (1) the tactics concerning convocation or disruption of formal disarmament conferences, (2) the formal proposals put forward by the Soviet Union, (3) the general thrust of Soviet disarmament propaganda, and (4) decisions, or what appear to be decisions, by the Soviet Union to negotiate seriously for an agreement. I recognize that these categories overlap and that one can easily devise a different set. Perhaps more seriously, this categorization leaves out the area of tacit arrangements, unilateral action, reciprocal unilateral actions — the whole question of how the Soviet Union disposes its forces, how it manages its command and control, how it manages crises, and so on, all of which may somehow be affected by the Chinese factor. But to consider these aspects of Soviet disarmament or arms control policy would vastly complicate an already difficult and obscure set of problems and I shall therefore leave them out of the present discussion.

Disarmament Conferences

Turning, then, to the first aspect of Soviet disarmament policy, I am intuitively inclined to think that the Chinese factor has played a considerable part in the way the Soviet Union has manipulated various conferences. But I believe some rigorous research is still needed to substantiate this supposition. In this connection, one should examine especially the Soviet disruption of the five-power U.N. disarmament subcommittee in September 1957, the agreement to constitute the Ten Nation Disarmament Committee in September 1959 (the committee actually convened March 15, 1960) and the Soviet disruption of that body in June 1960, the agreement to constitute the Eighteen Nation Disarmament Committee (ENDC) in September 1961, and, finally, the Soviet maneuvers around the reconvening of the ENDC in 1965.

One could perhaps add to this list the Soviet decisions in the spring of 1958 to agree to hold meetings of experts on the inspection of a possible nuclear test ban and on the prevention of surprise attack. The former, however, perhaps falls more properly into the fourth of the categories suggested because it seems to be part of a whole series of Soviet decisions that eventually led to the limited test ban agreement in 1963.

Of the cases listed, the Soviet walkout of September 1957 seems the least persuasive example of the operation of the Chinese factor. One might argue that because of the then pending negotiations with the Chinese and other Communist parties (culminating in the Moscow Declaration of Communist Parties in November) the Soviets considered that they should scuttle a disarmament forum from which the Chinese were excluded and in which issues clearly affecting the Chinese — such as that of conventional force levels — had been under discussion. While considerations such as these might have played a role, they seem farfetched, especially since the Soviet move can be plausibly explained in other ways. Thus, Moscow had long bridled at this particular forum with the line-up of four NATO allies against the solitary Soviet Union. In its mood at that moment — when the first ICBM test had just succeeded and the first Sputnik was being made ready — Moscow insisted on parity in disarmament forums and refused to join in talks again until parity in one form or another had been achieved. Moreover, Moscow's repeated expressions of frustration over the U.N. subcommittee's lack of accomplishment, although smacking of hypocrisy, may in fact have reflected its judgment that that particular body had run its course. In any event, termination of its existence fitted in well with the generally more demanding stance of Soviet policy in the autumn and winter of 1957–1958, resulting apparently from a view that the balance of forces was shifting significantly "eastward."

Nevertheless, there remain puzzling aspects to Soviet disarmament policy at this time. We know from the Chinese that some sort of nuclear aid agreement was reached between Moscow and Peking in October 1957. What its terms were is still unclear (although the Chinese claimed that it involved turning over a sample weapon at some point), but it is conceivable that the agreement was intended to compensate the Chinese should a test ban agreement be reached. Yet at this very moment the Soviets scuttled the forum in which such an agreement would have been negotiated. Did they do it, perhaps, to make the possibility of an agreement even more remote than it already was in order to deflect Chinese demands for rapid nuclear assistance? I have no answer to the question nor, indeed, any evidence bearing on it. To compound the puzzle, at the very moment the Soviets made their nuclear deal with the Chinese (whatever its precise content) they also, for the first time, made a proposal for nonproliferation of nuclear weapons at the U.N. General Assembly. The move may simply have been disingenuous to mask a disseminatory agreement with the Chinese. Or it may in some way have been part of the bargaining process between Moscow and Peking.

I raise these questions to emphasize that while I am reasonably sure that Moscow's disruption of the U.N. subcommittee was largely independent of the Chinese factor, there remain enough intriguing uncertainties to warrant further inquiry.

The next instance in the conference category that might merit further study is the Soviet agreement in early May 1958 to a conference of experts on inspection problems connected with a test ban. As already suggested, this decision probably belongs in the final category under my suggested scheme. In any case, I doubt that in this instance the Chinese factor played a role one way or the other in any active sense. At this stage, the Soviets and the Chinese seem to have been in general accord on how to pursue the test ban issue, particularly if one assumes that the 1957 nuclear assistance agreement was drawn up as part of such general accord.

Similarly, the Soviet agreement in July 1958 to talks on surprise attack is difficult to connect in any clear way with China. Moscow's objective in this move, as became apparent when the conference convened in the autumn, was to exert pressure on Western military arrangements in Europe.

Still, even if it is correct that the Chinese factor played no discernible role in the Soviet decisions to attend the experts' meeting of 1958, it is perhaps worth observing that these meetings helped establish the practice of East-West contacts on disarmament issues to the exclusion of China and probably contributed to some degree to Sino-Soviet difficulties.

Turning next to the agreement, announced in September 1959, to establish the Ten Nation Disarmament Committee, I again come to the disappointing conclusion that an active Chinese role is hard to discern in the Soviet decision. Still, we know from subsequent Chinese disclosures that Sino-Soviet relations had by this time encountered serious problems, and indeed the Chinese had claimed that Khrushchev had deliberately reneged on the nuclear assistance agreement in order to propitiate the United States. So it is possible that Peking considered as invidious the establishment of a new disarmament forum from which it was excluded and that it made its displeasure known to the Soviets. If so, the Soviet decision to go ahead with the Ten Nation meetings may have been taken without regard for Chinese objections. But this is pure speculation. What can be said with hindsight is that this committee and its eventual successor, the Eighteen Nation Disarmament Committee (ENDC), became the forums for discussions of general and complete disarmament (GCD), a subject on which the Soviets and Chinese were eventually to diverge sharply. But while it is likely that at the time the Soviets agreed to the establishment of the Ten Nation Committee they had already decided to launch their GCD proposal (September 17, 1959), it is doubtful that they already envisaged this proposal as a stick with which to beat Peking. Here again, it may be that additional research may turn up interrelationships not so far evident.

The Soviet bloc's walkout from the Ten Nation Committee on June 27, 1960, presents in some respects a more intriguing problem than the cases mentioned so far. On the face of it, there is a perfectly adequate explanation for the Soviet-inspired maneuver since this was the aftermath of the U-2 episode and the Soviets were generally making good their threat to halt further contacts with the U.S. government until President Eisenhower had been replaced in the forthcoming election. Moreover, the committee was getting nowhere and the West was about to make a new proposal that might have stolen some thunder from Moscow's own GCD panacea, which up to that point had been the focus of the committee's deliberations. So, to scuttle the meetings must have seemed a cheap but eye-catching way of underlining Moscow's indignation at Eisenhower's "perfidy."

What makes this event interesting in the present context is its coincidence in time with the Third Congress of the Romanian Workers' Party in Bucharest at which the Soviets and the Chinese for the first time openly crossed swords in earnest. Just how the Geneva walkout and the Bucharest altercation may have been related remains obscure. But it is possible that in anticipation of a period of intense intrabloc maneuvering Khrushchev wanted to disembarrass himself of the Geneva forum, where, apart from dealing with the United States, he also had to coordinate the positions of the Communist members, some of whom may have disappointed him by their lack of full support for his onslaught against the Chinese at Bucharest. In the ensuing weeks, during which occurred the haggling leading up to the eighty-one parties meeting, Khrushchev at any rate could concentrate on that important event, undistracted by Geneva and innocent of any Chinese charge that he was conniving with the American imperialists. Some day perhaps evidence will come to light to support an interrelationship such as this; for the moment I can base my suppositions on little more than a striking coincidence in dates.

Soviet agreement to the establishment of the ENDC, in September 1961, — as well as to the statement of agreed principles that was negotiated simultaneously — falls into the period of preparation for the Twenty-second CPSU Congress, preparation, that is, for the attacks on Stalin and Albania that were to occur at the Congress. It may be that at some time in this period Khrushchev decided to burn certain of his bridges, as far as catering to Chinese sensitivities was concerned, and was prepared to make an effort in the disarmament field, regardless of Chinese opposition to it.

The negotiations leading up to the agreement on the ENDC and the statement of agreed principles are a somewhat curious episode: they came at the height of the 1961 Berlin crisis. A U.S. delegation headed by John J. McCloy was actually in

Moscow (the talks had begun in Washington in June, then moved to Moscow in July and concluded in New York in September) when President Kennedy announced U.S. military moves to meet the Soviet challenge in Berlin. I have always thought that Moscow's willingness to proceed with these talks, and to make the adjustments in its initial position that were necessary for eventual agreement, may have involved some crisis management at this time of considerable tension: an effort to set some limit to the deterioration in American-Soviet relations. In addition, of course, the Soviets managed, in the agreement to set up the ENDC, to achieve the participation in disarmament talks of a number of nonaligned states, something Moscow had long advocated in hopes of appealing to sentiments in the third world and of getting from the latter support against the West. I would not rule out, however, the further possibility that the September 1961 agreements were, in Khrushchev's mind, in part directed against the Chinese at a moment when he was contemplating some quite serious steps against China and Albania at the Party Congress.[1]

I am inclined to think that Soviet maneuvering around the reconvocation of the ENDC in the spring of 1965 had a good deal to do with China. It seems clear — Soviet statements on this point may be taken more or less at face value — that the post-Khrushchev leaders had from the beginning of their tenure been engaged in reshaping the tactics to be followed in the dispute with China. They set out to reduce the cruder and more uncouth aspects of Khrushchev's approach; to tone down, if not to mute entirely, the virulence of open polemics; to remove as much as possible from the Soviet position the most vulnerable elements of Khrushchev's era; and certainly to eliminate the increasingly bitter personal element that Khrushchev had injected into the dispute. At the same time,

---

[1] I may add parenthetically that I have always found Khrushchev's performance at the Twenty-second Congress a bit baffling. When the Congress was first announced, it seemed intended as an occasion to glorify Nikita S. Khrushchev as the creator of the third Party Program. In the event, however, the Congress became caught up in the attack on Stalin and Albania, and one of its high points was Chou En-lai's premature departure. The Party Program barely caused a ripple and what had started as a testimonial to Khrushchev ended up as a resounding demonstration of Communist disunity.

they began to contest more actively with the Chinese in areas that Khrushchev by default had tended to leave to the Chinese. They sought, in short, to reverse the emphasis of their policy. Under Khrushchev there had come into being a curiously ambivalent strategy made up on the one hand of virulent polemics and even direct threats, and on the other of a certain defeatism (for instance, vis-à-vis the Japanese Communist Party). The new leaders now combined greater verbal civility, and even offers of better state relations, with active attacks on Chinese strongholds in the international Communist movement and in the third world — one reason, no doubt, why the dispute before very long broke out with renewed violence.

In this context, the Soviets may have considered the ENDC, and the disarmament issue generally, as expendable in the early months of their new line toward the Chinese. At any rate, the Soviets at this time tended to speak very softly on those aspects of their disarmament position known to be obnoxious to the Chinese and to make some show of supporting the Chinese positions on the disarmament front. It may thus be that the Soviets were prepared to postpone the ENDC indefinitely (it had recessed in September 1964) or perhaps even to scuttle it altogether. As an alternative, they requested the convocation of the U.N. Disarmament Commission, composed of all U.N. members, hoping presumably to obtain from it a series of resolutions favorable to themselves and, perhaps, a ringing call for a world disarmament conference that might make the ENDC superfluous. If these were their aims, the Soviets miscalculated rather badly: the Disarmament Commission produced an overwhelming vote in favor of resuming the ENDC, and largely because of that, I believe, the Soviets found it necessary to return to Geneva in July 1965.

In this instance the Chinese factor may have affected Soviet decisions in an unanticipated way. Precisely because of the new decision to contest Chinese influence more actively in the third world, the Soviets found it difficult to flout the overwhelming vote of the underdeveloped and nonaligned countries in favor of the ENDC. I do not mean to imply that the return to the ENDC caused excessive pain to Moscow: once back at Geneva the Soviets no doubt found issues worth pursuing (for instance, nonproliferation and NATO nuclear sharing); and by July relations with China had again soured. But earlier in the year, the ENDC may have seemed to be one irritant in the Sino-Soviet relationship that could be dispensed with.

I have perhaps belabored this aspect of the topic more than it deserves. I do think that some fruitful research remains to be done here. One might perhaps make a tentative case that in periods of Sino-Soviet tension the Soviets have some preference for disarmament talks, though this is by no means the only factor that affects the decision. Conversely, one might tentatively conclude that in periods when the Soviets are seeking to placate the Chinese, or, at any rate, to reduce their vulnerability to Chinese attacks, they are prone to back away from disarmament talks. Here again, obviously, other considerations also play their part.

Apart from the paucity or ambiguity of the available evidence, any such generalization should, however, be treated with caution for another reason. The mere convocation of a disarmament conference is not on the face of it proof that the Soviets are seriously interested in disarmament. After all, these forums are frequently used for abuse of the West, for appeals to neutrals — for a whole variety of things not really germane to possible disarmament agreements. And the Soviets are quite capable of trying to propitiate the Chinese, or to reduce their vulnerability to Chinese charges, by assuming a totally obstreperous, agitprop posture at Geneva. Nevertheless, there is a symbolic quality to the convocation or disruption of disarmament conferences, and I am persuaded that to a degree at least the Chinese factor has played and will play a role in how the Soviets manipulate such conferences.

Disarmament Proposals

We turn next to a consideration of the Chinese factor and its relationship to the launching of Soviet disarmanent proposals. As in the previous discussion, there is a great deal of uncertainty and ample room for caution. For one thing, the timing of Soviet proposals is often governed by the availability of a suitable forum, such as the U.N. General Assembly. The content of proposals is often closely attuned to the mood at these forums, to the course and content of the particular debates into which the Soviet proposal is injected, as well as to many other extraneous factors.

Perhaps the most interesting Soviet initiative to examine in the present context is the Soviet GCD proposals of September 1959. Whatever may have been Moscow's other purposes in launching this proposal, it came to represent something of a burning of bridges in the Soviet polemic with Peking. The Soviets could have used it simply as the Chinese would have wanted them to use it: to pillory the aggressors and to expose the imperialists. But while using it in that way to some extent, the Soviets also chose to build around the proposal certain doctrinal assertions on the nature of imperialism, the preventability of war, and related issues. It is possible that the Soviets had not expected the Chinese to make an issue of the GCD plan because at the outset it had all the earmarks of a typical agitprop scheme designed to show Soviet devotion to the cause of peace. But before very long the Chinese did choose to make an issue of the whole rationale of the proposal — the notion of a "world without arms, a world without war" — and Khrushchev seemed quite willing to argue with them on that very ground. He was prepared to picture the Soviets as wanting peace and the Chinese as wanting war, the Soviets as willing to concede the existence of certain "reasonable" forces among imperialists, the Chinese as taking an undifferentiated view of all imperialists.

As time went on, indeed, Khrushchev became increasingly willing to make the GCD proposal, and its doctrinal trimmings, one of the key issues in the polemics with the Chinese. He evidently believed that it was a profitable issue on which to contest with the Chinese because of its appeal not only among the Soviet population but within the international Communist movement and the third world. In the end, the GCD proposal became not so much a means of exposing the "imperialists" (who, beginning in 1960 but especially after 1961, declared their readiness to engage in negotiations on the subject) but one of belaboring the Chinese. Conversely, when the post-Khrushchev leaders sought to tone down the blatantly anti-Chinese aspects of the Khrushchev line, they muted their emphasis on GCD.

It seems clear that in the later Khrushchev years certain Soviet disarmament proposals were designed to demonstrate Moscow's readiness to take positions regardless of Chinese opinion. This was probably the case with the various Soviet proposals in the long-drawn-out test ban negotiations both before the conclusion of the 1963 treaty and in the subsequent discussions of a comprehensive ban. Here again one could note a certain Soviet reticence in the months immediately after Khrushchev's fall. The same applies to Soviet proposals on nonproliferation. Perhaps the most obvious case of a proposal that Khrushchev must have known would grate on Chinese ears was the so-called "nuclear umbrella" idea in late 1962. This was a modification of the original Soviet GCD plan, made ostensibly in response to Western criticism: instead of calling for total elimination of all nuclear delivery vehicles in the first stage of disarmament the Soviets proposed the retention by the United States and the Soviet Union of a limited quantity of such vehicles through the entire disarmament process. To the Chinese, this must have appeared a glaring example of Soviet readiness to collude with the United States toward the establishment of an atomic monopoly — though in fact, of course, the Soviet move did little to solve the differences and complexities of East-West disarmament negotiations.

The year 1962 seems to have been a watershed after which the Soviets became increasingly willing to make proposals that would probably be opposed by the Chinese, although the exact moment when Khrushchev decided on this tack remains obscure. As late as May 1962 there still appeared to be some desire to avoid affronting Peking: at that time the Soviets suddenly withdrew from an agreement that had been substantially reached in Geneva on a declaration banning war propaganda. Some of the language of this document could have been interpreted as condemning certain types of war hitherto proclaimed as sacred by the Soviet Union. The whole episode remains a murky one, and precisely what motivated the Soviets to go as far as they did in agreeing to potentially embarrassing formulations and then to reverse themselves is still obscure. Because the issues involved were highly charged in the context of the Sino-Soviet polemic, a last-minute decision to avoid offense to the Chinese — or at least to avoid giving them a target to shoot at — cannot be excluded. By September, however, Gromyko was prepared to offer the "nuclear umbrella"; and in December, after the Cuban crisis, Khrushchev accepted a limited number of on-site inspections to police a test ban, a move that, in his eyes at least, may well have represented a significant step toward an agreement known to be opposed by the Chinese.

Soviet disarmament proposals in the months after Khrushchev's fall seem, as already indicated, to have been framed with an eye to avoid giving obvious offense to the Chinese. During this period the Soviets endorsed a world disarmament conference, which the Chinese had also done after their first nuclear test in October 1964; they disinterred once again their old proposal to ban the general use, but particularly the first use, of nuclear weapons, which, again, had been advocated by the Chinese. On the other hand, their advocacy of a comprehensive test ban, GCD, and the "nuclear umbrella" was soft-pedaled, and the West seemed to display greater activity on the question of nonproliferation than did the Soviets. This pattern held fairly constant until the summer of 1965. It is probable that with the deterioration of Sino-Soviet relations in 1965 the Soviets again felt fewer inhibitions in advancing positions known to be objectionable to Peking, though this did not of course mean that they were necessarily constructive from the point of view of reaching East-West agreements.

As a very general proposition, it seems safe to conclude that disarmament proposals have at various times played a role in Moscow's tactical conduct of the dispute with the Chinese, sometimes as a stick, sometimes as a carrot.

Disarmament Propaganda

The third category, Soviet disarmament propaganda, can be dealt with briefly. This is the aspect of Soviet disarmament policy in which the Chinese factor can be seen most plainly, because it is here that Moscow has actually taken on Peking directly and explicitly. Especially during the 1963–1964 period, when the dispute reached its most overt and virulent stage, Soviet propagandists took to defending Soviet disarmament positions against Chinese attack. This was true of the Soviet GCD proposal and then, pre-eminently, of Soviet participation in the test treaty and advocacy of a nonproliferation agreement. Soviet propagandists also actively defended the "hot line," the U.N. resolution against placing nuclear weapons into orbit, and the parallel U.S. and Soviet announcements of April 1964 regarding a cutback of nuclear production. In conducting the polemic, Moscow sought, in particular, to stress the danger of modern war, as against Chinese indifference to it; the resultant need to work toward agreements, as against Chinese opposition to them; the desirability of checking nuclear proliferation even within the socialist camp (the latter on the grounds both that Soviet nuclear weapons would defend their allies and that such proliferation would lead to proliferation in the West), as against Chinese thirst for nuclear weapons and indifference to the dangers of their further spread; the benefits of a test ban agreement, including those of halting contamination of the atmosphere, as against Chinese callousness on these matters.

These points are fairly obvious and well documented. It is perhaps worth observing, however, that in the course of the polemic Soviet statements tended to become increasingly harsh and categorical in their advocacy of a "prodisarmament" position and, under Chinese attack, provided lengthy rationalizations of the Soviet approach. The effect was to create, on occasion, overly optimistic assessments in the West of the prospects of reaching disarmament agreements with the Soviet Union, and to generate rather oversimplified notions of the Soviets "turning to the West." While the significance of Moscow's propeace and pro *détente* rhetoric in the context of the Sino-Soviet dispute should not of course be written off, its importance in practical terms must be measured against the actual positions that the Soviet Union was prepared to take on concrete issues in disarmament negotiations. And on this score the post-test ban period was not very encouraging: most of the long-standing disarmament issues, including, notably, the inspection problem, remained essentially deadlocked. Moreover, it must be recalled that throughout this period, and even more after Khrushchev's fall, the Soviets exempted revolutionary and "liberation" wars from the categories of conflicts that should be avoided. Indeed, precisely because the Sino-Soviet conflict involved to an important degree a contest for influence among revolutionary movements in the third world, Soviet moderation on direct East-West issues was largely offset by a high degree of militancy in regard to the "national liberation movement" — militancy not only in Soviet pronouncements but to some extent in Soviet actions. In this sense, the Chinese factor tended to inhibit Soviet disarmament policy, and this continues to be the case. (It is only fair to observe that just as Soviet polemics against the Chinese in favor of disarmament tended to create an exaggerated impression of actual Soviet willingness to come to terms in negotiations, Soviet verbal militancy about "national liberation" did not exclude a good deal of Soviet caution in particular third world crises and conflicts.)

Finally, it should be noted that as part of the revised Soviet tactics toward China after Khrushchev's fall, Soviet propaganda substantially muted explicit disarmament polemics. Thus, as previously suggested, statements tended to tone down Soviet advocacy of various disarmament measures obnoxious to the Chinese and stopped altogether the attacks on Chinese opposition to them. Moscow made no critical comment on Chinese nuclear tests: the Soviet press simply carried brief unobtrusive announcements of them; and Soviet discussions of nonproliferation focused almost exclusively on the evils of West German acquisition of nuclear weapons, a tactic that served to draw attention away from Chinese acquisition of such weapons (to which Moscow itself had contributed by its assistance program of earlier years). Even when the Chinese, later in 1965, resumed their open attacks on the Soviet role in the ENDC's nonproliferation negotiations, Moscow did not revert to Khrushchev's line but steadfastly bore down on the German angle. Some Soviet statements, indeed, made a point of stressing that any proposed agreement would be intended to prevent the spread of nuclear weapons to additional countries but would not affect the possession of nuclear weapons by existing nuclear powers — one of which China had meanwhile become.

Disarmament Agreements

We consider, last, the role of the Chinese factor in Soviet decisions to negotiate seriously on a particular issue and to reach agreement. This is undoubtedly the most crucial area to examine, because it is here that one can attempt to test the theory that a basic Soviet change of front in international affairs is occurring under the impact of the Chinese challenge, and that it involves, *inter alia,* an increasing recognition of parallel interests with the United States.

I do not propose here to undertake a review of the several negotiations that resulted in agreements in the disarmament field, nor of those that have not been consummated but that the Soviets may have been quite serious about. Others have attacked this formidable task and have attempted to correlate Soviet tactics in these instances with developments in the Sino-Soviet relationship.

My own general conclusion, on the basis of experience to date, is that it would be overdrawing the case to say that the Chinese challenge has driven the Soviet Union "westward" in its orientation. The most that seems warranted is that in several instances the Soviets have been prepared to conclude an agreement or arrangement that they judged to be in their national interest even though they knew it to be objectionable to the Chinese and realized that they would come under attack from Peking.

None of the agreements that the Soviet Union has so far concluded (the limited test ban treaty, the hot line, the U.N. resolution on nuclear weapons in orbit) can be said to be directly injurious to Chinese interests. The same is true of the parallel U.S. and Soviet declarations of April 1964 concerning a cutback in nuclear production. The two agreements that actually provide for prohibitions of certain military actions do not in practice affect the Chinese because they simply have not been adhered to; the other two arrangements apply solely to the United States and the Soviet Union.

It is conceivable that the Soviets intended to use the limited test ban in an effort to isolate the Chinese politically, on the assumption that Chinese failure to sign would produce resentment among substantial numbers of countries favoring the agreement. Any such Soviet calculation did not, however, prove to be valid: in the 1963–1964 period immediately following the test ban treaty the Chinese were recognized by more countries than in any other two-year period since 1950. Moreover, the Chinese failure to adhere to the treaty and their subsequent nuclear testing in defiance of it had no visible negative effect on voting trends in the U.N. General Assembly on the question of Chinese representation. Thus, even if one were to view Soviet signature of the test ban treaty as in part designed to injure Chinese interests indirectly, the effort came to nothing and was not, moreover, pursued in any active sense by the Soviets. I have heard of no instance where the Soviets might have urged a country to withhold recognition from Peking because the latter was boycotting the treaty.

Similarly, while the Chinese have made clear their opposition to the nonproliferation negotiations that have from time to time been held between the Soviet Union and the West, the Soviets can hardly be said to have engaged in these negotiations with any realistic expectation of injuring Chinese interests. Had an agreement been achieved before the first Chinese test, the Chinese would simply have refused to adhere to it, just as they refused in the case of the test ban treaty. And if the Chinese chose to adhere to a possible nonproliferation treaty once they became a nuclear power, they would only be obligating themselves not to disseminate nuclear weapons to others. It might be argued that if potential recipients of Chinese assistance were persuaded to adhere to a nonproliferation treaty, the Chinese would be deprived of possible objects for their attentions. But it is difficult to believe that any country seriously interested in receiving nuclear weapons assistance from the Chinese would sign a nonproliferation agreement. In sum, it is difficult to view Soviet participation in negotiations in this field as directly aimed at injuring

Chinese interests; and, indeed, it is reasonably clear from Soviet conduct that Moscow's principal concern was with the European, and more specifically the German, aspects (real or alleged) of the problem.

If one wanted to argue that the East-West arms control agreements so far reached reflected a Soviet decision to make common cause with the West against China, one would have to demonstrate that the Soviets were prepared to join with the West in forcing the Chinese to adhere to the agreements or in applying sanctions against them when they failed to adhere to them or when they acted in violation of their terms. But the experience of the test ban treaty does not point to any Soviet willingness, either unilaterally or in conjunction with others, to coerce or otherwise pressure the Chinese. It is conceivable that at some future time if China flouted the terms of some disarmament agreement to which the Soviet Union was a party, the Soviets might acquiesce in the application of sanctions by others. But this is a wholly speculative contingency and hardly a realistic one at present. What seems much more likely in the foreseeable future is that only arms control arrangements that the powers involved consider useful without Chinese participation, or in which Chinese participation is not relevant (for instance, the hot line), will be agreed upon. This does not, of course, preclude the possibility that the Soviets may enter an agreement for the additional purpose of making a political demonstration of their readiness to deal with the West in defiance of Chinese opposition.

In the present context it is also worth making the historical observation that really serious East-West disarmament negotiations have occurred for only relatively brief periods since the Sino-Soviet dispute became a fact of international life. Allowing for differences of opinion as to when that dispute seriously began, one would have thought that if it were driving the Soviet Union "westward," the process of serious bargaining, negotiation, and consideration of actual agreements between the Soviet Union and the West would have been more prominent than it has in fact been.

At the same time, it is of course suggestive that the 1963–

1964 period, which was the most virulent in the Sino-Soviet dispute, was also the most productive in U.S.-Soviet disarmament negotiations.[2] Nevertheless, it seems that, so far at least, a great many other elements apart from the state of Sino-Soviet relations must fall into place before the Soviets are prepared to join in conclusive negotiations on one or another arms control agreement or arrangement. In any event, the gathering momentum of understandings in the arms control field failed to be maintained in the period following the April 1964 announcements on nuclear materials production, a period that encompasses both the end of Khrushchev's rule and the beginning of that of his successors.

It must be noted again, too, that the Chinese challenge can have an inhibiting effect on Soviet willingness to negotiate seriously with the West. Undoubtedly Moscow's impulse to outdo the Chinese in striking a revolutionary posture in the third world serves to make certain arms control arrangements more difficult. And the fact that the Chinese challenge, in addition to other factors, has made Moscow more responsive to East European sensitivities has probably also inhibited Soviet disarmament policy. Thus, the concerns of the East Germans may have served to make the Soviet Union even more demanding in nonproliferation negotiations than it would have been of its own volition. In particular, it is conceivable — and there is tenuous evidence to be derived from a close reading of Soviet and East German statements in 1964 — that the Soviets might have taken a slightly less adamant view of the MLF if there had not been violent East German opposition to it.[3]

In sum, while it is possible to conclude that the dispute with the Chinese has made the Soviet Union more willing to consider arms control agreements in disregard of Chinese objections, it must also be noted that one can trace to the Chi-

[2] It should not be overlooked, however, that important agreements with arms control implications were achieved in earlier years, for instance, the statute of the International Atomic Energy Agency in 1956 and the Antarctic Treaty in 1959.

[3] It is clear, at any rate, that the Polish proposals in 1964 for a nuclear freeze in Europe, which the Soviets supported, would not have precluded formation of an MLF.

nese factor certain inhibitions on Soviet flexibility in disarmament negotiations with the West.

I emphasize that my purpose has been to indicate avenues
for further inquiry. Such conclusions as I have suggested are
highly tentative, and it is my hope that further study may
add clarity to what still remains a quite obscure subject, although one of considerable significance as both the Sino-Soviet
dispute unfolds and East-West disarmament talks proceed.

PART II

SINO-SOVIET NUCLEAR RELATIONS

5

Sino-Soviet Nuclear Relations, 1957–1960 [1]

MORTON H. HALPERIN

Since 1957 there has been a close and continuing interaction between the progressive worsening of Sino-Soviet relations and the policies of the two countries toward the development and control of nuclear weapons. This relation has been manifest over a number of different issues but most directly in the interaction between Soviet nuclear aid to China and Soviet efforts to negotiate a nuclear test ban treaty in the period 1957–1960.

The first possible divergence in the outlooks of Peking and Moscow toward the suspension of nuclear testing came in February 1956, when Khrushchev, in the words of the Chinese, "divorced the cessation of nuclear tests from the question of disarmament."[2] The Chinese add that from then on they supported Khrushchev when he was right and opposed him when he was wrong. However, the evidence suggests that it is only in retrospect that the Chinese became uneasy about the 1956 Soviet action. Prior to 1956 the two countries had

---

[1] This chapter has benefited from detailed substantive comments from A. Doak Barnett, William Gleysteen, William Griffith, Harold Hinton, Alice Langley Hsieh, Malcolm Mackintosh, Dwight Perkins, Helmut Sonnenfeldt, and Thomas Wolfe.

[2] "Statement by the Spokesman of the Chinese Government of August 15, 1963." Text in William E. Griffith, *The Sino-Soviet Rift* (Cambridge: The M.I.T. Press, 1964), p. 352.

agreed on a propaganda position that emphasized the need
to eliminate nuclear weapons. Neither China nor Russia
seems to have expected that these proposals would lead to
any agreements with the West, nor did they particularly desire any agreements except perhaps a ban on the use of nuclear weapons.

During the next three years, the Soviets were to emphasize
the desirability of a cessation of nuclear tests as a first separate
step.[3] The Chinese while accepting and endorsing test suspension tended to stress rather more than the Russians did
that the primary value of the test ban was as a first step
toward *total* nuclear disarmament. The period 1957–1960 was
also marked by extensive Soviet assistance to the Chinese nuclear weapons program. The relation between these policies
is explored in this chapter.

On January 14, 1957, the Soviet Union introduced a resolution in the U.N. General Assembly calling for a separate
ban on the testing of nuclear weapons.[4] At the London Disarmament Conference the Soviets began to press for a separate treaty banning the testing of nuclear weapons and
stressed the value of this measure, not only on humanitarian
(health) grounds but also as a means to halt the spread of
nuclear weapons. For example, the Soviet delegate to the
Conference, Zorin, described the value of a test ban as follows:

> The situation will be complicated by any increase in the num-
> ber of states in possession of atomic and hydrogen weapons.
> Clearly this complication will likewise affect the United States
> of America.
> If atomic and hydrogen weapons' tests are prohibited, the re-
> sult will be that, even if a country not now in possession of atomic
> or hydrogen weapons learns the secret of their manufacture and
> has access to the necessary materials, it will be unable to test
> these weapons effectively. Hence the prohibition of tests will
> seriously hinder the production and stockpiling of atomic and
> hydrogen bombs in other states. Obviously the security of all

---

[3] Lincoln P. Bloomfield, Walter C. Clemens, Jr., Franklin Griffiths,
*Khrushchev and the Arms Race: Soviet Interests in Arms Control and
Disarmament, 1954–1964* (Cambridge: The M.I.T. Press, 1966), pp. 93–97.
[4] U.S. Department of State, *Documents on Disarmament 1945–1959*
(Washington, D. C.: Government Printing Office, 1960), Vol. II, 1957–1959,
pp. 736–737. (Hereafter cited as *Documents on Disarmament 1945–1959.*)

states, including the United States of America, will gain from this.[5]

On the following day the Soviets publicly announced that they would be willing to accept a temporary suspension of nuclear tests.[6] On June 1, a Chinese spokesman on disarmament matters, Kuo Mo-jo, announced Chinese support for Soviet efforts to negotiate an international pact to end nuclear weapons tests.[7]

On June 14, 1957, the Soviets submitted to the London Disarmament Conference a formal proposal for an "immediate cessation of all atomic and hydrogen weapon tests if only for a period of two or three years."[8] At the same time the Soviets in a major concession to the Western position accepted the principle of international control over a possible test ban agreement. On July 11 the *People's Daily* supported a temporary ban on nuclear tests as a first step toward universal disarmament and complete prohibition of nuclear weapons. It condemned the United States' attempts to link the test ban with other issues as "hopelessly complicating the question."[9]

Several days later at the London Disarmament Conference, commenting on American questioning as to whether other "essential states" would in fact join the test ban treaty, Zorin specifically stated that China would adhere to such a treaty. He told the London meeting that he had checked a map and

> I found a great country — The People's Republic of China; and a great Asian power — India. I reflected whether there was any real reason why these two great countries, which in truth are

[5] United Nations Disarmament Commission, Subcommittee of the Disarmament Commission, Verbatim Record No. 91, March 25–26, 1957.

[6] Ciro E. Zoppo, "The Test Ban: A Study in Arms Control Negotiation," Ph.D. thesis, Columbia University, 1963, mimeographed, p. 431.

[7] Kuo Mo-jo at Peking rally, June 1, 1957, as reported by New China News Agency (NCNA), Peking, in English, June 12, 1957; reprinted in *Survey of the China Mainland Press (SCMP)*, (Hong Kong: U.S. Consulate General), No. 1544, p. 30. (NCNA English language dispatches datelined Peking are cited as "NCNA, date, in *SCMP*." Any deviation, such as a different dateline, is noted.)

[8] *Documents on Disarmament 1945–1959*, p. 791.

[9] *People's Daily*, Commentary, NCNA, July 1, 1957, in *SCMP*, No. 1571, p. 40.

among the "essential states in the world," should not accede to a treaty which halted atomic weapon tests for two or three years.

I do not think anyone, even our opponents, could have any grounds for such an assertion. Neither have I. For the People's Republic of China and the Republic of India have repeatedly proclaimed their whole-hearted support for a suspension of atomic and hydrogen tests. . . . What reason is there, then, to think that these two states would not accede to the agreement? I am aware of none. If Mr. Stassen has any in mind I should like to hear what they are.[10]

By mid-July 1957, the Soviets had taken a number of steps toward an agreement with the West for a treaty banning nuclear tests. They had accepted the need for international controls of a test suspension and had limited their demands to a moratorium of several years. In fact they had succeeded in convincing even the usually skeptical American Secretary of State, John Foster Dulles, that they seemed to be desirous of arriving at an agreement.[11] China was publicly supporting Soviet initiatives in this period, and Zorin, with only minimal probing from the American delegate, Harold Stassen, had assured the London Disarmament Conference that China would sign a test ban agreement. The Chinese made no move, as they were to do in 1960, to disabuse the West of this belief.

During mid-1957 there were also extensive Sino-Soviet discussions about nuclear weapons. The Chinese officer corps had focused, at least since 1955, on the importance of Soviet aid in the modernization of the Chinese army, and in particular in the development of nuclear weapons and modern delivery systems.[12] In early 1957 the Chinese apparently pressed the Soviets for an increase in assistance to the indigenous Chinese nuclear production, which apparently started in 1955. According to the account of the Chinese Communists, which was indirectly confirmed by the Soviets on October 15, 1957,

[10] United Nations Disarmament Commission, Records of the London Disarmament Conference, Verbatim Record No. 135, July 12, 1957, p. 16.

[11] See comments by Dulles in U.S. Department of State Bulletin, July 15, 1957, p. 101 (hereinafter cited as DSB), as quoted in Zoppo, op. cit., p. 62.

[12] Malcolm Mackintosh, Chapter 8. See also Ellis Joffe, Party and Army: Professionalism and Political Control in the Chinese Officer Corps 1949–1964 (Cambridge: East Asian Research Center, Harvard University, 1965).

the two countries signed an agreement to share new technology for defense.[13] Neither government has made clear the precise Soviet commitments under this agreement or what aid the Soviets actually gave to the Chinese. Judging from the current state of Chinese weapons capability, it appears that the agreement led to Soviet assistance in the development of an indigenous Chinese weapon production capability and was related to Soviet aid to an indigenous Chinese capability for the production of missiles, as well perhaps as submarines and other delivery systems. Despite a number of disagreements during the rest of the decade, Soviet aid to the Chinese nuclear program appears to have continued until mid-1960 and resulted in substantial assistance to the construction of a gaseous diffusion plant and several reactors, as well as the beginning of a missile production capability.[14]

There is very little mystery about China's motivations in seeking increased Soviet assistance for its effort to develop an indigenous nuclear weapons production capability. The Chinese had reached an industrial and scientific level where they could contemplate an acceleration of their nuclear production program, particularly if they could count on substantial Soviet assistance. Moreover, the Chinese were on the verge of launching their "Great Leap Forward" and were already in a mood to develop ambitious plans for industry, technology, and science. Given their long-standing desire to make China a great power, the Chinese leaders were anxious to press ahead as quickly as possible in developing nuclear weapons and, hence, would have welcomed substantial Soviet aid provided it did not involve Soviet controls. Khrushchev's motives in yielding at least partially to these demands and stepping up Soviet assistance to the Chinese program are much more obscure. In general the Soviet leadership was probably not happy about giving China the independent capability to launch a nuclear war. However, there were at least six factors that may have combined to make Khrushchev feel that it was desirable for

[13] Chinese government statement of August 15, 1963, in Griffith, *op. cit.*, p. 351; Soviet government statement of August 21, 1963, in Griffith, *op. cit.*, p. 365.

[14] Morton H. Halperin, *China and the Bomb* (New York: Praeger, 1965), pp. 78–82.

him to acquiesce in Chinese demands for aid to their nuclear program:

1. Khrushchev was faced with the fact that the Chinese were determined to go ahead with the development of nuclear weapons whether or not they received extensive Soviet assistance. Hence, Khrushchev's choice was not between a China equipped with nuclear weapons or a China dependent on the Soviet Union for nuclear deterrence. Rather it was between a Chinese nuclear program carried out in defiance of, or at least without the aid of, the Soviet Union, or a nuclear program carried out in cooperation with the Russians. In the latter case Soviet technicians would be involved in the program, giving the Russians considerable information about what the Chinese were doing and some degree of control over the evolution of the Chinese weapons development program.

2. During 1957 Khrushchev was engaged in a power struggle for the leadership of the Soviet Communist Party that was to see him purge first the anti-Party group in June and then Marshal Zhukov in October. Khrushchev undoubtedly was interested in securing at least the neutrality, and if possible the support, of the Chinese Communist Party in his effort to deal with opposition in the Soviet Union. His willingness to grant nuclear aid to China might have been part of his effort to ensure Chinese neutrality and possibly to convince the Peking leadership that their own security would be enhanced if Khruschev emerged the dominant figure in the Soviet hierarchy.

3. The Chinese had played a critical role during the latter part of 1956 and in early 1957 in helping to resolidify Soviet influence in Eastern Europe following the events in Hungary and Poland. Nuclear aid might have been in part a repayment for Chinese favors and support.

4. The Sino-Soviet agreement on advanced technology for defense was signed on the eve of the Moscow Conference, at which the Soviets hoped to have a manifesto approved that would form the basis for the unity of the international Communist movement. It was clear that there were some issues on which the Chinese and the Russians disagreed, and the Chinese had made it clear that they were prepared to argue

for their own position. Stepped-up nuclear aid could have been part of the price that Khrushchev paid to the Chinese to secure at least their partial cooperation at the November conference and their willingness to compromise on key issues in dispute.

5. Khrushchev was seeking closer military cooperation with Communist China during this period, and was to propose, in 1958, various kinds of joint military arrangements, including, it will be suggested later in this section, an agreement to station Soviet nuclear weapons on Chinese territory. It is possible that he viewed the granting of aid to the Chinese nuclear weapons production program as a useful backdrop with which to negotiate closer military cooperation with Peking.

6. Although there was a hiatus in negotiating forums in October 1957, Khrushchev had already taken the first steps toward a nuclear test ban agreement with the United States, and was to take further steps in 1958. A test ban at this time required the active participation of China. Khrushchev must have recognized that the Chinese would be suspicious of his effort to negotiate a test ban treaty if it appeared to preclude Chinese nuclear tests. He may have concluded that the most effective way to secure Chinese public and private support for the test ban treaty was to make such support a precondition for the granting of nuclear assistance.

Each of the considerations just presented probably contributed to Khrushchev's decision to yield to Chinese pressure and to accelerate aid to the Chinese nuclear weapons production program. It is possible that even at the time the agreement was signed, in October 1957, the Chinese had doubts about how much aid Khrushchev would really be willing to give them. They may have known that his decision to grant this aid was taken reluctantly and because of the pressures already discussed rather than because of any Soviet desire for an independent Chinese nuclear capability. The Chinese may, however, have had an interest of their own in a compromise at the November conference, and may have decided that public support for the test ban treaty was a reasonable price to pay for Soviet nuclear assistance.

There remained a dilemma of relating the Chinese determination to get nuclear weapons, and hence the need to carry out nuclear tests, with the Soviet desire to negotiate a suspension of nuclear tests to which China would be expected to adhere. It is possible to speculate that, as a result of discussion, a "test ban clause" was inserted into the Sino-Soviet nuclear agreement. The clause might have involved some specific further commitments by the Russians in case the Chinese were precluded from testing by an international agreement. More likely, it may simply have been an understanding that the Soviet Union would render such assistance as would be necessary to permit the Chinese to accept the test ban agreement.[15]

With substantial Soviet assistance, the Chinese could now look forward to the detonation of their first nuclear device, perhaps in 1960, and the development of an operational capability during the following years. This left the question, which was to be intensely debated in China during late 1957 and early 1958, of whether or not it would be desirable to have an interim arrangement under which Soviet nuclear weapons might be stationed on Chinese territory, presumably under joint Soviet-Chinese control. Such an agreement appears to have had the support of the Chinese military and to have had the acquiescence at least of Soviet Premier Khrushchev. The events surrounding this proposal, which will be discussed later, leave it unclear whether this was a Soviet initiative accepted by the Chinese military, or an initiative of the Chinese military accepted by the Soviet leadership. Mackintosh has suggested that Khrushchev sought closer military cooperation with China during this period and may himself have proposed the sharing of nuclear weapons under joint control.[16]

---

[15] It will be argued further on that the Chinese demands for increased assistance in June 1959 were related to the possibility of an impending test ban treaty. This argument lends some plausibility to the notion that there was a test ban clause in the 1957 agreement. Moreover, the existence of such a clause would be one way of making compatible the Chinese launching of a stepped-up nuclear weapons program with Soviet aid concurrent with the support of both countries for a test ban treaty. However, there was the further problem of reconciling whatever understandings were reached with the Soviet proposal for an agreement, submitted to the U.N. General Assembly in September 1957, that would ban the transfer of weapons.

[16] Mackintosh, *op. cit.*, pp. 12–20.

The Chinese military, for its part, may have been uneasy about the hiatus in nuclear protection until China had its own operational capability and may have sought to enhance the Soviet commitment by having Soviet weapons actually stationed in China. Whatever the origins of the proposal, it appears to have been discussed between the two countries and intensively within China itself, leading to a debate between the army leadership and the Party.

In October 1957, three Chinese delegations were in Moscow. Most publicized was the attendance of Mao Tse-tung and other Chinese leaders at the celebration of the Soviet Revolution and at the meeting of the ruling Communist parties. A Chinese military delegation led by P'eng Teh-huai was present with Mao and remained for a series of meetings after Mao's departure.[17] A scientific delegation led by Kuo Mo-jo, President of the Chinese Academy of Sciences, carried on negotiations, from October 18, 1957, to January 19, 1958, on scientific cooperation.[18] It is possible that the scientific groups concentrated on discussions of the implementation of the agreement on Soviet aid to the indigenous Chinese nuclear program and also other aspects of Sino-Soviet scientific cooperation. But there seems to be little doubt that Mao himself and particularly the military delegation discussed various nuclear sharing arrangements including, perhaps, the stationing of Soviet-made nuclear systems on Chinese territory, presumably under some form of joint control.

Public statements by Chinese military leaders calling for the utilization of Soviet technology began in late October 1957, just prior to the departure of the military delegation to Moscow on November 6.[19] On October 31, 1957, the *People's Daily* published an article by Marshal Liu Po-ch'eng, Vice Chairman of the National Defense Council. The article entitled "The Soviet Army is the Example for the People's Armies of the World" touched on both aspects of what the Chinese People's Liberation Army (PLA) might learn from

---

[17] NCNA, November 28, 1957, in *SCMP*, No. 1663, pp. 48–49.
[18] NCNA, Moscow, January 18, 1958, in *SCMP*, No. 1696, pp. 34–35.
[19] Donald Zagoria, *The Sino-Soviet Conflict, 1956–1961* (Princeton: Princeton University Press, 1962), p. 170.

the Soviet Union: political control and advanced technology. The question of whether the Soviet army should provide an example for improved political control of the army (presumably advocated by Mao and his political associates), or whether it could also provide the basis for a quick improvement in Chinese military capability, (as advocated by the professional army) was to be the major thread in the conflict evolving over the next six months. Marshal Liu felt that much could be learned from both aspects of Soviet accomplishments and stressed the up-to-date nature of the Soviet armed forces including their development of intercontinental ballistic missiles. He declared that the Chinese army would learn from "*all* Soviet advanced experience."[20] The nature of the conflict within China at the time was demonstrated in a statement by Chien San-chiang, perhaps China's most distinguished nuclear physicist, who on the same day, according to NCNA, discussed Soviet nuclear accomplishments. He pointed out that the Soviet Union had been the first to produce a hydrogen bomb that could be delivered and the first to launch an ICBM and an earth satellite, and he declared that the Soviet Union was leading the United States by a large margin. However, Chien argued not that China could borrow wholesale Soviet technology as the army was suggesting but rather that it must build up its own scientific capability following the pattern of Soviet scientific development. He declared:

> We must follow the Soviet pattern with scientific development and strive to build a scientific and technical force of the working class equipped with Marxism-Leninism, and to catch up with the advanced world levels in a period of two or three five year plans, helped by the Soviet Union.[21]

P'eng Teh-huai, the Chinese Defense Minister, apparently the leader of the group urging the acceptance of finished Soviet weapons, came out explicitly in favor of borrowing Soviet technology. He too reviewed Soviet military, scientific, and technological accomplishments and declared that the Soviets

[20] Marshal Liu Po-sheng, "The Soviet Army is the Example for the People's Army of the World," *People's Daily*, October 31, 1957, NCNA, October 31, 1957, in *SCMP*, No. 1647, pp. 26–30. Italics added.
[21] NCNA, October 31, 1957, in *SCMP*, No. 1645, pp. 27–28.

were now the world leaders. But from this he drew the conclusion that the Soviet armed forces could be the great example for the modernization of Chinese armed forces and "a modernization of our army may thus be accomplished with a reduction of roundabout ways."[22]

On the following day, two domestic radio broadcasts stressed the fact that the Chinese army would not be able to progress as fast as it had without Soviet help and without learning from Soviet experience. One of the broadcasts, quoting from an article by Marshal Ho Lung in *Red Star,* pointed out that Soviet experience would save the Chinese army time and effort in modernizing.[23] The same theme was reflected in a speech by Marshal Chu Teh on November 7 when he pointed out that the Soviet Union had done its utmost to render assistance to other socialist countries.[24] On November 30 the military delegation left the Soviet Union. P'eng Teh-huai, its leader, declared that

> The Chinese Communist Party and Comrade Mao Tse-tung had constantly told us to learn from the Soviet armed forces and learn all their advanced experiences. This aspiration of ours is being realized step by step through the immense aid of the Soviet people and the Soviet army.[25]

What appears to be the last indication in the Chinese press that China might soon get finished nuclear weapons from the Soviet Union, came on January 16, 1958, when the Chinese *Liberation Army Daily* published a report indicating that a new training program had been distributed to the troops and would finally be approved in June 1958. The

22 Marshal P'eng Teh-huai, "Learn from the Heroic Soviet Army," NCNA, November 4, 1957, in *SCMP,* No. 1649, pp. 28–30. See also Harold P. Ford, "Nuclear Weapons in the Sino-Soviet Estrangement," *The China Quarterly,* No. 18 (April–June 1964), pp. 160–173; and Alice Langley Hsieh, *Communist China's Strategy in the Nuclear Age* (Englewood Cliffs: Prentice-Hall, 1962). This interpretation while differing in important respects from both of these studies draws extensively on their research.

23 Ho Lung, "The Great Friendship and Shining Example," *Red Star,* broadcast on Chinese Home Service, Peking, November 5, 1957; Hsia Hua, "Long Live Solidarity Between the Armed Forces of the Chinese and Soviet Peoples," Chinese Home Service, Peking, November 5, 1957.

24 Speech at Soviet Embassy banquet, Peking, NCNA, November 7, 1957, in *SCMP,* No. 1651, cited from Ford, *op. cit.,* p. 161.

25 NCNA, Moscow, November 30, 1957, in *SCMP,* No. 1664, p. 51.

draft, according to the newspaper report, incorporated Soviet advance experience and prepared the army for training under "the modern conditions of atomic bombs, chemical warfare, and guided missiles."[26] It is possible that the training was related to enemy nuclear weapons, but in any case, the program was apparently dropped.

The decision to reject nuclear sharing arrangements seems to have been taken by early February 1958 when the Chinese line began to change; while it continued to stress the need to learn from the Soviet army, it emphasized the learning of political control. At the same time the press began to stress the need to build modernized weaponry based on Chinese industrial development. These changes reflected the settlement of a general Party-army dispute of which the nuclear weapons issue was only one facet.

On February 3, 1958, the first clear sign of the switch in emphasis came in a *People's Daily* article; reflecting the "Great Leap Forward," it declared that national construction at top speed was necessary if China's security was to be guaranteed, and that the building of modern industry would be a "prerequisite for modernizing our national defense," and it attacked the notion of depending on other people.[27] On February 14, Liu Ning-yi, Vice President of the Sino-Soviet Friendship Association, while stressing the importance of learning from the Soviet Union declared that in the not too remote future China would be an advanced, prosperous, powerful, industrialized nation. This would be necessary, he said, before military modernization could take place.[28]

On February 27, 1958, P'eng, speaking at a rally celebrating the fortieth anniversary of Soviet Army Day in Peking, signaled the retreat of the professional army group under his leadership from the effort to have the Chinese government agree to accept Soviet nuclear weapons. His speech made a passing reference to the up-to-date nature of the Soviet army

[26] "New Training Program Promulgated by General Department of Supervision of Training," *Liberation Army Daily*, January 16, 1958, in *SCMP*, No. 1786, quoted in Ford, *op. cit.*, p. 162, and Hsieh, *op. cit.*, p. 110.
[27] *People's Daily*, February 3, 1958, cited from *SCMP* in Ford, *op. cit.*, p. 166.
[28] NCNA, February 14, 1958, in *SCMP*, No. 1716, p. 18.

and its modern military equipment and indicated that the Chinese army must learn from the Soviet. However, what he felt China could learn had changed dramatically since his statements, and those of his associates, in the fall of 1957. Now he stressed that what was to be learned from the Soviets was their experience "in solving questions related to the building of the armed forces by means of Marxist-Leninist theories," and he went on to point specifically to Soviet experience in the relationship between the army and the Party, the army and the masses, and relationships within the army. P'eng made no mention in the statement of borrowing Soviet technology or advanced weapons equipment. In fact, he now emphasized the need to build up Chinese industry first. Thus he concluded:

> We are convinced that in coordination with the new leap forward in our national economy we will certainly build our army faster than ever into a modernized revolutionary army as excellent as the Soviet army.[29]

Three weeks later Kuo Mo-jo, in a major speech on the strengthening of Sino-Soviet cooperation in science, stressed the need for China to make active progress of its own in the newest branches of science and technology, including the atomic field.[30] On the following day an academy of military science of the PLA was set up to guide the army's study of military science. Marshal Yeh Chien-ying declared that the academy would make full use of the latest scientific and technical developments and carry out research in a planned way. He declared that the academy would combine the advanced Soviet military science with a study of the concrete situation in China.[31]

With the new line clearly established, the Chinese press began to carry discussions on what apparently was the heart of the issue whether or not to accept Soviet nuclear weapons, namely the question of how to deter an American attack on China before the latter had its own nuclear weapons capa-

---

[29] NCNA, February 22, 1958, in *SCMP*, No. 1717, pp. 26–30.
[30] Kuo Mo-jo, "A Realization of a Big Leap Forward in Science," in *SCMP*, No. 1714, pp. 5–14.
[31] NCNA, March 16, 1958, in *SCMP*, No. 1736, p. 2.

bility. The campaign was to reach a climax with the publication of the collection of Mao's articles entitled "Imperialism and All Reactionaries are Paper Tigers" and the drive to establish a militia in August 1958.

The *Liberation Army Daily*, on March 16, 1958, pointed out that Mao had drawn a basic conclusion in his writings: to defeat a better equipped army with inferior weapons depends on the reliance on revolutionary warfare. The article continued:

> In case "a motherland-defense" war were to break out in the future, the equipment of our armed forces would be inferior to that of the imperialist forces within a certain period. The principle of defeating a better equipped army with inferior weapons, therefore, would still apply to future war which would utilize atomic bombs, missiles and chemical weapons.[32]

On March 30, apparently attacking the position that he had held until very recently, P'eng declared that China must systematically arm itself with new technical equipment but that "in the light of our industrial capacity we can do so only gradually." P'eng pointed out that "some comrades," presumably including himself, had "failed to appreciate that the modernization of our army must be established on the basis of our national industrialization, thus tending to expect too much of our modernization too soon."[33]

Thus by March the notion of a quick modernization of the Chinese army, by accepting equipment from the Soviet Union, had been firmly rejected by the Peking leadership. There is, as has been indicated, uncertainty as to what triggered the discussion by the PLA leadership on the possibility of quick modernization and whether their hopes were dashed by Peking or by Moscow.[34] The weight of the evidence would suggest that it was Mao who rejected the proposals being espoused by P'eng

32 Joint Publications Research Service (JPRS), Washington, D. C., Translation Study No. 1687, June 9, 1959, quoted from Ford, *op. cit.*, p. 163.

33 P'eng Teh-huai, "Build Our Army into an Excellent Modernized Revoluntary Force," *Chien-Sang-Chu Pao*, March 30, 1958 (JPRS, Translation Study No. 764-D), quoted from Hsieh, *op. cit.*, p. 110.

34 Ford for example suggests that the Soviet Union was unwilling to give the kind of aid that the Chinese leaders had hoped for. See Ford, *op. cit.*

and his colleagues and by Khrushchev. There is considerable evidence that Khrushchev proposed various kinds of cooperative schemes with China, including a joint naval command and a joint radar network, with his pressure reaching a peak in April 1958 after the Chinese rejection had been made clear at least in their public statements.[35] It is these overtures, perhaps pressed as rejection became more likely, that the Chinese declared that they firmly opposed:

> In 1958 the leadership of the CPSU put forward unreasonable demands designed to bring China under Soviet military control. These unreasonable demands were rightly and firmly rejected by the Chinese Government.[36]

Beginning in May 1958, presumably after the final firm rejection of Khrushchev's various proposals for joint command and the decision not to accept nuclear weapons under joint control, the Chinese press published several articles that for the first time publicly announced China's intentions to manufacture nuclear weapons but at the same time condemned those who had urged too great a reliance on foreign techniques and on copying the Soviet Union. The statements emphasized that industrial development would have to precede modernization of the armed forces.[37]

The willingness of the leadership to commit itself publicly to the development of atomic weapons and missiles might have resulted from its confidence that Khrushchev would continue his assistance to the indigenous Chinese nuclear program despite the rejection of his "unreasonable" demands. By May 1958 Soviet aid may have been sufficiently advanced to give Peking this confidence. The message that the political leadership was giving to the army and to the Chinese people, as well as to the Soviets, was that China would depend on cautious action, the umbrella of Soviet nuclear power, and its own capability for revolutionary war to deter or defeat an Ameri-

---

35 For a discussion of the evidence emphasizing the Khrushchevian initiative reaching a climax in April 1958 see Mackintosh, Chapter 8.

36 "The Origin and Development of the Differences Between the Leadership of the CPSU and Ourselves — Comment on the Open Letter of the Central Committee of the CPSU," September 6, 1963, *Peking Review* (September 13, 1963), reprinted in Griffith, *op. cit.*, p. 399.

37 These statements are summarized in Ford, *op. cit.*, and Hsieh, *op. cit.*

can attack until China could develop its own indigenous nuclear capability. This capability would be developed as quickly as possible utilizing as much Soviet assistance as was available.

On May 22, the military committee of the Central Committee of the Chinese Communist Party convened for a session that was to last through July 22. This meeting, according to the official communiqué, "reviewed the over-all strengthening of the PLA since the founding of the People's Republic, and defined the lines of policy for the future. At the same time, taking cognisance of the present world situation, it discussed the country's national defence and made decisions accordingly."[38] The conference apparently discussed and formally ratified the decisions of the top leadership, which were then expressed in a major statement on "People's Army, People's War" by Chu Teh and released on July 31, 1958. The article accepted that emphasis must be given to modern technological equipment but reminded its readers that China was not an advocate of the sole importance of arms. It declared that there are some people, presumably those around P'eng Teh-huai, who advocate an exclusively military viewpoint and who pay attention only to national defense and do not realize the significance of economic construction to defense. Chu Teh declared that China must base its military development on its own military experience and situation.[39] On the next day, in the guise of discussing causes of the failure of the Nanchang uprising of 1927, Marshal Ho Lung expressed the error of the military professionals:

> We tried to solve our problem purely from the military point of view, and hoped for outside aid instead of relying on mobilisation of the masses.[40]

[38] *Peking Review*, No. 22 (July 29, 1958), quoted from John Gittings, "China's Militia," *The China Quarterly*, No. 18 (April–June 1964), p. 105.

[39] Chu Teh, "People's Army, People's War," NCNA, July 31, 1958, in *Current Background*, No. 514 (August 6, 1958), pp. 1–4. The article was reprinted in *Pravda*, August 3, 1958 (See *Current Digest of the Soviet Press* (*CDSP*), Vol. X, No. 31, weekly index, p. 61.)

[40] *People's Daily*, reprinted in *Current Background*, No. 514, quoted, with this implication of the meaning of the remark, from Ford, *op. cit.*, p. 163.

The shift in policy was also reflected in the promotion of Lin Piao to a position as a member of the Standing Committee of the Politburo on May 25, 1958.[41] It is possible that he began to direct the PLA at this time, replacing P'eng Teh-huai who was dismissed in September 1959. An editorial in the *Liberation Army Daily* on August 1, 1958, declared that some comrades had neglected the revolutionary nature of the people's army. It continued:

> Based on the principle of military operations, they one-sidedly stressed the part of atomic weapons and modern military techniques and neglected the role of the people. Instead of proceeding from the actual conditions of the enemy and our own side, and studying strategy and tactics suited to the peculiarities of our country, they followed the book formulas. They encouraged mechanical and stereotyped movements and rigid application and looked upon flexibility with disfavor. In their attitude toward study, they stood for mechanical application of foreign experience and looked upon with disfavor the combination of study with initiative and selective study.[42]

Through August and into the fall, the Chinese press contained stories attacking those comrades who had overemphasized the possibilities of borrowing from the Soviet Union. Reflecting the general spirit of the Great Leap, increased emphasis was put on the revolutionary tradition of the army, including the need to rely on the masses as, for example, when the *Liberation Army Daily* on September 20 declared: "If only we can rely on the masses and base everything on reality, we will surely work out something which is suitable for our own forces."[43] In August 1958, the Chinese proclaimed the "everyone a soldier" movement vastly expanding the People's Militia.[44] In an NCNA statement discussing an "Important Statement by Chairman Mao" following a provincial tour, Mao was reported to have linked the militia to the prevention of invasion or the defeat of such an invasion if it should occur.[45]

[41] *Current Background*, No. 519, p. 9.
[42] *Liberation Army Daily*, in *SCMP*, No. 1881, pp. 1–3.
[43] JPRS, No. 1357 (March 16, 1959), quoted from Ford, *op. cit.*, p. 164.
[44] Gittings, *op. cit.*, p. 103.
[45] NCNA, October 1, 1958, quoted in Gittings, *op. cit.*, p. 105.

Thus in less than a year the Chinese had come full circle and returned to their reliance in the short run on the People's Army reinforced by an expanded militia. The proposals for joint nuclear arrangements with the Soviet Union had been firmly rejected. Nevertheless China had, with confidence, publicly committed itself to a nuclear weapons program and was in the process of receiving large-scale assistance from the Soviet Union.

The inference that Soviet nuclear aid to China continued during this period and was the basis of Chinese support for the test ban is reinforced by the fact that public support for Soviet efforts to negotiate a test ban treaty were not shaken by the events of 1958. The Chinese did have other reasons to support a test ban (including its popularity in Japan) but they are unlikely to have given public support if they saw the test ban as an anti-Chinese measure. As will be indicated, the Chinese did back away from the test ban as such in 1959 while continuing to emphasize nuclear disarmament.

In early September 1957 the London Disarmament Conference came to an end as a result of Soviet pressure,[46] but on September 20, 1957, the Soviet Union introduced in the General Assembly a resolution calling for a discontinuance of nuclear tests for two or three years as of January 1, 1958. The draft resolution first called upon nuclear powers not to carry out any tests during this period and then called on "other states" to accede to the agreement.[47] Four days later the *People's Daily* reported that the Chinese government supported the Soviet proposal.[48] During the remainder of 1957 and into 1958 the Chinese continued to support, within four or five days time, Soviet statements calling for a suspension of nuclear tests. The Soviets in turn reprinted some of these Chinese statements.[49]

46 *The New York Times*, September 7, 1957, p. 1.

47 *Documents on Disarmament 1945–1959*, pp. 884–885.

48 *People's Daily*, September 24, 1957, reported by NCNA, September 24, 1957, in *SCMP*, No. 1619, p. 50.

49 For example *Izvestia* on January 17, 1958, reprinted a *People's Daily* article calling for the ending of nuclear tests: cited in *CDSP*, Vol. X, No. 3, weekly index, p. 40.

On March 31, 1958, the Soviet Union announced that it was unilaterally suspending nuclear tests and that it would not test again unless the United States and the United Kingdom continued testing. On the next day the *People's Daily* supported the Soviet unilateral suspension of nuclear testing. At the same time it did note that the United States was willing to equip German armed forces with nuclear weapons and declared, as had the Soviet note, that if the United States and the United Kingdom did not stop testing the Soviet Union would have to resume its tests.[50] The Soviet move was reported to have received wide support in Communist China.[51] Perhaps Peking was pointing out to Moscow that Washington did not view a test suspension as incompatible with nuclear sharing. On April 4, 1958, Khrushchev dispatched notes to a number of heads of government including President Dwight D. Eisenhower and Chinese Communist Premier Chou En-lai. In these notes he pointed out that the Soviet Union had unilaterally renounced testing and urged rapid agreement:

> Today only three powers — the U.S.S.R. the U.S.A. and Great Britain — possess nuclear weapons; therefore agreement on the discontinuation of nuclear weapons tests can be achieved relatively easily. If the tests are not stopped now, within a certain time other countries may have nuclear weapons, and in such a situation it would, of course, be much more difficult to obtain an agreement.[52]

Ford has pointed out that Peking did not send a formal response to the Soviet note until ten days later and draws from this the conclusion that Peking may not have been happy about Soviet efforts to negotiate a test ban. However, the total Chinese reaction to the Soviet note suggests a different interpretation. On April 7, a *People's Daily* editorial supported the Soviet proposal and in paraphrasing it declared:

> In fact, an agreement can be reached with relative ease on the discontinuance of nuclear tests, as at present only the Soviet

---

[50] *People's Daily*, April 1, 1958, reported by NCNA, April 1, 1958, in *SCMP*, No. 1746, pp. 37–38.

[51] NCNA, April 1, 1958, in *SCMP*, No. 1746.

[52] Message from Nikita S. Khrushchev to Dwight D. Eisenhower, April 4, 1958, printed in *Pravda*, April 6, 1958, p. 1, translated in *CDSP*, Vol. X, No. 14, p. 26.

Union and the United States and Britain possess atomic weapons.[53]

On April 9, NCNA reported Chou En-lai as saying that the Chinese government had been informed of the Soviet decision to suspend nuclear tests and that the Chinese people gave it their enthusiastic support.[54] And on April 10 the Chinese attacked the United States for rejecting the Soviet proposal to suspend tests.[55]

The formal Chinese response, dated April 13, in response to Khrushchev's letter of April 4, declared that the Chinese government

. . . fully supports the decision of the Soviet Government to first discontinue the test of all kinds of atomic and hydrogen weapons and the proposals concerning this question made by the Soviet Government to the governments of the United States and Britain.[56]

Even in April 1958, at the time of the Chinese rejection of Khrushchev's proposals for nuclear sharing, Khrushchev was sufficiently confident of a Chinese positive response to dispatch a letter publicly to the Chinese government asking its views on the nuclear test suspension. In fact, Chinese support for Soviet proposals in the test ban area and Soviet confidence that China would support efforts to end nuclear weapons tests were to continue into 1959.

On May 9, 1958, Khrushchev took a major step toward a test ban when in a letter to Eisenhower he accepted the Western proposal for a conference of experts to examine the feasibility of a controlled system for the detection of nuclear weapons tests.[57] In taking this step Khrushchev must have known that a treaty, and even a control system, would be unacceptable unless China participated and the control system included Chinese territory. In fact Khrushchev's letter reflected his confi-

[53] *People's Daily*, editorial, April 7, 1958, reported by NCNA, April 7, 1958, in *SCMP*, No. 1749, pp. 43–44.

[54] NCNA, April 9, 1958, in *SCMP*, No. 1750, p. 51.

[55] Reported by NCNA, April 10, 1958, in *SCMP*, No. 1751, p. 36.

[56] NCNA, April 14, 1958, in *SCMP*, No. 1753, pp. 43–46.

[57] Letter from the Soviet Premier to President Eisenhower, May 9, 1958, in *Documents on Disarmament 1945–1959*, p. 1038.

dence that China would participate. In a follow-up letter on May 30 Khrushchev agreed to the American proposal that scientists from Great Britain and France should participate in the Conference of Experts and indicated that Czech and Polish scientists would also participate. The letter went on to state:

> Nor does the Soviet Government consider that the work of the experts should be confined to this group of countries. Therefore it seems advisable to invite experts from India also, and possibly *from certain other countries,* to participate in the conference.[58]

The American government apparently took Khrushchev's letter, and perhaps other informal Soviet indications, to mean that the Soviets wished to propose the inclusion of Chinese scientists at the Conference of Experts. According to one press report, Washington's tentative decision was to accept the presence of Chinese scientists.[59] Whether in fact such a proposal was actually made and rejected by the American government is not clear from the public record.

Chinese support was indicated on June 27, 1958, the eve of the conference, when NCNA noted that the talks between experts should help facilitate an agreement on the cessation of nuclear weapons tests. However, it warned that the United States would use the talks to cover up its ambitions for a nuclear arms race.[60] While Chinese statements continued to point to American preparation for nuclear war, they did give support to the conference. They also pointed out that the United States was on the verge of increasing its exchange of nuclear weapons information with Great Britain and, apparently, with France to gain their adherence to the test ban. These comments as well as those already cited in regard to Germany may have been intended as a reminder by Peking to Moscow that nuclear sharing was also being accelerated by the United States, and hence was presumably looked upon by both countries as compatible with and even apparently neces-

---

[58] Letter from the Soviet Premier to President Eisenhower, May 30, 1958, in *Documents on Disarmament 1945–1959,* pp. 1050–1051. Italics added.

[59] *The New York Herald Tribune,* June 5, 1958.

[60] NCNA, June 27, 1958, in *SCMP,* No. 1803, p. 49.

sary for gaining the concurrence of its principle allies in negotiating a test ban treaty.[61]

At the Conference of Experts the Communist delegates made no effort to resist proposals for a controlled network covering the entire world, including China. In fact, on the second day of the conference, the Czechoslovak delegate spoke of a controlled network "spread out over the whole world."[62] The report of the conference proposed a control network that included eight stations in mainland China.

On August 31, 1958, NCNA declared that the United States and the United Kingdom should suspend all tests since "the experts at Geneva have found detection possible" and that an "agreement must be negotiated for a permanent ban on the testing of all atomic and hydrogen weapons by all powers."[63]

With the opening of the political conference to draft a nuclear test ban treaty, the Soviets continued to act as if the Chinese would certainly adhere to such an agreement. Thus, at the opening session of the conference on August 31, 1958, Soviet delegate Tsarapkin, while proposing that the original agreement be signed only by the three nuclear powers, declared:

> It stands to reason that if the Soviet Union, the United States and the United Kingdom cease nuclear weapons tests on the basis of such an agreement [i.e. an agreement on control posts in the three countries] and any other countries did the opposite, that is to say, worked on the production of nuclear weapons and began testing them, that would undoubtedly frustrate the idea of agreement on the universal discontinuance of nuclear weapons tests. In order to prevent this from happening, the draft agreement should contain a provision to the effect that the governments of the three powers, i.e. the Soviet Union, the United States, and the United Kingdom, undertake to promote the assumption by all other states in the world of an undertaking not to carry out tests of atomic and hydrogen weapons of any type.[64]

[61] See for example, *People's Daily*, July 5, 1958, reported by NCNA, July 5, 1958, in *SCMP*, No. 1807, p. 50; and *People's Daily*, July 5, 1958, in *SCMP*, No. 1811, pp. 36–40.

[62] Conference of Experts to Study the Possibility of Detecting Violations of a Possible Agreement on a Suspension of Nuclear Tests, Verbatim Records, Second Meeting, July 2, 1958, p. 22.

[63] NCNA, August 31, 1958, in *SCMP*, No. 1846, p. 3.

[64] Conference on the Discontinuance of Nuclear Weapons Tests, Ver-

And the Soviet draft agreement included an article which declared that

> The three governments undertake to promote the assumption by all other states in the world of an undertaking not to carry out tests of atomic and hydrogen weapons of any type.[65]

On the next day, the *People's Daily* indicated China's support for the permament suspension of nuclear tests, and at the same time supported the Soviet decision to resume testing in light of the refusal of the Western powers to accept a temporary moratorium.[66] Through the end of 1958 the Chinese continued to support the Soviet position at the Geneva Conference. Tsarapkin in Geneva resisted Western proposals to have the test ban treaty negotiated by all of the countries in the world. He declared that asking every country to sign the initial treaty would "liberate a genie from a bottle" and that various countries would propose various changes and reservations. However, on other occasions he reiterated his belief that all other countries would adhere to the treaty once it had been signed and ratified by the three nuclear powers.[67]

During the first half of 1959, while Sino-Soviet relations were worsening on a number of counts, the Soviets pushed ahead toward negotiation of a test ban treaty, apparently still acting on the assumption that China could be brought into the agreement. For example, the Soviet proposal for membership in the commission governing the disarmament control organization proposed that "three seats [be allotted] to the Soviet Union and *states friendly* or allied with the Soviet Union,"[68] and the preamble to the treaty accepted by all three powers on April 17, 1959, expressed the hope that all other countries would "also join in undertakings not to carry out nuclear weapons tests and to ensure the satisfactory operation" of the international control organization.[69]

batim Transcript, First Plenary Meeting, October 31, 1958, p. 25 (cited as UN/GN/DNT/PV1).

[65] *Ibid.*, p. 26.

[66] *People's Daily*, November 1, 1958, NCNA, November 1, 1958, in *SCMP*, No. 1889, pp. 44–45.

[67] See for example, UN/GN/DNT/PV12, November 24, 1958, pp. 9–12; and UN/GN/DNT/PV11, November 21, 1958, pp. 21–22.

[68] UN/GN/DNT/PV52, February 11, 1959. Italics added.

[69] Zoppo, *op. cit.*, p. 318.

In February 1959, British Prime Minister Harold Macmillan was in Moscow for talks with Soviet Premier Khrushchev and proposed a compromise on what then appeared to be the major stumbling block to a test ban treaty. Macmillan suggested that the number of on-site inspections to examine possible violations of the test ban treaty be negotiated politically between the three powers and that they settle on some specified number of annual inspections that would be veto free. On April 23, in letters to Eisenhower and Macmillan, Khrushchev alluded to and accepted the Macmillan proposal.[70]

On May 12, 1959, Harold Macmillan told the House of Commons that on the basis of his agreement with Khrushchev in Moscow he expected a nuclear test ban treaty to be signed within several months. In a letter to Eisenhower on May 14, Khrushchev noted with satisfaction the willingness of the United States to study what was now in effect a joint British-Soviet proposal for a politically agreed number of veto-free inspections and declared:

> We continue to be of the opinion that this proposal constitutes a good basis for a solution of the most difficult problem — the problem of sending inspection teams for investigations on the spot. Obtaining agreement on this proposal would open the way to the conclusion of an accord on the cessation of all types of tests.[71]

On June 9, a *New York Times* report from Geneva indicated that the Soviets appeared to be moving toward acceptance of the notion of international staffing of control posts in the Soviet Union.[72]

Thus by early June 1959 it must have seemed to the Chinese as if the Soviet Union were close to signing a test ban treaty with the United States and Great Britain. At the same time Khrushchev appeared to be aiming at a general improvement of his relations with the United States; the Chinese must have known, as the Western powers did, that he was seeking an

---

[70] *Documents on Disarmament 1945–1959*, pp. 1396–1400.

[71] "Letter from the Soviet Premier [Khrushchev] to President Eisenhower Regarding Nuclear Test Suspension, May 14, 1959," in *Documents on Disarmament 1945–1959*, p. 1409.

[72] *The New York Times*, June 10, 1959.

invitation to visit that country. In this context of increased suspicion of Soviet motives, it would have been quite natural for the Chinese to reopen discussions with the Soviets about the price that the latter were prepared to pay to ensure Chinese adherence to the test ban treaty. The Chinese reported that on June 20, 1959, the Soviet Union refused their request for "a sample of an atomic bomb and technical data concerning its manufacture."[73] The statement declared that the Soviets rejected the Chinese request and "unilaterally tore up the agreement on new technology for national defense" as a "presentation gift" at the time the Soviet leader went to the United States for talks with Eisenhower in September.[74] This statement, even if accepted, would not explain why the Chinese made these demands but only the reason for the Soviet rejection. Moreover, it is now clear from Eisenhower's memoirs that the invitation to Khrushchev to visit the United States was not given until July 1959, and then only as the result of a misunderstanding between Eisenhower and Under Secretary of State Robert Murphy.[75]

A possible explanation for the Chinese demands at this time was their belief that a test ban was about to be signed. The Chinese may have stated their conditions for adhering to the treaty. The particular items that the Chinese say they requested in June 1959 are "a sample of an atomic bomb and technical data concerning its manufacture." It is at least plausible that these demands would be made as the price for restraint from nuclear testing. Alternately the Chinese may have demanded a bomb that they could not test before a test ban treaty went into effect. Unless they believed that a test ban was imminent they would not have any reason to make these particular demands at this time. The state of the public literature on bomb design, and the Chinese confidence in their nuclear physicists, would have led the Chinese to view a sample bomb (whatever that may be) as less important than, for example, stepped-up help to their own production facilities or,

---

[73] "Statement by the Spokesman of the Chinese Government," August 15, 1963, in Griffith, *op. cit.*, p. 351.

[74] *Ibid.*

[75] Dwight D. Eisenhower, *Waging Peace* (New York: Doubleday, 1965), pp. 405–408.

perhaps, advice on methods of handling weapons-grade pluto-
nium. The Chinese themselves relate their demands to the
nuclear test ban but in a negative way. They say that "as far
back as June 20, 1959, when there was not yet the slightest sign
of a treaty on stopping nuclear tests," the Soviets refused their
demands. This description of the situation in June 1959 is not
accurate; in fact, there were expectations that a test ban treaty
would shortly be signed. Both the Soviet government and the
British government had made statements indicating that they
thought a test ban treaty might be signed shortly, and stories
from Geneva indicated that compromises were about to be
made on a number of the major issues.[76] It is not impossible
that the Chinese statement should be read as saying: "As far
back as June 1959 when on a previous occasion a test ban treaty
appeared imminent the Russians refused to pay our price for
signing." The Chinese themselves have offered no explanation
for making demands at this particular time, nor has any been
offered thus far in the public literature.

The deterioration of Sino-Soviet relations in 1959 may explain both China's pressure for increased aid to its nuclear
program before it became committed to a test ban treaty and
Soviet reluctance to grant the aid. Moreover Khrushchev's
motivation for turning down the Chinese request may simply
have involved his feeling that there was not yet sufficient certainty of a test ban treaty to justify a formal commitment as
to the price the Russians would pay to bring in the Chinese.
Khrushchev was undoubtedly becoming increasingly disturbed
about the unwillingness of the Chinese to go along with his
efforts to improve relations with the United States. He was
at this time hoping for an invitation to visit Washington and
may have concluded that the transfer of nuclear weapons to
China, particularly if the Chinese tested the weapons, would
reduce the chances of his being able to arrange such a visit.
The charge by the Chinese that Khrushchev intended his
turning down of the Chinese request as a present to the United
States during his visit is contradicted by the information that

---

[76] There were of course a number of differences remaining between
the parties but it was not the case that there was "not the slightest
sign" of a treaty.

he had not yet received an invitation. Moreover, there is nothing to suggest that he told American leaders about either the nuclear aid agreement or the fact that it had been broken. After turning down the Chinese request for increased nuclear aid in June 1959, Khrushchev was faced with the fact that the signing of a test ban treaty would now mean a break with China. There were divergent trends in Soviet policy following June 1959, which may have indicated uncertainty as to whether or not Russia should proceed with the test ban in the face of likely Chinese opposition and, perhaps, increased pressure to test from the Soviet military. The test ban negotiations did continue, and at least for several months the Soviets appeared to be presenting serious proposals and negotiating in an effort to arrive at an agreement. At the same time Khrushchev, during his visit to the United States in the fall of 1959, introduced a major new element into the disarmament negotiations, namely, the proposal for general and complete disarmament. While he implied that the test ban could still be negotiated separately, the emphasis of Soviet policy from September 1959, was on the efforts to promote general and complete disarmament. In January 1960 the Chinese made clear in a public statement what they must already have indicated to the Russians:

> . . . any international agreement concerning disarmament, without the formal participation of the People's Republic of China and the signature of its delegate, cannot of course have any binding force on her.[77]

Soviet aid to the Chinese nuclear program appears to have continued at least at a modest level until mid-1960, when all Soviet technicians were withdrawn from China.[78]

By this time the Soviets had drawn away from serious efforts to negotiate a test ban treaty. Khrushchev's effort to produce a test cessation agreement to which China would adhere had ended in failure. The Soviets were to return to the test ban in 1962–1963 but were then to view it as an effective move in their bitter dispute and competition with China.

[77] Resolution of the National People's Congress, January 21, 1960, reported by NCNA, January 21, 1960, in *SCMP*, No. 2185, p. 4.
[78] Cf. speech by President Lyndon Johnson in *The New York Times*, October 19, 1964, p. 14.

6

The Nuclear Test Ban
and Sino-Soviet Relations[1]

WALTER C. CLEMENS, JR.

The impact of the 1963 test ban treaty on world politics and, more narrowly, on Sino-Soviet relations extended far beyond the immediate arms controls it provided. Looking back over the years, we see in retrospect that the issues surrounding the possibility of a ban on nuclear testing became, perhaps as early as 1956, a prime factor in the deterioration of Soviet-Chinese relations. Whether one believes the Sino-Soviet dispute hinges on differences of national interest, or ideology, or both, the prospect of a nuclear test ban has clearly been of profound substantive as well as symbolic importance to the "fraternal" regimes in Moscow and Peking.[2]

Prelude to Schism

During the years 1957–1958, the government of Mao-Tsetung moved away from the Bandung spirit to a more bellig-

[1] The author wishes to express his thanks to William E. Griffith and Morton H. Halperin for their helpful suggestions and criticisms of the manuscript.

[2] For a discussion of the interplay between national interest and ideology in Sino-Soviet differences on arms control, see Walter C. Clemens, Jr., "The Sino-Soviet Dispute — Dogma and Dialectics on Disarmament," *International Affairs* (London), Vol. XLI, No. 2 (April 1965), pp. 215–219.

erent stance; at the same time Khrushchev's regime was expressing increasing dedication to peaceful coexistence as the main line of Soviet foreign policy. Given this context, a Soviet-U.S. agreement to ban nuclear tests could be viewed only with the gravest concern by Peking. From China's perspective, a Soviet decision to sign any major agreement with the United States suggested that Moscow was turning westward, away from alliance with Peking. Ideologically, such a turn would serve to reinforce Mao's growing belief that the Khrushchev government was abandoning world revolution to concentrate on raising to new levels the Soviet Union's *embourgeoisement*. Strategically, a Soviet accord with the West would tend to confirm the Kremlin's unwillingness to support China's external policies, particularly in the Taiwan Straits. In specific terms, a nuclear test ban treaty could threaten China's security on several levels: at the least it could bring a halt to Soviet aid to Peking's nuclear program and create some legal or moral restraint upon China's future capacity to test nuclear weapons; a test ban might well lead to a U.S.-Soviet nonproliferation agreement, thus increasing the pressures against Chinese entry into the nuclear club; more ominously, a U.S.-Soviet understanding could lead to joint measures to eliminate China's incipient nuclear plant. For all these reasons, any sign of Soviet interest in a nuclear test ban tended, along with other irritants, to undermine the Peking-Moscow axis.

The revelations of the Sino-Soviet dispute point to the nuclear test ban issue as a major factor exacerbating relations between Moscow and Peking as early as the Twentieth Congress of the CPSU in February 1956, when Khrushchev — in Peking's apt expression — "divorced the cessation of nuclear tests from the question of disarmament."[3] After 1956 the Soviet leaders "were wrong on certain [disarmament] issues and correct on others," according to Peking, and China "supported them in all their correct views."[4]

While one cannot take at face value these restrospective Chi-

---

[3] Chinese government statement of August 15, 1963, in William E. Griffith, *The Sino-Soviet Rift* (Cambridge: The M.I.T. Press, 1964), p. 352. (Hereinafter cited as Statement of August 15, 1963).
[4] *Ibid.*

nese judgments, it seems likely that — for reasons just outlined — Moscow's first steps toward a nuclear test ban as a negotiable "partial measure" of disarmament did in fact cause China serious concern. The fact that Peking's declaratory policy generally supported Moscow's disarmament line until 1959 is no proof that the Chinese shared the Kremlin's reasons for making those proposals.[5] It is more likely that China toed the Soviet line only while Peking's leadership doubted that anything would come of the East-West negotiations and while China received substantial Soviet military and economic aid. The Khrushchev government, on the other hand, seems to have been interested by mid-1957 at the latest in a cessation of nuclear testing, if not a formal treaty banning such tests, and appears to have been sanguine that such an arrangement could be achieved by negotiation with the West.[6] While the extent of Soviet assistance to China's nuclear program was probably substantial, it came to a jarring halt in 1959–1960.[7]

From 1959 until 1962 Sino-Soviet relations continued to spiral downward, troubled by disagreement on many issues, one of these being the issue of a nuclear test ban. Did the Soviets appreciate the grave consequences for their relations with Peking that would ensue from formalization of a limited test ban? Surely the answer is affirmative. Moscow must have known that the Chinese would regard the signing of a U.S.-Soviet test ban as a step that could and probably would lead to a superpower conspiracy to keep China out of the nuclear club. According to Peking, China received word from Moscow on August 25, 1962, that the Soviet government had responded "affirmatively" to Secretary of State Rusk's proposal for a non-proliferation agreement. His proposal stipulated that (1) the nuclear powers should refrain from transferring nuclear weap-

---

[5] For a contrary interpretation, see Morton H. Halperin, Chapter 5.

[6] Lincoln P. Bloomfield, Walter C. Clemens, Jr., Franklyn Griffiths, *Khrushchev and the Arms Race: Soviet Interests in Arms Control and Disarmament, 1954–1964* (Cambridge: The M.I.T. Press, 1966), pp. 151–157.

[7] According to the Chinese statement of August 15, 1963, Moscow on June 20, 1959, "refused to provide China with a sample of an atomic bomb and technical data concerning its manufacture," and unilaterally tore up the agreement on new technology for national defense concluded between China and the Soviet Union on October 15, 1957.

ons and technical information concerning their manufacture to nonnuclear countries; and (2) that nonnuclear countries should refrain from manufacturing nuclear weapons, seeking them from nuclear powers, or accepting technical information concerning their manufacture.[8]

Moscow's expression of some "affirmative" interest in a non-proliferation agreement came in private negotiations at the same time that the Kremlin was making concessions in the open negotiations in Geneva to narrow the gap separating Moscow and Washington from an agreement to end nuclear testing. (As if to prove the existence of a private understanding between Moscow and Washington on *nonproliferation,* Peking has printed the public documents recording the narrowing gap between the Soviet and U.S. *test ban* proposals.[9]) On August 27, 1962, the U.S. delegate to the Eighteen Nation Disarmament Conference (ENDC) stated his government's willingness to agree either to a comprehensive test ban involving on-site inspection or a ban excluding underground tests but without on-site inspection. The Soviet delegate replied on August 29 and again on September 3, 1962, announcing Moscow's readiness to sign a three-environment ban with a moratorium on underground testing "while continuing negotiations on the final prohibitions of such explosions." A similar proposal had been made by Moscow on November 28, 1961, but with the provision that inspection over the underground test moratorium could take place only in the context of a comprehensive disarmament agreement. Moscow's position of August 29–September 3, 1962, seemed no longer to be contingent upon GCD measures. But on September 5, Soviet representative Vasily V. Kuznetsov clouded the issue by reiterating Moscow's support for its stand of November 28, 1961.

In any event, the Western delegates rejected the new Soviet overture on principle because — after the sudden Soviet test resumption in 1961 — the West would no longer consent to an unpoliced moratorium.[10] But the shift in Moscow's position

---

8 *Ibid.,* p. 351.

9 See appendixes to *People of the World, Unite, for the Complete, Thorough, Total and Resolute Prohibition and Destruction of Nuclear Weapons!* (Peking: Foreign Languages Press, 1963), pp. 127–135.

10 ENDC/PV. 76, August 29, 1962, pp. 14–23; ENDC/PV. 79, September 3, 1962, pp. 78–80. See also Verbatim Records of September 5, 1962.

on August 29, 1962, was described by *Pravda* on the following day as "opening the way to agreement" and was soon thereafter similarly featured by the Soviet publication *New Times*.[11] On October 1, 1962, in Ashkhabad, Khrushchev reiterated Soviet willingness to sign an agreement on a partial test ban on the terms articulated by Kuznetsov on August 29 and September 3.[12]

People's Daily charged on September 12, 1962, that the United States was obstructing the progress of the ENDC by demanding on-site inspections. But the article went on to indicate a deeper concern. The U.S.-British statement on testing, said *People's Daily,* declared that the

> . . . treaty would make it easier to prevent the spread of nuclear weapons to countries not now possessing them. . . . The reason U.S. ruling circles are so interested in preventing what they call nuclear proliferation is not secret. . . . Washington is anxious to tie China's hands in developing nuclear weapons.

People's Daily went on to say that

> . . . only a complete ban on nuclear weapons and the unconditional destruction of all existing nuclear weapons can prevent a nuclear war. . . . The discontinuance of nuclear tests . . . should under no circumstances become a means by which the United States may achieve and maintain nuclear superiority.[13]

Peking's response to the reported U.S.-Soviet understanding in nonproliferation was to send three memoranda to Moscow — on September 3, 1962, October 20, 1962, and June 6, 1963. Their substance held:

> It was a matter for the Soviet Government whether it committed itself to the United States to refrain from transferring nuclear weapons and technical information concerning their manufacture to China; but that the Chinese Government hoped the Soviet Government would not infringe on China's sovereign rights and act for China in assuming an obligation to refrain from manu-

11 September 8, 1962 (Russian edition).
12 *Pravda,* October 2, 1962.
13 New China News Agency (NCNA) in English, Peking, September 12, 1962 (*Survey of China Mainland Press* [SCMP] No. 2820, September 18, 1962, pp. 30–31). This policy statement crowned a series of declarations on disarmament in which nuclear test cessation was generally made dependent on the banning of nuclear weapons. See Ciro E. Zoppo, "The Test Ban: A Study in Arms Control Negotiation," unpublished Ph.D. dissertation, Columbia University, 1963, p. 385.

facturing nuclear weapons. We solemnly stated that we would not tolerate the conclusion, in disregard of China's opposition, of any sort of treaty between the Soviet Government and the United States which aimed at depriving the Chinese people of their right to take steps to resist the nuclear threats of U.S. imperialism, and that we would issue statements to make our position known.[14]

This "earnest counsel," Peking professed to hope, would lead the Soviet leaders to "rein in before reaching the precipice" so as not to "render matters irretrievable. Unfortunately," the Chinese statement goes on, Moscow "did not pay the slightest attention" to China's advice but proceeded to conclude the limited test ban, "thereby attempting to bring pressure on China and force her into commitments."[15]

Shortly after the Kremlin's message to Peking on nonproliferation, two other events seriously affected Soviet-Chinese relations: the Cuban missile crisis and the Chinese-Indian engagement in the Himalayas. From these points in time until the signing of the nuclear test ban treaty in July 1963 the tensions between Moscow and Peking seemed to escalate in three stages amounting to quantum jumps in the dispute. These stages corresponded roughly with Moscow's rejection of Peking's thrice-proffered "earnest counsel" to desist from negotiating a nonproliferation agreement. While the evidence is far from complete, it is possible that a cause and effect relationship existed between the general deterioration of Sino-Soviet relations and China's mounting concern that Moscow would reach an entente with Washington on the spread of nuclear weapons.

The first stage in the escalation ran from October 1962 to April 1963, when a series of Communist Party congresses and front meetings provided a forum for Soviet and Chinese delegates to assail one another openly, and readers of *People's Daily* saw Khrushchev criticized by means of attacks on Togliatti and Thorez.[16] After a relative lull in April and May

14 Statement of August 15, 1963, pp. 351–352.
15 The Chinese statement hinted that Moscow's views had been criticized many times before 1962, at least by silence.
16 See the materials in Alexander Dallin, ed., *Diversity in International Communism: A Documentary Record, 1961–1963* (New York: Columbia

1963, Peking let loose its broadside of June 14, to which Moscow replied in kind on July 14. While this exchange added a new dimension to the dispute, particularly in "naming names" instead of using surrogates like Albania or Italy, it was qualitatively surpassed by the polemic initiated by China on July 31, commenting on the test ban initialed on July 24. In William E. Griffith's words, "Peking now opened an overt and all-out attack on Moscow: the Sino-Soviet schism had now clearly occurred."[17] Moscow's reply came quickly — on August 3 — and a new chapter began in which both sides released detailed, if distorted, accounts of their hitherto secret conflicts on political, military, and economic affairs. In Communist parlance, not only "Party" but "state" relations became an issue.[18]

University Press, 1963), pp. 664–829. For discussion of the Bulgarian, Hungarian, Czechoslovak, Italian, and East German Party congresses and the Sino-Soviet ideological exchanges of December–January and February–March, 1963, see Griffith, *op. cit.*, pp. 67–104.

[17] *Op. cit.*, p. 162.

[18] As early as February 1963, however, *People's Daily* charged that Khrushchev's unilateral abrogation (at some unspecified time) of "hundreds" of agreements and contracts concluded with China constituted an extension of "ideological differences to state relations. . . ." (*The New York Times*, February 27, 1963, p. 1.)

The major exchanges over the test ban treaty were attributed to the Soviet and Chinese "governments" rather than to the respective "parties." See the Chinese statements of July 31, August 2, August 15, and September 1, 1963. (The texts are given in *People of the World, Unite . . .*, *op. cit.*) Of course Party newspapers and mass meetings in both the U.S.S.R. and China reiterated the lines of their "governments."

The flavor of the controversy may be seen from the title of Peking's communication of August 15, 1963: "Statement by the Spokesman of the Chinese Government — A Comment on the Soviet Government's Statement of August 3." The CPR note was characterized by the government as "slanderous and hostile." *The New York Times*, August 22, 1963, p. 15, cited in Morton H. Halperin, *China and the Bomb* (New York: Praeger, 1965), p. 80.

In contrast to the *People of the World, Unite . . .*, cited above, two other books published by Peking's Foreign Languages Press include primarily "Party" statements: *Workers of All Countries, Unite, Oppose our Common Enemy!* (1963), and *The Polemic of the General Line of the International Communist Movement* (1965). The latter work gives the June 14, 1963 letter, the nine replies made by the Chinese Party to the CPSU letter of July 14, 1963, and the November 21, 1964 statement, "Why Khrushchev Fell." The Soviet Party letters of March 30 and July 14, 1963, are given as appendixes. One difference between the 1965 and

If we trace the relationship in time between these stages and Peking's concern over a U.S.-Soviet nonproliferation treaty, we note that the Kremlin told Peking on August 25 that it had responded "affirmatively" to the U.S. proposal and China replied privately to Moscow on September 3, 1962. In the next weeks — even while Soviet missiles were being unloaded in Cuba — the Kremlin made concessions to the Western position not only on the test ban but also on general disarmament issues.[19] The second Chinese comment on the Soviet nonproliferation message came on October 20 — two days before the U.S. quarantine of Cuba, and almost two months before Khrushchev announced his government would accept "two to three" on-site inspections per year for the control of a comprehensive test ban treaty.[20] The third "earnest counsel" from Peking, that Moscow should desist from negotiating a nonproliferation agreement, came on June 6 — four days before President Kennedy's address at American University and

the 1963 documentary collections was that the former used surrogates (e.g., Italy or Yugoslavia) instead of "naming names."

[19] On September 21, 1962, Foreign Minister Gromyko modified the Soviet GCD proposal (to China's disfavor) by allowing for a limited nuclear umbrella to be retained by the two superpowers in Stage I instead of insisting upon the complete destruction of all such weapons at the very outset of the disarmament process. (United Nations Document A/PV. 1127, September 25, 1962, pp. 38–40.)

Moscow's concessions in the arms control negotiations still left the Soviet Union and the United States far from agreement, even on a test ban. Perhaps the concessions were to parallel other moves designed to tranquilize official Washington before it woke up to the *fait accompli* of Soviet missiles emplaced in Cuba. Alternatively, Moscow may have conceived of a complementarity: compromise arms control agreements in exchange for U.S. acquiescence in a more credible parity resulting from Soviet MRBM's along the coast of Cuba. In any event we are left with this puzzling situation: Moscow chose to alienate Peking further by the message concerning nonproliferation at the very time the Kremlin most needed to bolster its alliance prior to the Cuban showdown. A partial answer may lie in internal contradictions within the Kremlin that precluded any completely logical strategy either toward the East or the West.

[20] The announcement came on December 19, 1962. (*Documents on Disarmament*, 1962 [2 vols.; Washington: U.S. Arms Control and Disarmament Agency, 1963], Vol. II, pp. 1239–1242.) It was preceded on December 3 and 10 by Moscow's public espousal of the idea of utilizing automatic seismic stations — "two or three" on the territory of the states possessing nuclear weapons, particularly in areas prone to earthquakes. (ENDC/PV. 90, December 10, 1962, pp. 23–25.)

one week before Peking issued its June 14 open letter. While the American University speech no doubt helped to pave the way to the Moscow Treaty, private talks among representatives of London, Moscow, and Washington had already led to a three-power agreement that enabled Kennedy to announce on June 10 that "high-level discussions will begin shortly in Moscow looking toward early agreement on a *comprehensive* test ban treaty."[21] Ten days later — on June 20 — the "hot line" agreement between Washington and Moscow was signed in Geneva.[22]

21 Italics added. Peking may well have inferred from President Kennedy's June 10 announcement that the Soviets had decided to sign a treaty with the West. However, the Chinese claim to have been informed by Moscow "as late as June 9, 1963 . . . that the Western powers' position on the halting of nuclear tests could not yet serve as a basis for agreement, and that whether negotiations could yield any results depended entirely on the Western powers." A similar statement by Khrushchev on June 15, 1963, in a press conference, is also cited in the same Chinese document, but its mention suggests that the Soviet communication of June 9 was merely intended to inform Peking before the announcement by President Kennedy of the impending negotiations, and implied no particular Soviet commitment to China. (Statement of August 15, 1963, p. 341.) While Peking later referred to the American University speech as "Kennedy's Big Conspiracy" (*Peking Review*, June 28, 1963, pp. 12–14), the first Chinese report on the address was neutral. The Peking Home Service toward the end of its bulletin on international news at 15:00 GMT, June 11, 1963, reported briefly that, according to TASS, Khrushchev, Kennedy, and Macmillan had agreed to a meeting in Moscow in mid-July with representatives of their three countries to resume talks on banning nuclear tests.

For discussion of W. Averell Harriman's role in encouraging the President to make an effort toward *détente* and a test ban, see Robert F. Kennedy, "Foreword," in Walter C. Clemens, Jr., ed., *Toward a Strategy of Peace* (Chicago: Rand McNally, 1965), pp. xiii–xiv. For an analysis of the speech and the Soviet response, see the editor's introduction, especially pp. 10–11. For additional background on the American University speech and U.S. policy prior to the Moscow test ban negotiations, see Arthur M. Schlesinger, Jr., *A Thousand Days* (Boston: Houghton Mifflin, 1965), pp. 889–923; and Theodore C. Sorensen, *Kennedy* (New York: Harper & Row, 1965), pp. 719–746.

22 But Moscow's representative had declared already on April 5 that his government agreed to this U.S. proposal "immediately without waiting for general and complete disarmament." (ENDC/PV. 118, April 5, 1963, p. 52.)

The Chinese reaction to the hot line agreement was not especially hostile. On June 21, 1963, NCNA at 15:30 GMT and the Peking Home Service at 16:00 GMT both reported the agreement without any comment. (BBC FE/1282/i, June 24, 1963.)

Significance of the Test Ban Issue

The precise role that the approaching test ban agreement played in the deterioration of Soviet-Chinese relations is probably impossible to disentangle from the web of other key elements such as Soviet aid to India. But the importance of the test ban issue to the Sino-Soviet schism has been noted by Soviet and East European as well as Western commentators. China's complaint that Moscow refused her a sample bomb in 1959 led *Pravda* to declare on August 21, 1963:

> It looks as if annoyance with this policy of the Soviet Union and other socialist states of not spreading nuclear weapons *explains* the attacks of the C.P.R. leaders on the U.S.S.R.'s foreign policy measures aimed at lessening international tensions and consolidating peace, especially their attacks on the nuclear test-ban treaty....
>
> The Chinese leaders abuse the Soviet Union in every way because it has nuclear arms, while the C.P.R. does not have them.[23]

The Soviet journal *New Times* used even stronger language in 1963 and linked Chinese opposition to the "Moscow Treaty" with the Kremlin's refusal to transfer atomic weapons to Peking. It argued that "the desire to get hold of the bomb by every available means seems to be the underlying motive of Peking's attitude to the test-ban treaty and of the clamorous campaign against the Soviet Union now being conducted in the Chinese press. . . ."[24]

The possibility that the nuclear test ban talks could lead to a major change in the thrust of Soviet foreign policy was suggested by the presence of a high-level Chinese delegation as well as a Western one in Moscow in July 1963. The dramatic parallel with the period of June to August 1939 was striking.[25] In 1963 as in 1939 the Kremlin seemed prepared

[23] Italics added. Also, in *Izvestia*, August 22, 1963. For a similar reaction by officials in Washington, see *The New York Times*, August 16, 1963, p. 1. Interviews with leading Communists from Italy and Yugoslavia in 1961 and 1962 specified disarmament as a fundamental area of disagreement between Moscow and Peking. See interview with Velio Spano in *L'Unita* (Rome), December 23, 1961, quoted in William E. Griffith, *Albania and the Sino-Soviet Rift* (Cambridge: the M.I.T. Press, 1963), and interview with Marshal Tito by Drew Pearson in *Review of International Affairs* (Belgrade), September 1962, p. 32.

[24] September 4, 1963, p. 1.

[25] See, e.g., Max Beloff, *The Foreign Policy of Soviet Russia* (2 vols.; London: Oxford University Press, 1949), Vol. I, pp. 249–270.

to throw its lot with one camp or the other, and received delegations from two opposing alignments. The analogy with 1939 fails in that Stalin gave both delegations — the Anglo-French and the German — a hearing before he had Molotov sign with Ribbentrop. The 1963 decision, by contrast, was probably struck before the Chinese or Western diplomats arrived in Moscow, as evidenced by the tit-for-tat Soviet response on July 14 to the vitriolic Chinese letter of June 14 and by the contrast in the reception accorded the Chinese and Western delegations. The 1939 pact led to much more active collaboration between its signatories than did the 1963 Moscow Treaty, but it ended in war between the two parties. The test ban treaty, on the other hand, served as a reminder — even after the Moscow "spirit" dissipated — that its signatories feared a nuclear engagement.

If one sought to compare the importance of the nuclear test ban with other issues exacerbating Sino-Soviet relations prior to July 1963, it would be difficult to point to any other that so consistently gnawed at what both sides regarded as their vital interests, whose symbolic and material significance was so great in itself, or whose ramifications penetrated so many other areas of the dispute. The issue of a nuclear test ban — in form and substance — drove to the very heart of the political, ideological, military, and even the economic factors in the rift. Hence it was not surprising that the signing of the Moscow Treaty seemed to hurtle the two giants of world communism onto a new and qualitatively more serious plateau of controversy.

Personality differences, as between Mao and Khrushchev, could be overlooked if broader common concerns brought the two governments together. Domestic policies — the denunciation of the personality cult in the Soviet Union and the "Great Leap Forward" in China — triggered major disagreements, but the threat each side posed to the other's internal stability remained quite remote, even when Moscow backed Defense Minister P'eng Teh-huai against the central hierarchy in 1959. Territorial disputes could be shelved, as they had been for the most part since Mao's pretensions over Outer Mongolia in his 1954 meeting with Khrushchev.[26] Soviet leadership of

---

26 As described in the article, "Concerning Mao Tse-tung's Talk with

the Communist movement could be tolerated by Peking so long as China received a sufficient payoff, for instance, nuclear and other aid. Similarly, disagreements over risk taking in foreign affairs could usually be contained because in most instances neither Peking nor Moscow had a direct stake in the areas contested by the other. The weaker party, China, was hardly in a position to do more than complain if the Kremlin refused to give unlimited support to Chinese aims in the Taiwan Straits or the Himalayas. Nor could Peking deter or effectively aid the Soviet Cuban gambit in 1962, except to denounce it after the fact as "adventurism" made worse by subsequent "capitulationism." Sino-Soviet competition for the allegiance of developing countries was fierce but offered inadequate grounds for a major break. The Soviets could live with Peking's rather leftist ideology and foreign policy, at least while the Chinese dragon's growl exceeded its bite. Similarly, Peking could stomach the Kremlin line on peaceful coexistence — "conflict *cum* collaboration" — so long as nothing came of U.S.-Soviet gropings toward entente.

All these and other factors severely strained the Sino-Soviet relationship, but none provided by itself either a necessary or sufficient cause for an overt schism. Taken together, however, their cumulative impact was such that a final straw could break the back of the alliance. The close connection in time between the escalation ladder of the dispute and Peking's protests against a Soviet entente with Washington regarding arms control suggested even in late 1962 and the spring of 1963 that a test ban agreement would have the gravest consequences for Chinese-Soviet relations. The violent Chinese response to the Moscow Treaty showed that its signing served at least as the occasion and perhaps also as the immediate

a Group of Japanese Socialists," *Pravda,* September 2, 1964, p. 2. Conflicts along the Central Asian frontier, though rumored earlier, were not admitted publicly by Peking or Moscow until 1963 after the signing of the Moscow Treaty. But already on March 7, 1963, *People's Daily* declared that Khrushchev's taunts about China allowing "imperialists" to remain in Hong Kong and Macao were opening the subject of all the old treaties imposed upon China in the nineteenth century by Russia as well as the Western countries. Peking stated it hoped to settle these "outstanding issues" with Russia by negotiation. (*The New York Times,* March 9, 1963, p. 1.)

cause — the final straw — that brought the schism into the open. The importance of the Moscow Treaty probably went still deeper. The test ban represented symbolically Moscow's decision to join what Peking deemed an imperialist conspiracy not only to try to block China's nuclear program but to oppose her political advance in the third world. The Chinese had known since 1959 that Moscow would not continue assistance to Peking's nuclear program. As the Chinese correspondence cited earlier indicates, Peking purported to fear (perhaps in part for propaganda reasons) that even a partial test ban might lead to a nonproliferation agreement and, what was worse, to coercive measures by the Soviet Union and the West to destroy the Chinese nuclear facilities. Finally, the Moscow Treaty confirmed for Peking that the Soviet regime had, to say the least, a quite different approach to world revolution than had Mao Tse-tung.

If we seek to determine the relative weight of the Moscow Treaty in bringing on the open schism, two sets of competing hypotheses must be considered. First, did Moscow sign the test ban because the Sino-Soviet dispute had become irreparable? Or did the dispute become irreparable because the Kremlin signed the test ban? There existed, in all likelihood, a vicious circle in which Soviet moves toward a test ban aggravated relations with the Chinese, thus leading Peking to adopt policies that heightened Moscow's interest in curbing China's nuclear potential and in mending fences with the West. On balance, however, it seems that military, political, and economic considerations led Moscow as early as 1957 to adopt a strategy aimed at halting nuclear testing while at the same time it hoped to keep China in the Soviet camp.[27] On

27 To be sure, the cessation or prohibition of nuclear testing would have to be on terms acceptable to Moscow, with little or no on-site inspection, if only because of Khrushchev's internal opposition. See Bloomfield, Clemens, Griffiths, *op. cit.;* also Jerome B. Wiesner, *Where Science and Politics Meet* (New York: McGraw-Hill, 1965), pp. 170–171. That Moscow broke the nuclear test moratorium in September 1961 does not contradict the foregoing argument, for that decision probably stemmed from a situation unexpected as late as 1959 or 1960, i.e., that U.S. ICBM production would far outstrip Soviet production, militating for Soviet tests of warheads much larger than those of the United States in order to

the other hand, it is also quite likely that the worsening state of Sino-Soviet relations after September–October 1962 ranked high among the reasons why Khrushchev agreed in July 1963 to a partial test ban that he had rejected in August 1962.[28]

A second set of hypotheses is a variation of the first. Did Moscow decide to sign the limited test ban treaty because it *wanted* to drive Sino-Soviet relations to the breaking point? Or did the Kremlin *dare* to go ahead with the treaty only because it believed the breaking point had already been reached? The second interpretation seems the more likely because of the evidence at hand and also because it conforms more with what is known of coalition patterns generally.

It was in Moscow's interest, so long as it could dominate the Communist movement, to have China's grudging and nominal support rather than to risk a split of the entire movement, with the splintering and polycentrism it would precipitate. As in the Atlantic Community, so in the Communist camp, the leading power has preferred to live with autonomy on the part of a major ally rather than lose him — and others — altogether. The vanguard power by his general weight within the alliance can usually get his way: hence his appearance of being more tolerant of diversity than the challenger to his pre-eminence. Paris (since 1958) like Peking (since 1959) seems to have become increasingly rebellious because of the

offset the latter's numerical advantage. This line of thinking was reinforced by the Berlin crisis in the summer of 1961.

[28] Among the other considerations were the lack of any prospect after the Cuban debacle to alter radically the balance of strategic weapons; Kennedy's apparent resistance to domestic pressures to exploit further the Soviet retreat; the mounting economic troubles facing the Soviet leadership; Khrushchev's need to have a tangible victory for his coexistence line, coupled with the incapacitating illness in mid-April 1963 of one of its major opponents, Frol Kozlov.

The partial test ban treaty that Moscow agreed to in July 1963 was quite similar to one of two alternative proposals the United States offered on August 27, 1962. As noted earlier, Moscow's counterproposal on August 29, 1962, called for a partial test ban with an unpoliced, indefinite moratorium on underground testing, a proviso unacceptable to the United States. It should be noted that, even though the August 29, 1962, Soviet proposal was rejected by the West, Soviet propaganda treated it as a major concession, and Peking claims it was informed on August 25, 1962, of Moscow's intention to sign a nonproliferation treaty.

reluctance of the alliance leader to ease its entry into the nuclear club or share its weapons.[29]

For Moscow, of course, much else was at stake in 1963 than the shaky and perhaps doomed alliance with China. The failure of the Cuban adventure, the increasing U.S. strategic lead, the faltering Soviet economy, along with the challenge from Peking, all dictated that Moscow should seek a breathing space, at least temporarily, in its political-military competition with the West. If Moscow therefore moved toward accommodation with the United States, it was more in spite of Chinese opposition than because of it. Soviet leaders would have preferred to retain China as an ally and follower, if only nominally. Since the Chinese seemed determined to challenge Soviet hegemony rather than submit to it, Moscow had little to lose and something to gain by coming to terms with Washington rather than attempting to deal with frontal pressures from East and West simultaneously.

Once Peking openly challenged Moscow's leadership, the Kremlin had additional incentives to ostracize if not excommunicate China from the Communist movement. That Khrushchev strove to do this in the year following the Moscow Treaty does not contradict the assertion that he would have preferred to avoid this course. Once the die was cast, both Moscow and Peking endeavored to win support — both in the Communist and in the third world — by their interpretation of the war/peace issue.

This analysis of what Peking and Moscow stood to gain or lose by pushing for an open break is corroborated by their respective tactics during the six to eight months prior to the signing of the test ban treaty. During this period it was usually China rather than the Soviet Union that intensified the public polemic, for example, by the strong criticism of the Soviet withdrawal from Cuba;[30] the thinly veiled attacks on Khrush-

[29] For comparative analysis and documents, see Walter C. Clemens, Jr., ed., *World Perspectives on International Politics* (Boston: Little, Brown, 1965), pp. 41–47, 57–155.

[30] The Soviet action was likened to "another Munich." *Peking Review*, November 9, 1962, pp. 12–13.

chev through criticism of Italian and French surrogates;[31] most important, the June 14 letter three weeks before Sino-Soviet negotiations were to begin in Moscow; the open Chinese attack on the Soviet line of peaceful coexistence at the World Congress of Democratic Women that met in Moscow on June 24–29, 1963 (where the Soviet delegation stressed *unity* as well as peace);[32] and the Chinese motion to "suspend" the party negotiations in Moscow on July 20, 1963.[33]

But if the Chinese were usually the first to escalate the public polemic, Soviet deeds often served as the catalyst. Peking's analysis of the Sino-Soviet axis naturally became darker as Khrushchev, after Cuba, not only moved toward an understanding with the Kennedy administration but began to supply India with more military aid than did the United States.[34] Then, at the East German Party Congress in January 1963, when the Chinese spokesman attacked Yugoslav revisionism, "his voice was drowned out by whistles, boos, shouts and feet-stamping — an insult carefully staged, one must assume, by Khrushchev, who was ostentatiously absent. . . ."[35]

The Rubicon was crossed on June 25, 1963, when the partial test ban was initialed. The last bridge, if one still existed, burned on August 5 when dignitaries from Britain, the Soviet Union, and the United States formally signed the document. A photograph of Khrushchev hugging the U.S. representative the day after the initialing ceremony was printed by Peking with the explanation: "Khrushchev Embraces Harriman."[36]

For almost a decade — with the possible exception of the period from the May 1960 summit meeting to the Cuban missile adventure — Khrushchev had staked the success of his

---

[31] *Ibid.*, January 4, 1963; March 1, 1963; March 15, 1963.

[32] See articles on the congress in *Pravda,* June 24, 25, 27, 29, 30, and July 1, 2, 1963; *Izvestia,* June 24 and 28, 1963; *Peking Review,* July 5, 19, 26, 1963.

[33] The Chinese delegation received a hero's welcome when it returned to Peking. *People's Daily* of July 22, 1963, pictured Mao Tse-tung himself at the airport, and listed the names of many other officials who attended the reception, some of them having been in semiexile until then. However, the jet aircraft pictured in the background bore the conspicuous Cyrillic marking "CCCP."

[34] *The New York Times,* May 13, 1964.

[35] Griffith, *The Sino-Soviet Rift, op. cit.,* p. 101.

[36] *People's Daily,* July 29, 1963, p. 3.

foreign policy on a gamble. He had calculated that Moscow could reach an understanding with "sober forces" in the Western governments, particularly in Washington, that would permit both sides to compete by measures short of war. From roughly 1955 to 1959 the Soviet First Secretary seemed confident that this competition would rapidly "bury" the West, shrinking its sphere of influence by winning the third world for the Soviet camp. By 1963, however, Moscow seemed satisfied merely to stabilize the political-military situation with the West and cut losses within the international Communist movement, accepting (even after Khrushchev's removal) the defection of China. Soviet acquiescence in these limited objectives stemmed from the narrowing of alternatives open to Soviet policy following the Cuban debacle. Rather than essay some other quick fix to overcome strategic inferiority, Moscow grasped the opportunity implicit in President Kennedy's refusal to exploit the Soviet retreat aggressively. Mounting tensions with China and the Soviet Union's stagnating economy made it the more desirable to reach some accommodation with Washington. While the Kremlin had no prospect of overturning the military balance, it could nevertheless rest secure behind its minimum but adequate deterrent.

The significance of the Moscow Treaty extended on many planes far beyond the immediate purpose of prohibiting nuclear testing in three environments. (It was precisely because the three signatories' interest in such tests had declined that the ban became militarily and politically feasible.) The treaty gave a boost to efforts to reach other arms controls agreements and, as a result, created a "spirit of Moscow" that has proved less transient in East-West relations than the "Geneva spirit" eight years before. But future historians might well decide that the treaty's greatest impact was registered upon international communism. For the signing of the test ban unleashed a torrent of words and some deeds within the Communist movement that left it not only divided but, at least in Europe, shattered both in structure and strategy. The now open struggle for power between the Soviet Union and Communist China within the movement spilled over into the third world, into relations with the West, and even into overt interferences in one another's domestic politics. The net impact was to supplant what some had seen as an age of ideology with a vivid return to the classic struggle of national interests — historically unique, however, in its global scale.

The Struggle Within World Communism

As Moscow sought to stabilize its Western front, its left flank became increasingly vulnerable to Chinese attacks. After mid-1963 it could no longer be doubted that Peking intended to challenge the Soviet Union's vanguard position in the Communist movement. Since Moscow had "sold out" to imperialism, its leadership had to be supplanted — both at home and in the revolutionary movement. The withdrawal of Soviet military and technical aid in 1959–1960 had left China with little incentive to abide by Soviet policies which, given China's historical development, conflicted with her perceived interests and, probably, her genuine convictions. Despite China's opposition and to a large extent *because* of troubles with Peking, the Soviet government opted to signify dramatically its common political and military interests with the United States. The 1963 Moscow test ban treaty provided the last straw, and Peking threw down the gauntlet.

The struggle for power between the protagonists of international communism thus became more intense, dominating their relations with other Communist parties, undermining what remained of the Sino-Soviet alliance, and eroding further the myth of Communist unity.

Numerous factors operated to wear down and break the bonds between Moscow and Peking. The role of the nuclear test ban, however, was unique. Not only did it help to signal and then to produce the open schism, it also became a major point of contention around which both parties tried to rally support and to "expose" their ideological adversary's errors.

The test ban was hailed by Soviet propaganda as proof of the validity of the peaceful coexistence line. It served as a kind of proof that it was possible to deal with "sober forces" in the West. Cooperation as well as collaboration was dictated "by life itself." True, "ideological coexistence" remained taboo, and Moscow rejected any suggestion of "convergence" of the Soviet system and Western capitalism.[37] But *Pravda* on April 12, 1964, published a hitherto unknown letter by Lenin urging Soviet diplomats at the 1922 Genoa Economic Conference to isolate and flatter the pacifist wing of the bourgeoisie and

> . . . to declare permissible and . . . desirable an agreement with them — not only on trade but also on policy (as one of the few chances for the *peaceful evolution* of capitalism to a new structure, [an event] that we, as Communists have little faith in, but are willing to help test and consider it our duty to do so, as representatives of one power confronting others in a hostile majority).[38]

While Khrushchev's government sought legitimation for its moves toward coexistence with the "class" adversary, Moscow's deteriorating relationship with Peking made the concept of a "fraternal bond" based on common ideology vacuous and sterile.[39]

Both the Soviets and the Chinese attempted to exploit the Moscow Treaty to win support in the Communist world. That the test ban agreement was even possible was hailed in Moscow as proof that the Soviet line was "correct" and Peking's "wrong." Moscow held that China's opposition to the treaty linked the latter's leadership with "madmen" such as Adenauer, de Gaulle, and Goldwater. Peking, of course, held

[37] See, for example, G. Frantsov, "What Lies Behind the Slogan 'Ideological Disarmament,' " *Kommunist*, No. 13 (September 1962), pp. 110–119; also Ven. Motylev, "The Prevention of War and Contemporary Reformism," *Mirovaia Ekonomika i Mezhdunarodnye Otnosheniia*, No. 12 (1963), pp. 127–139. The Motylev article explicitly criticizes John Strachey's *On the Prevention of War* (London: Macmillan, 1962) for offering as an ideological justification for disarmament the convergence of capitalism and socialism.

[38] See Walter C. Clemens, Jr., "Lenin on Disarmament," *Slavic Review* (September 1964), p. 512 (Italics added). The "pacifist wing," according to Lenin, consisted of "petty bourgeois, pacifist and semipacifist democracy, of the type of the Second International or the Two-and-one half International, and then of the Keynes type, and so on. . . ."

[39] Even for domestic audiences Soviet propagandists portrayed Chinese strategy as a kind of yellow peril menacing all civilization. Cf. Radio Moscow's Domestic Service, August 2, 1963; also the TASS statement broadcast in English to Europe on August 5, 1963, reporting on the Sino-Soviet disputations in Hiroshima at the Ninth International Conference for Outlawing Atomic and Hydrogen Weapons.

that Moscow's entente with the West allied the Soviet leaders with "imperialism." The issue of the nuclear test ban forced Communist parties — like governments — to be "for" or "against."

In the first six months to one year following the Moscow Treaty, the West European and North American parties remained basically pro-Soviet, although some were extremists and others moderate. While splinter groups arose siding with Peking, only in Belgium did the pro-Chinese detach a significant following. In Latin America, the struggle developed more between Havana and Moscow than between Moscow and Peking. The old guard of most Latin parties adhered to the Soviet line, but Castro declared Cuba's neutrality in the Soviet-Chinese dispute while at the same time refusing to sign the Moscow Treaty on the ground that it involved the United States. All East European parties, except the Albanian, sided with Moscow but managed to gain more autonomy in the process. The Australian party lined up with the Kremlin, while New Zealand's party identified with Peking. The Malaysian, Thai, and Burmese parties remained pro-Chinese extremists. Elsewhere in Asia only two parties stood clearly with the Soviets — the Outer Mongolian and the Ceylonese, joined by part of the Indian. Four parties that had attempted neutrality — the North Korean, Vietnamese, Indonesian, and Japanese — drew closer to Peking, as the test ban foreclosed the possibility of nonalignment in the Sino-Soviet rift.[40]

The embarrassment of having to "choose" between the Soviet Union and China was particularly acute in Japan, where popular sentiments against nuclear testing run high. In part for that reason, a pro-Soviet faction later appeared in the Japanese Party. When two of its deputies voted in the Diet for ratification of the Moscow Treaty, they were expelled by the pro-Peking majority, thus setting in motion an exchange of letters between the Soviet and Japanese Communist parties exacerbating their already strained relationship.[41]

[40] See Griffith, *The Sino-Soviet Rift, op. cit.,* pp. 177–202. For a comprehensive listing of parties with their respective allegiances and factions as of late 1964, see "International Communism: The End of an Epoch," *Survey,* January 1965, pp. 190–196.

[41] The expulsion is reported in *Akahata,* May 23, 1964, translated in

The role of the nuclear issue in the general deterioration of Sino-Soviet relations was suggested by a Chinese statement in November 1965 charging that "the signing of the partial nuclear test ban treaty by the Soviet Union, the United States, and Britain was an important landmark in Khrushchev's alliance with the United States against China." The new Soviet leadership that succeeded Khrushchev was accused not only of having accepted his legacy but of plotting new deals with the United States for the prevention of nuclear proliferation and other so-called disarmament measures to perpetuate the U.S.-Soviet nuclear monopoly "against China and all other independent countries."[42]

The Future

The record of China's diplomacy and propaganda since its first nuclear test in October 1964 suggests that the Moscow Treaty remains a major irritant in Sino-Soviet relations. But the substance of the treaty may in time be less important to Peking than its symbolic meaning. As China's nuclear program advances, the threat of Soviet or U.S. moves to destroy the Chinese plant probably diminishes.[43] Even in 1964–1965 the political cost to China of testing in contempt of the Moscow Treaty was not onerous. With each Chinese test — as with each increase in Chinese strength generally — fewer criticisms of Peking's experiments will be heard, although Japan and India may provide vigorous exceptions to this tendency. If

Peking Review, May 29, 1964, pp. 17–21. For the exchange of correspondence, see *Partiinaia zhizn'*, No. 14 (July 1964), pp. 8–9; and *Akahata*, August 8, 1964, and September 2, 1964, in *Peking Review*, September 11, 1964, pp. 27–28, and September 18, 1964, pp. 12–19. For a sample of the Japanese Communist Party's intransigent position vis-à-vis the CPSU, see Kenji Miyamoto's report to the Ninth Congress of the JPC, in *Akahata*, November 25, 1964.

[42] Editorial in *People's Daily* and *Red Flag*, November 11, 1965, translated in *Peking Review*, November 12, 1965, pp. 13–14.

[43] The assumption is that Moscow and Washington will be increasingly resigned to China's membership in the atomic club, for which they may try to compensate by developing an ABM system or by other measures. However, there may be a period of several years before China weds nuclear tips to MRBM's when the temptation to pre-empt this capability will be high, especially if tensions in Southeast Asia increase.

other states "go nuclear," the criticism of China's atomic program will become still thinner. But Peking all the while can continue to exploit the propaganda theme that the Moscow Treaty represents a U.S.-Soviet attempt to perpetuate their atomic hegemony. And if one of the other signatories should repudiate the treaty, that would only serve to strengthen China's claim to political prescience.

Should either the United States or the Soviet Union denounce the treaty — an event that now seems quite unlikely — there would be more room for some *rapprochement* between Moscow and Peking. But if the partial ban were made comprehensive by U.S.-Soviet agreement, the ties between those two countries would become firmer, and the charge that they were free to carry on advanced testing underground would be negated.

Even the partial test ban provides some barrier to proliferation of atomic weapons, since signatories such as Israel, Sweden, Japan, and India would have to withdraw from the Moscow Treaty in order to test without violating the agreement — unless they should test underground only. Should China decide to oppose nuclear spread to additional countries, it might want to support a test ban, whether partial or comprehensive. But without a larger package deal of interest to China, its support for any version of the Moscow Treaty would entail high political costs. This is so not only because of its past criticism of the treaty but also because it still seeks to utilize the treaty for anti-Soviet, anti-imperialist propaganda.

It may be argued that China's "objective" interests require it to pay this cost in order to foreclose the prospect of Indian or Japanese membership in the atomic club. Furthermore, while the third world may not protest loudly against its atomic tests, it seems likely that China would be more influential among the established governments of Asia and Africa if its image were less militant and its propaganda thrust aimed more toward promises of peace and prosperity. The essential consideration would be that China stands to lose from allowing further nations to "go nuclear." At best it is likely to run a treadmill, attempting to stay ahead of India and Japan while trying to create a force that will penetrate U.S. and Soviet defenses.

Should Peking come to reason along these lines, however, it might have to decide upon strategic as well as propaganda sacrifices. For to shut the door to India and other potential nuclear powers may require agreement in the near future on nonproliferation. The timing could be inopportune, since China would not yet have become a nuclear power except in name. India's maximum condition for such a pact could include a freeze or reduction of nuclear armaments by the five existing nuclear powers. At a minimum, it would probably demand security guarantees from the United States and the Soviet Union that would seem to hang a Damocles' sword above China indefinitely — with little prospect that Peking could develop a first- or second-strike force capable of directly threatening the nuclear superpowers.

For all these reasons, material and symbolic, the test ban issue promises to remain an important factor in Sino-Soviet relations and in U.S. policy toward the two countries.

PART III

SINO-SOVIET RELATIONS IN A U.S.-CHINA CRISIS

7

The Chinese Attitude

HAROLD C. HINTON

It is common knowledge that Communist China tries to exploit its largely self-created adversary relationship with the United States, and the real or alleged inadequacy of Soviet support in this connection, for political advantage. It should not be imagined, however, that there is nothing more to this question than Chinese propaganda. China, unlike the Soviet Union, is a divided country, and the non-Communist portion of its territory is governed by a regime allied with the United States. As a disadvantaged and anti-*status quo* power fearful of American aggressive or retaliatory attack, and as the weaker partner in the Sino-Soviet alliance, Communist China has clearly felt entitled to make demands on the Soviet Union for aid, support, and protection, particularly in crisis situations. The Chinese have naturally but vainly hoped that such help could be had at the cost of minimum Soviet interference. The probable key to this, as to many other seemingly unrealistic aspects of their foreign policy, is the simple proposition that when one holds fairly low cards one must nevertheless play the best cards available for what they are worth.

Chinese Strategic Demands on the Soviet Union

The subject of Chinese strategic expectations of the Soviet Union is extremely complex and, largely no doubt because of its great sensitivity, obscure. Published documents are of course helpful to an effort at reconstruction, but they must be heavily supplemented by analysis of concrete events and the contexts in which these have occurred.

One important category of Chinese expectations is what might be called the demand for Soviet maintenance of a favorable (not necessarily quantitatively superior) East-West balance, both political and military. The Chinese appear to have demanded in this connection that the Soviet Union observe a proportionality in the distribution of its strategic attention between Europe and the Far East;[1] that the Soviet Union build up its strategic forces to a level sufficient to exert effective politico-military pressures on the West on behalf of the world Communist cause, China of course included;[2] and that the Soviet Union deter the United States, which the Chinese claim to regard as a strategic "paper tiger," from launching general war through such means as a blackmail threat against Western Europe, a blackmail threat (since 1957) against the continental United States,[3] and support within limits for the "national liberation movement."[4] In the Chinese view, such

[1] The Chinese phrase for this concept is the "indivisibility of peace." For documentation see Alice Langley Hsieh, *Communist China's Strategy in the Nuclear Era* (Englewood Cliffs, N.J.: Prentice-Hall, 1962), pp. 40ff.

[2] One of the expressed Chinese objections to the nuclear test ban treaty was that it would "ensure that the United States and its allies will gain nuclear superiority over the Soviet Union and further develop it." Statement of August 15, 1963, cited in William E. Griffith, *The Sino-Soviet Rift* (Cambridge: The M.I.T. Press, 1964), p. 343.

[3] The idea of a blackmail threat against the United States is implicit in the concept that "the East wind has prevailed over the West wind," announced by Mao Tse-tung in 1957. Note the high-risk conditions specified by the Chinese for nuclear disarmament: "We believe that it is possible to attain a complete ban on nuclear weapons in the following circumstances: The socialist camp has a great nuclear superiority; the people's struggles in various countries against nuclear weapons and nuclear war become broader and deeper; having further forfeited their nuclear superiority, the imperialists are compelled to realize that their policy of nuclear blackmail is no longer effective and that their launching of a nuclear war would only accelerate their own extinction." ("The Differences Between Comrade Togliatti and Us," *People's Daily*, December 31, 1962.)

[4] The Chinese have insisted that support by the Soviet Union and the rest of the "socialist camp" for "wars of liberation" must not include the use of nuclear weapons. See "Two Different Lines on the Question of War and Peace," *People's Daily* and *Red Flag*, November 19, 1963.

a strategy would clearly require the maintenance of a united "socialist camp led by the Soviet Union." Unfortunately for Communist China, the United States took a similar view and announced in 1959 that it would hold the Soviet Union "partially responsible" for Chinese actions;[5] Khrushchev thereupon disavowed both "partial responsibility" and, since leadership implies responsibility, Soviet leadership of the "socialist camp."[6]

A second category of Chinese demands relates to Soviet political and military support for Chinese national objectives, of which one of the most important is obviously the "liberation" of Taiwan. Speaking before the U.N. Security Council on November 28, 1950, Wu Hsiu-ch'üan pointedly reminded the Soviet Union that it had adhered to the Cairo and Potsdam Declarations, which promised to return Taiwan to China, and demanded that the Security Council take action to terminate the American "occupation" of Taiwan.[7] The Soviet Union, however, showed itself generally unresponsive on this score.[8] The disappointing (to the Chinese) Soviet performance during the 1958 Taiwan Strait crisis, Soviet nonendorsement of

[5] Speech by Under Secretary of State Douglas Dillon, October 7, 1959 (text in *The New York Times,* October 8, 1959).

[6] A speech by Khrushchev to the Supreme Soviet, October 31, 1959 (excerpts in *The New York Times,* November 1, 1959), explicitly disavowed "partial responsibility"; the Moscow statement (text in G. F. Hudson and others, *The Sino-Soviet Dispute* [New York: Praeger, 1961], pp. 177–205) implicitly denies Soviet leadership of the "socialist camp"; Khrushchev explicitly denied Soviet leadership of the "socialist camp" shortly afterward: "The role of the Soviet Union does not lie in the fact that it leads other socialist countries. . . ." Speech of January 6, 1961 (text in *Kommunist,* No. 1, January 1961). For a statement of the Chinese view that Soviet leadership of the "socialist camp," were the Soviet Union willing to accept it, would imply responsibility rather than power, see "The Leaders of the CPSU Are the Greatest Splitters of Our Times," *People's Daily* and *Red Flag,* February 4, 1964; the last Chinese statement in which I have found a quasi-factual reference to the "socialist camp led by the Soviet Union" is "Hold High the Red Banner of the October Revolution, March from Victory to Victory," *People's Daily,* November 7, 1960.

[7] Text in *The New York Times,* November 29, 1950.

[8] There was little mention of Taiwan in the Sino-Soviet joint communiqué of October 11, 1954 (text in *The New York Times,* October 12, 1954), none in the Chou-Bulganin declaration (text released by TASS, January 18, 1957), and none in the Mao-Khrushchev statement of August 3, 1958 (text in *The New York Times,* August 4, 1958).

Mao Tse-tung's thesis that "Imperialists and All Reactionaries Are Paper Tigers,"[9] and the obvious caution that Khrushchev displayed in waiting until the crisis had subsided before serving his "ultimatum" on the West with respect to West Berlin (in November 1958), seem to have led to a Chinese failure to exploit for propaganda purposes an important article, "Chairman Mao on the October Revolution," which had evidently been intended as a companion piece to the one on "Paper Tigers." It included a number of statements made by Mao during the 1930's to the effect that the Soviet Union would give support to "people's wars of liberation."[10] After this episode a highly belligerent statement of support for Communist China on the Taiwan issue, made by Khrushchev for political effect in 1959,[11] evidently seemed incredible in Peking and was not publicized there.[12]

On a related issue, the prevention of "two Chinas," the Chinese have also apparently expected more Soviet support than they have received. In fact, they have charged Khrushchev with advising them in 1959 to accept indefinitely the existence of a separate Taiwan, on the analogy of Soviet Russia's temporary toleration (actually, maintenance) of the former Far Eastern Republic.[13] The Chinese have also interpreted Soviet acceptance of Nationalist Chinese adherence to the nuclear test ban treaty as indicative of Soviet acquiescence in "two Chinas."[14]

Communist China also seems to have expected more Soviet

[9] Text released by New China News Agency (NCNA), October 31, 1958.

[10] Text in *Shih-chieh chih-shih* (World Knowledge), November 1, 1958. The principal statements may be found in *Selected Works of Mao Tse-tung* (New York: International Publishers, 1954), Vol. 2, p. 176, and Vol. 3, p. 47. In the latter passage, the statement in the original (*Mao Tse-tung hsuan-chi*, Manchuria Publishing House, 1948, p. 458) to the effect that the Soviet Union "will surely help in wars beneficial to the security of the Soviet Union" (*pao-wei Su-lien*) has been altered to read: ". . . to the defense of peace."

[11] See Averell Harriman, "My Alarming Interview with Khrushchev," *Life*, July 13, 1959, pp. 34, 36.

[12] Hsieh, *op. cit.*, p. 165.

[13] Chinese statement of September 1, 1963 (cited in Griffith, *op. cit.*, p. 382).

[14] Chinese statement of September 1, 1963 (Griffith, *op. cit.*, pp. 382–383).

support than it has received on the question of removing American bases, and of course nuclear weapons, from the Far East and the western Pacific (especially Japan and Okinawa), and to have rejected Soviet endorsement of a proposal, essentially Japanese in origin, for an "atom-free zone" in the region that would preclude Chinese as well as American and Soviet nuclear weapons.[15] The main practical requirement for the removal of American bases would be a termination of the American-Japanese mutual security treaty. Since pressures toward this end, such as those exerted in 1960, have failed, only blandishments offer any prospect of success. These must come mainly from the Soviet Union, since although the main utility of American bases in Japan and Okinawa lies in their serving to contain Communist China, it is the Soviet Union rather than China of which the Japanese are afraid. Soviet conciliation of Japan, to be effective, would require the return of at least some of the disputed islands in the north and the removal of Japan from the wording of the Sino-Soviet alliance, and the result would presumably be to focus increased Japanese attention on the American presence in Okinawa. The Soviet Union has failed to take any significant steps toward these ends, and the Chinese seem to have concluded that the Soviets are more than willing to see them continue to be contained by the United States.[16]

Finally, Communist China has felt entitled to expect Soviet support, of a political kind at any rate, in the Sino-Indian border dispute and has, not unreasonably, interpreted the actual Soviet policy toward the dispute as being pro-Indian.[17]

---

15 Cf. "The [Afro-Asian People's Solidarity] Conference called for the immediate cessation of nuclear weapons tests and held that Asia and Africa should be a peace zone in which no *foreign* country should deploy nuclear and rocket weapons" (Chou En-lai, report to National People's Congress, text released by NCNA, February 10, 1958. Italics added). The original proposal endorsed by the conference had not included the qualification "foreign."

16 In an interview of January 17, 1965, as reported in Tokyo *Asahi*, January 18, 1965, Chen Yi charged that Khrushchev had ignored repeated Chinese requests to return the Kurils to Japan, because he (Khrushchev) did not want to disturb the American position in the Ryukyus and Bonins.

17 The Chinese have described the Soviet statement of September 9, 1959, on the Sino-Indian border dispute as the occasion when "the internal differences among the fraternal parties were first brought into the open"

A third category of Chinese demands on the Soviet Union relates to military aid. In the conventional field, the Soviet Union initiated weapons shipments to China, on a reimbursable basis, after the latter's entry into the Korean War, made important new commitments in 1952 and assisted in the creation of Chinese defense industries in the mid-1950's, but virtually terminated military deliveries in 1960 as an act of political pressure.[18] In the nuclear field, the Chinese seem to have demanded nuclear weapons unsuccessfully from the Soviet Union in the early months of 1953[19] and are known to have received a Soviet commitment in October 1954 to aid in "peaceful" nuclear research and development.[20]

In February 1956, at the Twentieth Congress, Khrushchev announced that he was in favor of a nuclear test ban even in the absence of a general disarmament agreement, and two months later the Soviet Union committed itself to supply China with a nuclear research reactor (not delivered, however, until mid-1958). This sequence of events, as well as evidence of a later date, strongly suggests a Sino-Soviet bargain: limited Soviet aid for an independent Chinese nuclear weapons program in exchange for Chinese acquiescence in a nuclear test ban, the main purpose of which in Soviet eyes was probably the discouragment of any thought of a West German nuclear weapons capability.

In the second half of 1957 the Chinese began to press the Russians for greater concessions. Their general rationale was that the "East wind has prevailed over the West wind" as the result of the psychological climate created in the United States by recent Soviet successes in space and missilery. No doubt they cited in addition such developments as the decision to station American nuclear weapons in NATO countries, and later in South Korea, and the beginning of increased

("Whence the Differences?" *People's Daily*, February 27, 1963). Cf. "The Truth About How the Leaders of the CPSU Have Allied Themselves with India against China," *People's Daily*, November 1, 1963.

18 Raymond L. Garthoff, "Sino-Soviet Military Relations," *The Annals of the American Academy of Political and Social Science*, Vol. 349 (September 1963), pp. 81–93.

19 Harold C. Hinton, *Communist China in World Politics* (Boston: Houghton Mifflin, 1966), pp. 222–229.

20 See the 1954 joint communiqué cited in footnote 8.

American military aid to Nationalist China. There is no question that the Chinese demanded and were granted, at the end of 1957, a substantial increase in the level of Soviet aid to their nuclear program, including a gaseous diffusion plant and aid in the development of medium-range surface-to-surface missiles. In addition, they evidently requested the transfer of finished nuclear weapons by the Soviet Union as a stopgap measure to protect themselves, if necessary, pending the fruition of their own development program. The Soviet Union evidently posed as a precondition a counterdemand for the virtual integration of the Chinese armed forces with those of the Soviet Union under a relationship of the Warsaw Pact variety, with the Soviet Union in effective control. The Chinese rejected this arrangement and gave up their demand for finished nuclear weapons, evidently in the spring of 1958, but their more limited agreement of support for a test ban in exchange for a now accelerated program of Soviet nuclear technical assistance remained in effect for the time being.

In the first half of 1959, however, in an episode probably related to the obscure Sino-Soviet military interplay connected with the fall of Defense Minister P'eng Te-huai, the Chinese demanded yet another increase in the level of Soviet aid to the Chinese nuclear program; but the Russians refused, probably because of concern over mounting Chinese militancy, the possible effect on the incipient partial *détente* between the Soviet Union and the United States, and above all the problem of a nuclear West Germany. Soviet nuclear aid to China seems to have been almost completely terminated in 1959–1960. The Chinese thereupon felt relieved of any obligation to support a nuclear test ban and began to revert to the pre-1956 Soviet position that such a ban would be acceptable only as part of a complete ban on nuclear weapons.[21]

21 On this obscure episode, see Alice Langley Hsieh, "China's Secret Military Papers: Military Doctrine and Strategy," *The China Quarterly*, No. 18 (April–June 1964), p. 93; Morton H. Halperin, *China and the Bomb* (New York: Praeger, 1965), pp. 80–81; Harold P. Ford, "Modern Weapons and the Sino-Soviet Estrangement," *The China Quarterly*, No. 18 (April–June 1964), pp. 160–173; Chinese statement of August 15, 1963. The foregoing interpretation differs significantly from that in any of these sources.

The most important, in the short run, of all Chinese strategic demands on the Soviet Union has been one for protection, meaning mainly protection in case of an American, or Nationalist Chinese and American, attack, whether aggressive or retaliatory, on Communist China. It is likely that at the time of the signing of the Sino-Soviet alliance (February 14, 1950), the Chinese and the Russians were afraid, on the basis of General MacArthur's New Year's Day message to the Japanese people,[22] that having lost its bet on the Chinese Nationalists the United States might proceed to rearm Japan and that, despite Secretary Acheson's seemingly reassuring speech of January 12,[23] the United States might retaliate for the planned Communist military operations in Korea and the Taiwan Strait.

Although Stalin's behavior during the Korean War came fairly close at times to meeting Chinese expectations, the same could not be said for his successors. The first major shock to the Chinese after the Korean armistice came in the wake of the enunciation of the Dulles doctrine of "massive retaliation," which was first expressed at a time of serious tension over Indochina. In the Far Eastern context the doctrine came to signify a determination to hold the Soviet Union at arm's length with the threat of thermonuclear war and, if necessary, to chastise the Chinese with tactical atomic weapons, which became part of the American arsenal in 1954.[24] By introducing a sharp differentiation into what had previously been a comparatively undifferentiated American threat to both the partners in the Sino-Soviet alliance, "massive retaliation" provided the Soviet Union with a powerful incentive to stay out of Sino-American crises. In a strategic dialogue conducted on the eve of the siege of Dien Bien Phu, Malenkov appeared to say that the Soviet Union should act on this incentive and defend only itself, while Khrushchev stated that it should, if necessary, defend China as well.[25]

22 Text in *The New York Times*, January 1, 1950.
23 Text in *Documents on International Affairs, 1949–1950*, pp. 96–108; see especially p. 103.
24 Extracts from speech of January 12, 1954, in *Documents on International Affairs, 1954*, pp. 265–267.
25 Cf. Hsieh, *Communist China's Strategy in the Nuclear Era, op. cit.*, pp. 24–25.

If, as seems probable, the Chinese were favorably impressed by Khrushchev's stand, they can only have been cruelly disappointed by his retreat during the next few years. The main reasons seem to have been the admission of West Germany to NATO and a resultant fear that a situation might arise in which the United States would feel tempted to launch a strategic surprise attack on the Soviet Union.[26] Soon afterward came Khrushchev's enunciation at his Twentieth Party Congress of the doctrine of the "noninevitability" of war, that is, of general war, meaning apparently that the chances of general war were sufficiently great, and its probable consequences for the Soviet Union and world communism were so terrible, that it could not be risked, although efforts would be made to find ways of exerting pressure on the United States without creating undue risk of general war.[27]

[26] On May 10, 1965, the day after West Germany's formal admission to NATO, the Soviet Union unveiled a major new disarmament proposal stressing the prevention of surprise attack (text in *Documents on International Affairs, 1955*, pp. 110–121). Note also other relevant Soviet moves during this period, such as the Austrian state treaty, the return of Porkkala to Finland, the formation of the Warsaw Pact, and the Geneva summit conference. On the discussion in Soviet military journals at this time of the problem of surprise attack, see H. S. Dinerstein, *War and the Soviet Union* (rev. ed., New York: Praeger, 1962), Chapter 6.

[27] Text of Khrushchev's report to the Twentieth Congress in *Pravda*, February 15, 1956. Among the evidence that could be cited in support of the proposition that Khrushchev's frequently warlike posture and "rocket rattling," although convincing to many, were essentially bluff designed among other things to compensate for Soviet strategic inferiority to the United States, to disguise the fact (which should have been obvious to all after the U-2 episode) that the U.S. government was aware of the actual strategic balance, and to justify to his colleagues his own preference for missiles over conventional forces, are the following: his rejection of the relatively high-risk strategy proposed by the Chinese and of the "East wind over West wind" and "paper tiger" concepts (as he remarked in his December 12, 1962, speech to the Supreme Soviet, the "paper tiger has nuclear teeth"); the stress in the Soviet discussions at the 1957 Moscow conference on the avoidance of war; Khrushchev's usual reluctance to confront the United States directly and his preference for trying to split the United States' allies through intimidation as well as blandishments; the careful timing even of his threats against American allies to achieve maximum psychological effect with minimum actual risk; his failure to intervene with more than threats in the Middle Eastern crises of 1956–1958; his apparently sincere espousal of "general and complete disarmament" (provided it could be achieved in a way that would not endanger Soviet security and that would result in an increase in comparative Soviet

Numerous acts of the Soviet Union during the next few years, and in particular its behavior during the Taiwan Strait crisis of 1958 and Khrushchev's trip to the United States in 1959, drove home to the Chinese that the Soviet Union was unlikely to assume any serious risks by confronting the United States on behalf of themselves. In addition, the Chinese apparently began to fear that the Soviet Union might try, within the framework of Khrushchev's proposal of September 1959 for "general and complete disarmament," to press China to reduce its conventional forces. Accordingly, Communist China formally denied the right of anyone else to bind it in the disarmament field without its own consent[28] and insisted that it would not reduce its conventional forces, which were allegedly needed to deter "imperialist" attack through the ability to invade other Asian countries.[29] The secret Chinese military papers seem to confirm the hypothesis that by 1961, if not earlier, the Chinese leadership was not counting on Soviet support or protection in any likely military crisis.[30]

The Kennedy doctrine of "flexible response," although adopted mainly in the face of expected Soviet rather than Chinese pressures, including increased Soviet involvement in "national liberation wars," was also of serious concern to the Chinese, particularly because of its emphasis on unconventional warfare and various statements by high American officials that the United States had both the nuclear weapons and the will to cope with the Soviet Union and Communist China simultaneously, or either of them separately, as the situation

influence) as a means of avoiding dangerous conflicts; and his rapid decision to withdraw his missiles and bombers from Cuba when faced with an unexpectedly determined American response. See Arnold L. Horelick and Myron Rush, *Strategic Power and Soviet Foreign Policy* (Chicago: The University of Chicago Press, 1966).

28 National People's Congress Standing Committee, resolution of January 21, 1960.

29 Cf. *Long Live Leninism* (Peking: Foreign Language Press, 1960), p. 34; K'ang Sheng's speech to the 1960 Warsaw Pact meeting (text in G. F. Hudson and others, *The Sino-Soviet Dispute* [New York: Praeger, 1961], pp. 72–77, note especially p. 74).

30 John Wilson Lewis, *Chinese Communist Party Leadership and the Succession to Mao Tse-tung: An Appraisal of Tensions* (Washington, D. C.: Department of State, Bureau of Intelligence and Research, January 1964), p. 28; Hsieh, *Communist China's Strategy in the Nuclear Era, op. cit.*, p. 81.

might require.[31] Clearly the Soviet Union was again being offered a powerful incentive to stay out of any Sino-American military confrontation. That the Soviet Union intended, under most circumstances at any rate, to do exactly that, was strongly suggested by an article in the Soviet press on the twenty-fifth anniversary of the Japanese attack on China, implying that now as then China could expect no more from the Soviet Union than arms and "volunteer" pilots and technicians.[32] Soviet behavior during the Cuban missile crisis can hardly have altered the Chinese view of Khrushchev's reluctance to run genuine, as contrasted with apparent, risks on behalf of "fraternal" regimes.

The nuclear test ban treaty, especially in view of what had happened between China and the Soviet Union in 1959, was virtually the last straw. *Détente* between the Soviet Union and the United States, whether in 1955 (the "spirit of Geneva"),[33] in 1959 (the "spirit of Camp David"),[34] or since 1963 (the nuclear test ban treaty and after),[35] has always been anathema to the Chinese for a number of reasons. One of the most important of these is a conviction that such a *détente* does not mitigate American hostility to Communist China and, regardless of what the actual chances may be that the Soviet Union will support China effectively in cases of a Sino-American crisis, diminishes the deterrent effect of the Sino-Soviet alliance by making it seem unlikely that the Soviet Union will in fact render such support.[36]

31 Cf. Jen Ku-ping, "A Scrutiny of the Counterrevolutionary Grand Strategy of U.S. Imperialism," *People's Daily,* July 22, 1962.

32 M. Domogatskikh and V. Karymov, "An Instructive Lesson," *Pravda,* July 7, 1962.

33 See Hinton, *op. cit.,* pp. 127–128, for an elaboration of the hypothesis that the Geneva summit conference of 1955 contributed to the acceleration of industrialization and socialization that began shortly thereafter in Communist China.

34 Cf. Donald S. Zagoria, *The Sino-Soviet Conflict, 1956–1961* (Princeton, N.J.: Princeton University Press, 1962), Chapter 9.

35 The Chinese attacked the test ban treaty on the ground, among others, that it fostered an "illusion of peace."

36 Chinese behavior at the time of the tenth anniversary of the signing of the Sino-Soviet treaty of alliance (February 14, 1960) suggests a desire to counter the effects of the "spirit of Camp David," which had not yet been exploded by the U-2 episode, and to evoke increased Soviet support at the time of the renewal of the mutual security treaty between the

The Korean War

The Korean War was clearly the most serious Sino-American military confrontation up to that time, and therefore constitutes what is probably the best case study in Chinese strategic demands on the Soviet Union in the context of such a confrontation.

As U.N. forces in Korea approached the 38th parallel in late September 1950, the Chinese warned (on September 25) that they would intervene if American (not South Korean) troops crossed the parallel.[37] Ratifications of the Sino-Soviet treaty of alliance were exchanged, rather belatedly and perhaps hastily, on September 30.[38] The main Chinese concern was unquestionably to keep American forces away from the Manchurian border, and to this end Chinese troops began to cross the Yalu River on October 15–16. Presumably Peking was counting on Soviet theater forces in Eastern Europe and the Far East to deter the United States from retaliating against Communist China, and in particular from using nuclear weapons. In addition, the Chinese may have attached some value to the attitude of the United States' European allies, who tended to agree with General Bradley that a major Sino-American war would be the "wrong war, at the wrong place, at the wrong time, and with the wrong enemy." In this connection, it should be noted that a vague statement by President Truman, on November 30, that the United States might use nuclear weapons in the Korean War[39] evoked a highly unusual hint from Moscow that the Soviet Union might involve itself directly in the war[40] and a hasty visit to Washington by Prime Minister Attlee, at the end of which Truman disavowed *implicitly* any desire to use

---

United States and Japan. For the documents, see *Sino-Soviet Alliance: Mighty Bulwark of World Peace* (Peking: Foreign Language Press, 1960); American Consulate General, Hong Kong, "Tenth Anniversary of Signing of Sino-Soviet Treaty of Friendship, Alliance, and Mutual Assistance," *Current Background*, No. 613 (February 26, 1960).

[37] Allen S. Whiting, *China Crosses the Yalu: The Decision to Enter the Korean War* (New York: Macmillan, 1960), p. 107.

[38] Chinese International Service broadcast, Peking, October 18, 1950.

[39] *The New York Times*, December 1, 1950.

[40] *Pravda*, December 3, 1950; cf. Max Beloff, *Soviet Policy in the Far East, 1944–1951* (London: Oxford University Press, 1953), p. 195.

nuclear weapons and *explicitly* any intent to invade North Korea again.[41]

The Chinese were probably disappointed, to say the least, at the virtual absence of Soviet support during the dangerous period embracing the relief of General MacArthur (April 11, 1951) and the disastrous failure of their own great offensives (April–May 1951). Instead, the Soviet Union on June 23 proposed armistice talks, on the basis essentially of the restoration of the *status quo ante* plus the retention of foreign troops in Korea. Although this proposal would leave unfulfilled the main Chinese demands in connection with the Korean crisis — the withdrawal of American forces from South Korea, the removal of American protection from Taiwan, and the admission of Communist China to the United Nations — Peking was left with no alternative but to agree to armistice talks, which it and Pyongyang did with probable reluctance on July 2.

In January 1952 the armistice negotiations were immensely complicated by the injection by the United Nations of the issue of voluntary repatriation of prisoners of war, a politically sensitive issue since it was expected that a large percentage of the Chinese and North Koreans taken by the United Nations would refuse repatriation. The Soviet Union seems to have involved itself in the ensuing outcry to the extent of helping to arrange the famous "germ warfare" campaign,[42] but when, in June, American aircraft began to bomb the Yalu dams for the first time the Chinese probably expected a stronger Soviet response. Instead, the Soviet ambassador left Peking for Moscow on July 1, and he was not replaced until early December. In the interval (in September) Stalin agreed to new commitments of conventional military aid to China and to the retention of the Soviet garrison at Dairen and Port Arthur beyond the originally envisioned terminal date, probably as a visible deterrent to American air attacks on Manchuria.

Late in the year, as the Chinese reinforced their troops in Korea, Stalin's willingness to confront the United States seems to have increased, for reasons of which some, such as his own

41 David Rees, *Korea: The Limited War* (New York: St. Martin's, 1964), pp. 166–171.
42 *Ibid.*, p. 359.

mental state, domestic political problems, and a crisis in his relations with Yugoslavia, were extrinsic to the Korean crisis. In addition, he was evidently concerned over the prisoner issue and angry at India for its pro-Western change of front in the course of its attempted mediation of the issue.[43] In February 1953, the United States, in its determination to have an armistice and to deter another possible Chinese offensive, threatened to extend the war to the mainland of China and use nuclear weapons.[44] Stalin must have been pondering this threat as he died, naturally or otherwise. That the Chinese were demanding further Soviet military support at this time is indicated by the strongly military composition of the Chinese delegation to Stalin's funeral on March 9; that they were also seeking nuclear weapons is suggested by the arrival on February 25 of a Chinese scientific delegation led by Ch'ien San-ch'iang, Communist China's leading nuclear physicist, and by the presence in the funeral delegation of Minister of Public Security Lo Jui-ch'ing, whose opposite number Beria was then in charge of the Soviet nuclear weapons program. By about mid-March it became clear to the Chinese that they would receive no effective support from Stalin's successors, and they accordingly had no choice but to sign a disadvantageous armistice on July 27. In 1958 they withdrew what remained of the "Chinese People's Volunteers" from North Korea, contrary to the wishes of the North Koreans, rather than leave them to face with questionable Soviet support the tactical nuclear weapons that the United States had recently introduced into South Korea.[45]

The Taiwan Strait

There can be no doubt that in late 1949 and early 1950 the Chinese Communists were preparing to "liberate" Taiwan by

[43] For elaboration, see Hinton, op. cit., pp. 219–221. For support for the thesis that Stalin at the end of his life was in a highly bellicose mood, see Boris I. Nicolaevsky, Power and the Soviet Elite (New York: Praeger, 1965), pp. 170, 247–249.

[44] Cf. Dwight D. Eisenhower, Mandate for Change, 1953–1956 (New York: Doubleday, 1963), p. 181; Sherman Adams, Firsthand Report (New York: Harper, 1961), pp. 48–49, 102 (quoted in Rees, op. cit., pp. 419–420).

[45] Hinton, op. cit., pp. 221–223.

means of an amphibious attack, and that this plan was frustrated by a series of setbacks of which the most important was the interposition of the U.S. Seventh Fleet on June 27, 1950.[46] Worse still from Peking's standpoint, General MacArthur's trip to Taiwan in July and his ensuing favorable remarks about Chiang Kai-shek seem to have roused the specter of an American and Chinese Nationalist military intervention on the mainland to strangle the Communist regime in its cradle, if possible.[47] In the autumn, as U.S. forces approached the 38th parallel, the center of gravity of this operation seemed to transfer itself to Korea, and it was essentially as a countermeasure to it that the Chinese then intervened. In addition, they probably hoped to acquire leverage that would be useful in connection with the Taiwan question. Their defeats in Korea in 1951 of course eliminated any such possibility.

The "unleashing of Chiang Kai-shek" by the United States in February 1953, in the hope of making Peking willing to sign an armistice, was an inadequate form of pressure and produced in itself no change of attitude on the crucial issue of prisoners.[48] This is not to say that in the tense atmosphere of those days the "unleashing" was ignored; on the night of February 17, in the course of his last interview with a foreigner (the Indian ambassador), Stalin warned in thinly veiled terms that he would use force if the United States employed Nationalist forces to attack the Chinese mainland.[49]

In 1954, a constellation of political factors and an increase in American military aid to the Chinese Nationalists seemed to suggest the distinct possibility of an attack on the China coast[50] and the advantages of some kind of spoiling or preemptive attack. Accordingly, the Communists made preparations for defense[51] and began immediately after the conclusion at Geneva of an Indochinese armistice to whip up a propa-

[46] Cf. Whiting, op. cit., pp. 21–22.

[47] Cf. ibid., pp. 81–82.

[48] Cf. Mao Tse-tung, speech on February 7, 1963, to National Committee of the Chinese People's Political Consultative Conference.

[49] K. P. S. Menon, The Flying Troika (London: Oxford University Press, 1963), pp. 28–29.

[50] Hinton, op. cit., pp. 258–261.

[51] Cf. Matthew B. Ridgway, Soldier: The Memoirs of Matthew B. Ridgway (New York: Harper, 1956), pp. 278–279.

ganda storm over the impending "liberation" of Taiwan. On September 3, Communist artillery began to shell Quemoy. As usual, it is difficult to infer exactly what the Chinese demanded of the Soviet Union at that time, but what they got was virtually nothing; it will be recalled that at this time the foreign policy consideration uppermost in the mind of the Soviet leadership was the impending admission of West Germany to NATO. On September 11, the Soviet Union proposed to Japan that they "normalize" their relations.[52] When Khrushchev visited China at the end of September, his published statements and the joint communiqué issued on October 11 said rather little about Taiwan. The Soviet Union displayed no significant reaction to the signing of a mutual security treaty between the United States and Nationalist China in December 1954 or to an implicit threat by Secretary Dulles on March 8, 1955, to take action against Communist China under the "massive retaliation" doctrine. Lack of Soviet support for Peking was probably an important reason why the situation in the Taiwan Strait eased in March–April.[53]

During 1958 there was a marked increase in American military aid to the Chinese Nationalists.[54] Chiang Kai-shek's recently published memoirs had implicitly repudiated the idea of an accommodation with the Chinese Communists and had explicitly advocated that the "democracies" launch a conventional war against Communist China.[55] The major danger for Peking in a Nationalist attack on the mainland lay, as always, in the possibility that the United States might involve itself voluntarily or involuntarily in the hostilities. Soviet protection already seemed a doubtful quantity, and Moscow had begun to display a seemingly unfavorable attitude toward the idea

52 James W. Morley, *Soviet and Communist Chinese Policies Toward Japan, 1950–1957: A Comparison* (New York: Institute of Pacific Relations, 1958), p. 9. The day before, the Soviet Union had received a note from the United States, Britain, and France indicating a definite intention to admit West Germany to NATO (text in *Documents on International Affairs, 1954*, pp. 55–57).

53 Cf. Hinton, *op. cit.*, pp. 262–263.

54 Joyce Kallgren, "Nationalist China's Armed Forces," *The China Quarterly*, No. 15 (July–September 1963), p. 38.

55 Chiang Kai-shek, *Soviet Russia in China: A Summing-up at Seventy* (New York: Farrar, Straus and Cudahy, 1957), p. 341.

of a Chinese nuclear deterrent. Among the indications of Chinese Communist concern, and of an intention to play the best cards available, even though not very good, were a renewal of the advocacy in the Chinese press of "armed struggle" against "imperialism" in underdeveloped countries, an upsurge of political indoctrination in the People's Liberation Army, and an important military conference (May 27–July 22, 1958) that "discussed and adopted decisions concerning the work of national defense in the light of the current international situation."[56] By the end of July, when Khrushchev flew secretly to Peking, the Chinese were probably demanding strong Soviet declaratory support in connection with their projected spoiling attack in the Taiwan Strait and also a Soviet diversion of some kind in the Middle East, which was then in the throes of a crisis.[57] Whatever Khrushchev promised was evidently something less; the joint communiqué did not even mention Taiwan.[58] The Soviet role during the ensuing crisis, which began on August 23, was, to put it briefly, not very impressive.[59] Khrushchev's statement of September 7, that "An attack on the People's Republic of China . . . is an attack on the Soviet Union," immediately followed American acceptance of a Chinese offer to resume Sino-American ambassadorial talks, which seemed to eliminate most of the risk of a major Sino-American war.[60] Khrushchev's statement of October 5, repeating the Soviet pledge to defend Communist China against the United States but adding that "we have not interfered in and do not

[56] NCNA dispatch, July 25, 1958.

[57] "Eisenhower Hoists the Pirate's Skull and Crossbones," *People's Daily*, July 21, 1958, which was published just as the Chinese were launching a propaganda offensive in connection with the Taiwan Strait, appears to urge the Soviet Union at least to send "volunteers" to the Middle Eastern countries allegedly threatened by American "imperialism."

[58] Text in *The New York Times*, August 4, 1958.

[59] Cf. John R. Thomas, "Soviet Behavior in the Quemoy Crisis of 1958," *Orbis*, Vol. VI, No. 1 (Spring 1962), pp. 38–64.

[60] On September 4, the Communist Chinese announced a twelve-mile limit on their territorial waters, in an obvious effort to keep the United States from convoying Nationalist ships headed for Quemoy as far as the three-mile limit. Secretary Dulles promptly responded with a threatening statement indicating a willingness to defend Quemoy if necessary (text in *The New York Times*, September 5, 1958). This was immediately followed by the convening of a Supreme State Conference in Peking and the issuing of an invitation to resume Sino-American ambassadorial talks.

intend to interfere in the civil war which the Chinese people are waging against the Chiang Kai-shek clique," was made the day before the expiration of a deadline imposed by the Nationalists for the cessation of Communist shelling of Quemoy — failing which the Nationalists would attack the Communist gun positions.[61] On October 6, the Communists announced the first of a series of cease-fires. It is not surprising that the Chinese, whether sincerely or for political advantage, have since ridiculed the Soviet performance during the Taiwan Strait crisis,[62] or that since 1958 the health of the already sickly Sino-Soviet alliance has shown a dramatic decline.

A somewhat similar sequence of events occurred in 1962. In the spring, the Communists thought they saw reason to fear a Nationalist attack on the mainland, and in June they heavily reinforced their garrison opposite Taiwan. At Warsaw, on June 23, the Communists received a pledge from the United States that it would not support a Nationalist attack on the mainland if one should occur,[63] and ten days later Khrushchev loudly announced Soviet support for Communist China if it were attacked.[64]

Indochina

The closest approach up till then to overt American threats against Communist China in connection with the Indochinese crisis occurred in 1954. In April, Secretary Dulles and some others seemed to be threatening retaliation if Communist

[61] On the deadline, see Tang Tsou, "The Quemoy Imbroglio: Chiang Kai-shek and the United States," *The Western Political Quarterly*, Vol. XII, No. 4 (December 1959), p. 1084.

[62] "In August and September of 1958, the situation in the Taiwan Straits was indeed very tense as a result of the aggression and provocations by the U.S. imperialists. The Soviet leaders expressed their support for China on September 7 and 19 respectively. Although at that time the situation in the Taiwan Straits was tense, there was no possibility that a nuclear war would break out and no need for the Soviet Union to support China with its nuclear weapons. It was only when they were clear that this was the situation that the Soviet leaders expressed their support for China." (Chinese statement of September 1, 1963, cited in Griffith, *op. cit.*, p. 382.)

[63] *The New York Times*, July 27, 1962.

[64] *The New York Times*, July 3, 1962.

China involved itself in the siege of Dien Bien Phu, some-thing it had no intention of doing. In June, Dulles again raised the possibility of American military action in view of the deadlock that had developed at the Geneva Conference over Vietnamese Communist demands that Vietnam, Laos, and Cambodia be treated on the same footing so that the Com-munist victory in the first of these countries would make itself felt in the others. It was probably Dulles' threat that led Chou En-lai to break the impasse by conceding on June 16 that Laos and Cambodia could be treated differently from Vietnam.[65] The Soviet Union, with its eyes mainly on Europe, did little for the Chinese at this time, nor did it seem unduly perturbed by the emergence of SEATO later in the year. Seven years later, at the Geneva Conference on Laos, the Soviet Union did not follow the Chinese example by trying to use the con-ference as a means of abolishing SEATO but contented itself with insisting on the withdrawal of SEATO protection from Laos.[66]

Communist China began to involve itself overtly in the second round of the struggle in Vietnam, although decidedly on a limited scale, when it sent a military delegation to Hanoi at the end of 1961. China's modest efforts on behalf of North Vietnam were rendered clearly inadequate by the massive American escalation that began in February 1965. On the other hand, the modesty of the effort, although presumably displeasing to Hanoi, does not so far seem to have created any serious risk of American retaliation against China. The United States has warned, however, that if China should intervene directly in the Vietnam war, it could not count on enjoying a "privileged sanctuary" again.

China has said that it would commit its ground forces to the war if the United States attacked China by land or air,[67]

---

65 Hinton, *op. cit.,* pp. 247–251.

66 George Modelski, *International Conference on the Settlement of the Laotian Question, 1961–1962* (Canberra: Australian National University, Department of International Relations, 1962), p. 31.

67 E.g., Chief of Staff Lo Jui-ch'ing, "Commemorate the Victory over German Fascism! Carry the Struggle against U.S. Imperialism through to the End!" *Red Flag,* May 10, 1965. The threat of a Chinese counterattack is missing from the better-known companion piece by Defense Minister

if the United States invaded North Vietnam or northern Laos,[68] or if the National Liberation Front with Hanoi's consent requested Chinese intervention.[69] None of these preconditions appears likely to materialize in the near future, and Chinese intervention is therefore improbable unless it should take the form of some sort of irrational spasm. There is no current sign that such a spasm is imminent.

The Soviet Union, for its part, while accusing the Chinese of obstructing the flow of Soviet arms to North Vietnam and of preventing "united action" by the Communist block on Hanoi's behalf, has been conspicuously silent as to what, if anything, it would do for China in the event of a Sino-American clash arising out of the war in Vietnam. The latest anniversary (February 14, 1966) of the Sino-Soviet alliance passed almost unnoticed in the Soviet Union; *Red Star* did not even mention it. The conclusion is inescapable that China can hardly count on Soviet support and protection in such a crisis. Does Peking even want it? Presumably it does but, as always in its dealings with the Soviet Union, on its own terms — which are very likely the undisputed authority to manage both the military and the political aspects of the Vietnamese crisis on behalf of all the Communist participants from behind the scenes, so that Hanoi's appearance of "self-reliance" remains as nearly unimpaired as possible. If so, the Chinese are demanding authority without responsibility, much as in the past they expected the Russians to assume responsibility without authority.

Conclusion: A Reconstruction and Prognosis

It seems likely that the Communist Chinese leadership believes, and is correct in believing, that the Soviet Union would

Lin Piao, "Long Live the Victory of the People's War," NCNA release, September 3, 1965.

[68] E.g., unattributed interview of Chen Yi with Dr. Hugo Portisch in *The New York Times*, August 7, 1964.

[69] A number of Chinese statements in March 1965 promised intervention if the "South Vietnamese people" requested it. The following month this was amended to read "Vietnamese people" (Standing Committee of the National People's Congress resolution, April 20, 1965, text in *The New York Times*, April 21, 1965).

intervene directly and militarily on its behalf only in extremely improbable contingencies, such as an unprovoked American strategic attack on China, American bombing of targets close to the Soviet frontier, or the landing of American ground forces in Manchuria or North China. It is very doubtful whether the Soviet Union would retaliate if the United States after appropriate provocation should attack Communist China's nuclear installations. The Soviet Union might be prepared to tolerate a loss of Communist control over South China if it should occur, as seems unlikely at present. Indeed, the possibility of Sino-Soviet hostilities, which have taken place on a local scale along the frontier since Khrushchev's last years in power, cannot be ruled out.[70]

As the magnitude of American power and the unreliability of Soviet support and protection have become progressively clearer, the Communist Chinese leaders have of necessity fallen back on crisis management techniques stressing, in their own phrase, strategic boldness and tactical caution. In particular they have stressed extreme caution when confronting the United States directly; threats designed to keep alive the belief that non-Communist mainland Asia is a hostage to China for American good behavior; informal contact with the American government combined with efforts to manipulate American public opinion in directions adverse to its policy; attempts to split the Western alliance on the Chinese question by means of trade and political ploys; and the maintenance of pressure on the United States from the direction of the third world by means of varying mixtures of diplomatic dealings with governments and the incitement of leftist revolutionary movements. Success to date has been limited, although not negligible, but, as has already been pointed out, the available cards must be played even if they are fairly poor.

As for the future, both political and military considerations argue against Communist China's success in gaining full Soviet strategic support and protection, let alone in gaining a share in the control over the Soviet strategic forces and in the plan-

[70] Cf. Malcolm Mackintosh, "The Sino-Soviet Dispute," *Survival*, Vol. VII, No. 7 (October 1965), pp. 246–251, where he advances a similar argument.

ning for their employment. It is by no means impossible that
Communist China, as its nuclear power grows, may engage in
at least tacit collaboration, for the purpose of putting pressure on the Soviet Union, with a West Germany that may
ultimately "go nuclear." In the opposite direction, it may well
try to compensate for the doubtfulness of Soviet protection
by using its nuclear force as a deterrent against the United
States, either directly by threatening the continental United
States or indirectly by holding American bases and allies in
Asia as hostages, or both. Effective or not, there is no reason to
suppose that the future of the star-crossed Sino-Soviet alliance
as it confronts the United States will be less interesting than
its past.

8

The Soviet Attitude

MALCOLM MACKINTOSH

The problem of analyzing the attitude of the Soviet Union in a major crisis between the United States and Communist China in the late 1960's or in the 1970's is extremely complicated because of the degree of secrecy involved in policy commitments between Moscow and Peking. It may be useful, therefore, to look first at some more general Russian attitudes toward China from the earlier years of this century. Like many other European powers, Russia had long regarded China as a decaying civilization that was a target for justifiable territorial expansion, yet many influential Russians who had dealings with the Chinese felt disquiet at the size of the country and the number of its people. The well-known Russian explorer and writer of the 1880's, General Przhevalski, underlined the poverty and inertia of Chinese life but still felt it necessary to end his book on China with an eloquent plea for a preventive war against the Chinese Empire "before it was too late." Vague fears of the "Yellow Peril" continued to haunt those responsible for the security of Russia's furthermost provinces in the East, which were connected to the West only by a single-track railway line with a limited capacity for the transport of armed men and military supplies. After the Russian defeat in the war with Japan in 1904–1905, it is true that the identification of the "Yellow Peril" became confused in Russian minds with

Japanese "Western" military skill, which became more dangerous than the less precise threat of Chinese manpower. The
Japanese element in this peril was increased by Japan's intervention in Siberia during the Russian civil war and by the
disappearance of effective central government in China after
the declaration of the Chinese Republic in 1911. In fact, the
Bolshevik Revolution in Russia ushered in a long period in
Russo-Chinese relations in which Russia, as an increasingly
homogeneous and powerful national state, found herself dealing with a steadily weakening China, split up between rival
war lords, plagued by civil war, or in the grip of foreign invasion. The conquest of the mainland by the armies of the
Chinese Communist Party in 1949 marked the first time that
the Soviet government had to deal with a united China; it
was a new and unpredictable situation for the Russians, in
which appreciations based on the experience of 1921–1948
were almost certainly bound to be wrong.

Both in their dealings with China as a state — or a series of
states — and with the emerging Chinese Communist Party,
the Russians seemed to waver between overconfident assumptions that the Chinese could not do without Soviet help and
advice and almost panicky resorts to hostile or even aggressive
actions; this vacillation suggested that the Russians' understanding of China, or Chinese communism, was severely limited. There is no evidence, during the period from 1921 to
1948, of skillful central direction of the Soviet Union's policy
toward China, and Stalin himself seems to have been singu-
larly hesitant in making decisions. When he succeeded Lenin
in 1924, Stalin committed Soviet aid and the young Chinese
Communist Party to the support of the Nationalist Kuomintang, planning, no doubt, to gain political control of the
movement in due course. But this first attempt to operate
through a "Popular Front" came to a disastrous end when the
anti-Communist majority of the Nationalist movement turned
on the Communists in 1927 and drove the Soviet advisers out
of the country. A small group of the tougher elements in
the Communist Party struggled free of the Nationalist trap
and founded a Communist base in south China, which sur-

vived until the Long March in 1934–1936 transferred the
base to Yenan in the north of the country. It is interesting to
note that Soviet prestige fell so low in China that one of the
northern war lords provoked a military conflict on the Sino-
Soviet frontier in 1929, which led to the establishment of the
Soviet Special Red Banner Far Eastern Army and a brief
Soviet military invasion of Manchuria designed to "teach the
Chinese a lesson."

Meanwhile, in the Chinese Communist Party, the failure of
the Soviet advisers to prevent or retaliate against the Nationalists' *coup d'état* of 1927 probably aroused strong anti-
Soviet feelings, and may also have led to a split between the
leadership in China and the Chinese representatives on the
Comintern committee in Moscow, many of whom were finding
themselves increasingly gripped by the Stalin terror and isolated from events in China. Nevertheless, there appears to have
been some contact between Moscow and the South China base
in the 1930's, for a disagreement broke out between Moscow
and some of the Chinese Party leaders on the destination of
the Long March. Mao Tse-tung, in opposition to some of his
colleagues, decided on a site in Yenan: he was ready for his
own "Popular Front" alliance, of a strictly tactical nature,
with the Nationalists and probably wanted to lighten Nationalist pressure by a common struggle against the Japanese.
Mao won his point, and the army settled in Yenan, an area
incidentally unsuited for easy land communications with the
Soviet Union.

When the main Japanese attack on China came in 1937, the
Soviet government sent some of its Far Eastern air squadrons
to central China to augment the Chinese Nationalist air force,
though none of their operations were carried out in support
of the sectors of the front line that were held by the Communists. The next two years, however, brought a series of
Japanese-Soviet clashes on the frontier, which led to two Soviet
local victories followed by a political truce between Moscow
and Tokyo, partially brought about by Japanese resentment
at Germany's deal with Stalin, behind Japan's back, in August
1939. In these maneuverings China was largely forgotten in

Moscow, a situation that became all the more marked after 1941, when Germany plunged the Soviet Union into a European war, and Mao Tse-tung was left to his own devices. Mao's concept of the dual war that he was fighting — against the Japanese and against the Nationalists (especially after 1941) — involved the retention of Yenan as a training and political base and the infiltration of picked guerrilla units into richer and politically more profitable areas of China-Shantung, the area north of Shanghai and in the Central Plains. A Nationalist ambush destroyed Mao's New Fourth Army north of Shanghai in 1941, but by the early part of 1945 the Communist Eighth Route Army was pressing in a southeasterly direction, apparently attempting to cut China in two on a West-East axis. In August 1945 the Soviet Union returned to the Far East in strength: she joined the war against Japan and occupied Manchuria and part of Korea. Once again Stalin and Mao showed that they had different plans for "Communizing" China though, while Stalin's military power and prestige was at such a high level, Mao appears to have moved cautiously. Politically, Stalin insisted that the Communists should call a halt to operations against the Nationalists and go to Chungking for talks on a coalition government — which the Communist leaders did. Militarily, Stalin's commander in chief in the Far East, Marshal Malinovski, rebuffed an early Chinese Communist attempt to establish a guerrilla foothold in Soviet-occupied Manchuria. Stalin, with his eye on the creation of a border enclave for the Chinese Communists under Soviet control, was not in favor of seeing Manchuria swarming with experienced Chinese partisans, and actually allowed the regular Nationalist army into southern Manchuria in 1946 and encouraged the Chinese Communists to concentrate north of the Sungari River, where a Soviet-trained Chinese Party leader, Li Li-san, was apparently already recommending the establishment of a Communist enclave.[1]

Stalin, however, badly miscalculated. The Communist-Nationalist coalition never materialized, and soon the Chinese

---

[1] See report on Li Li-san's views in *The New York Times,* October 11, 1946. Li Li-san at this time was political commissar of the Communist forces in Manchuria, later the Fourth Field Army under Lin Piao.

Red Army was locked in a full-scale civil war with the Nationalists, not only in Manchuria but all over northern and east-central China. Once Soviet troops had left Manchuria (by mid-1946) Mao concentrated on the defeat of the Nationalist army in that province, and once this was achieved (by December 1948) the Chinese revolution was beyond Stalin's control. Moreover, it was in the hands of a Chinese leader, Mao Tse-tung, whose experience of Soviet help and Soviet motives can hardly have been encouraging for future Sino-Soviet cooperation directed, as Stalin hoped it would be, on the basis of Soviet political supremacy.

The conquest of the mainland by the Communists was the precursor of a lengthy visit by the Chinese Party leaders to Moscow in December 1949, which began with the celebration of Stalin's seventieth birthday and ended in the signature of a series of Sino-Soviet treaties, including a defense treaty, on February 14, 1950. The defense commitment that the Soviet Union undertook was to go to the help of China if she was attacked directly or indirectly by Japan or any nation allied to Japan. The actual wording stated: "In the event of one of the Contracting Parties being attacked by Japan or any state allied to Japan, and thus being involved in a state of war, the other Contracting Party shall immediately render military and other assistance by all means at its disposal." This was a revolutionary step for the Russians: never before had they committed themselves to defend China, now in effect united as a mainland power. Moreover, China was still fighting a civil war that the Communist government was determined to finish by capturing the island of Taiwan. Further, the Russians signed the defense treaty with China at a time when they had already begun to plan military action in the Far East: the attack on South Korea in June 1950. There is evidence that the mobilization of the North Korean army began in February 1950, and that personnel of Korean origin serving in the Chinese Communist army were released and sent to Korea to join the North Korean army at about the same time.[2] The Russians must have

2 *Military Situation in the Far East,* Hearings before the Committee on Armed Services and the Committee on Foreign Relations, U.S. Senate, 82nd Congress (May 3–June 27, 1951), Part 5, p. 3403.

taken into account the backward state of China's armaments and communications, her total lack of an air force or air defense capability, and realized that if the defense treaty was to be invoked by the Chinese at this time and was to be honored, the Soviet army would have to bear the brunt of operations against the United States — the obvious "nation allied to Japan." Yet the Soviet government embarked on the planning of the Korean War apparently convinced that there would be no South Korean resistance and no American or U.N. aid for the South Koreans. In weighing up the factors involved in the situation Stalin probably took into account that the American army in 1949–1950 was reduced to one operational division (the Russians had thirty in the Far East alone) and Russia had already a small stock of atomic bombs. It seems possible that, in addition to the protection the Soviet defense guarantee would give to China in general terms, the treaty may have had a direct connection with Stalin's intention to launch a limited war in Korea. Stalin may have hoped that, whatever happened in Korea, the Sino-Soviet defense treaty would deter the United States from taking reprisal action against China as a result of the Communist attack on South Korea, and thus keep the military action necessary to conquer South Korea limited to the Korean peninsula.

The course of the Korean War showed that, for a variety of reasons, the Soviet deterrent was not challenged. But the original decision to force a limited war on the Far East probably cost the Chinese 400,000 casualties and revealed to the military leaders of the Chinese Communists that their shortcomings in weapons and training were frightening. Captured Chinese army documents revealed that in one artillery unit, in late 1950, 70 per cent of Chinese-produced artillery shells failed to explode, and even when Soviet arms became available Chinese troops were unable to make the best use of them. Three points of relevance to the Soviet commitment to China emerged from the Korean War. First, the United States was deterred from extending the war to China. Second, from the Soviet point of view, China was still a long way from great power status in the military field and would have to be supplied with arms and an armaments industry to enable her even to hold her own in the Far East; meanwhile she would have to be protected by a continuing deterrent guarantee. Third, from the Chinese point of view, while the professional soldiers were impressed by their complete dependence on the Soviet Union in the field of modern weapons, many Party leaders probably expressed anxiety at the miscalculations that Stalin had made over Korea. Both elements were probably inspired to achieve self-sufficiency in defense and foreign policy at the earliest possible moment.

Two years after the beginning of the Korean War a major Sino-Soviet conference was held in Moscow, which was attended by the deputy chiefs of the Chinese and Soviet General Staffs, Generals Su yü and Malinin, and representatives of the two air forces and navies, with the addition, in the case of the Chinese, of the deputy commander of the army's artillery directorate. The Chinese delegation stayed in Moscow for a month (the military representatives remained even longer), at the end of which an agreement was signed permitting the Russians to continue the military occupation of Port Arthur "until the conclusion of a peace treaty between Japan and the U.S.S.R. and China." In the circumstances, this meant indefinitely, since the United States had already ratified a peace treaty with Japan on March 20, 1952, and Nationalist China had signed a treaty with Japan on April 18 of the same year. The new agreement of September 15, 1952, returned the Manchurian railway to the Chinese.

The military implications of the Port Arthur decision reflected not only Soviet military thinking of the time but also Soviet intentions over the Sino-Soviet defense treaty of 1950. Soviet military thinking of the period 1949–1953 was dominated by Stalin's belief that a third world war would be waged on lines similar to those of 1941–1945, and the deployment of Soviet ground, sea, and air forces was regulated by an attempt to put an iron ring around the farthest frontiers of the Soviet Union. Garrisons of considerable strength were precariously perched in the Chukotski Peninsula and on the Kuril Islands, and Sakhalin Island was the headquarters of an entire Military District. With large forces in the Maritime Province, near Khabarovsk and in the Trans-Baikal area, the garrison in Port

Arthur completed a military ring around Manchuria as well as a chain of bases stretching from Port Arthur to the Bering Strait. This deployment suggests that Manchuria, in Stalin's eyes, was virtually a Soviet-protected area that could be occupied by the Russians at short notice. In the event of a Sino-American conflict in which military operations spread to north China, Port Arthur would be in an isolated position. But as an advanced base supporting a Soviet occupation of Manchuria, ostensibly in defense of China, Port Arthur in Russian hands seems to have made strategic sense to a Stalinist military thinker.

The argument in favor of a special Soviet interest in Manchuria is supported by the role of Kao Kang, the Chinese Communists' political, economic, and to some extent military boss of Manchuria from 1949 to 1953. Persistent reports from Yugoslav sources and accounts of the international meeting of Communist parties in Bucharest in June 1960 have mentioned that Kao Kang, independently of the central government in Peking, cooperated with the Soviet Union over and above the separate trade agreements on Manchurian industry. It is possible that Stalin was grooming Kao Kang to be a pro-Soviet replacement for Mao Tse-tung as leader of the Chinese Communist Party. Certainly Kao Kang, who was in charge of Manchurian affairs during the Korean War, must have seen at first hand the dependence of the Chinese forces on the Soviet Union for arms and equipment, and this may have led him into a readiness to accept a greater degree of Soviet tutelage than was thought necessary in Peking.[3] This was the period when Stalin was most rigorously imposing leaders of absolute loyalty to himself on all Communist parties, and it would be logical to expect him to attempt an intrigue in this direction with the Chinese, especially since Stalin's first apparent emissary, Li Li-san, had been "unmasked" and rendered innocuous by the Chinese leadership in the late 1940's.

[3] The same argument might apply to P'eng Teh-huai, the commander of the Chinese army in Korea, who fell into disgrace in 1959, probably partly because of his readiness to accede to Soviet ideological leadership in the interests of receiving more Soviet military assistance. See David A. Charles, "The Dismissal of Marshal P'eng Teh-huai," *The China Quarterly*, No. 8 (1961).

It seems possible to conclude, therefore, that the most important motive behind the Sino-Soviet defense treaty was deterrence of the United States. But the deployment of Soviet forces in the Far East and the decision to maintain a Soviet base in Port Arthur, taken together with the possibility that Stalin may have been intriguing with the political boss of Manchuria, suggest that the Russians may have had their own "national" plan of action in the event of hostilities between America and China: the military occupation of Manchuria under cover of denying the province to American forces. Stalin may have argued that in the circumstances of 1952 there was relatively little that the Russians could do to help the Chinese directly in hostilities in south or or southeast China that would not involve the danger of American nuclear attack on Soviet territory. But a swift occupation of Manchuria under the pretext of coming to China's help would offer many advantages to a regime concerned mainly with its own security, and which was still dominated by ground-force concepts of warfare and was unwilling to risk too much on behalf of even its largest ally. The Americans would be unlikely to oppose it, and in any ultimate settlement of a Sino-American war the Soviet Union would be in a useful bargaining position. Possession of an important Chinese province could permit the reconstruction of a pro-Soviet Communist regime modeled more closely on those of Eastern Europe at that time.

Such a policy of interpreting the Sino-Soviet defense treaty strictly in accordance with Soviet needs would not be inconsistent with a certain amount of Soviet help for China's armaments industry, which probably began slowly in 1950. By September 1956 the first jet fighters of Chinese manufacture were flown in China, and Chinese-made tanks and light naval craft made their appearance.[4] But the death of Stalin and the formation of the collective leadership, followed by the rise to power of Khrushchev and Bulganin in the spring of 1955, apparently coincided with a change in Soviet military policy toward China. In October 1954 a Soviet delegation visited

4 Raymond L. Garthoff, "Sino-Soviet Military Relations," *The Annals of the American Academy of Political and Social Science* (September 1963), p. 86.

Peking and agreed to hand back Port Arthur to China and to annul the 1950 agreement on the joint exploitation of uranium resources in China.[5] Both offers were clearly intended as concessions to the latter's national pride. In May 1955 the Chinese Minister of Defense, Marshal P'eng Teh-huai, was invited to attend the foundation ceremony of the Warsaw Pact in Warsaw, and then spent June in Moscow in discussions with Soviet military representatives. The Port Arthur decision and the association of China with the Warsaw Pact suggest that Khrushchev and Bulganin were prepared to put Sino-Soviet military relations on a new footing, which seems to have led to a greater Soviet effort to arm the Chinese effectively in return for Chinese acceptance of Soviet military planning, possibly on a joint force basis. In formulating this policy, the Soviet leaders may have counted on exploiting the Chinese army's lack of modern weapons to persuade the Party leaders to accept Soviet strategic planning for the defense of the Pacific area. In an interesting commentary in July 1955 on China's need for new weapons, one of the Chinese marshals, Yeh Chien-ying, criticized those in China who failed to appreciate the need to equip the army with modern weapons: "If a big war breaks out" he said, "we could not win without atomic weapons; pending the full establishment of our industry, within certain limits it is necessary for us to resort to the expedient measure of placing orders with foreign countries."[6] Visits to the Soviet Union of high-ranking Chinese soldiers suggest that considerable pressure was being put on the Russians for atomic and other advanced weapons in the period 1955–1957. Marshal Nieh Jung-chen, who was believed to be responsible for military-scientific development in China, paid two visits to Moscow in 1956 and 1957 and, according to the Soviet press, had talks with General Antonov, the officer in charge of military liaison with Russia's allies. Marshal Ho Lung also visited Moscow in January 1957 and met Soviet government and

5 The Soviet leaders' decision to withdraw from Port Arthur and to hand all military installations back to China was in line with a new Soviet defense policy that abandoned Stalin's insistence on holding on to outlying salients with military force. The Russians also withdrew from Porkkala in Finland and from eastern Austria in 1955.

6 New China News Agency (NCNA), Peking, July 27, 1955.

military leaders. In April 1956 Mikoyan visited Peking for talks with the Chinese Defense Minister Marshal P'eng Teh-huai and senior Party and economic officials.

Material on Soviet military aid to China is extremely difficult to obtain, but a study of the military personalities in the Soviet Ministry of Defense concerned with the Warsaw Pact alliance suggests that in 1956–1957 some kind of permanent Soviet military mission may have been established in China linked to the Warsaw Pact directorate of the Soviet General Staff.[7] While it is not suggested that Khrushchev was trying to bring China into the Warsaw Pact, this evidence may mean that he was considering the reorganization of Sino-Soviet military relations along the lines of a more integrated alliance somewhat similar to that being built up gradually in Europe within the Warsaw Pact.

In the absence of direct information on the type of military assistance offered by the new Soviet leaders in 1955–1960, recourse must be made to the evidence produced on this subject in the exchange of notes between Moscow and Peking since the Bucharest meeting in June 1960 and in accounts of this meeting that have been published in the Western press. First, there is the report of Khrushchev's speech at that meeting, on June 26, in which he complained that the Chinese had hampered Soviet defense measures on the Manchurian border by preventing the installation of a radio station (possibly a radar facility?) and hindering reconnaissance flights by Soviet aircraft.[8] Another report of the proceedings of the preparatory meeting for the conference of eighty-one Communist parties in 1960 mentions the refusal of the Chinese to allow arrangements to be made for the use of Chinese airfields by Soviet aircraft in time of war. The Secretary-General of the Sino-Japanese Friendship Association, Chang An-po, was reported to

[7] During Mikoyan's visit to Peking, in April 1956, among Soviet officials in the Chinese capital who conferred with him was A. V. Petrushevski, described as an "adviser." Petrushevski is almost certainly the colonel-general of that name who was closely associated with the Warsaw Pact, and may have been a senior Soviet military adviser in China. He was not the military attaché, a position held by the political Major-General A. I. Zudov.

[8] As reported in Edward Crankshaw, *The New Cold War: Moscow v. Peking* (Harmondsworth, England: Penguin Books, 1963), pp. 108–109.

have said in Tokyo on February 23, 1964, that Russia had tried to rule China by proposing in April 1958 a joint Sino-Soviet fleet and the construction of a long-range radar station on the Chinese mainland.[9] On the Chinese side, the article on the origin and development of the differences between the leadership of the Soviet Communist Party and the Communist Party of China, published in *Red Flag* and *People's Daily* in Peking on September 6, 1963, contained the statement that "in 1958 the leadership of the CPSU put forward unreasonable demands designed to put China under Soviet military control. These unreasonable demands were rightly and firmly rejected by the Chinese Government."[10]

If we add to these hints on the true nature of the Sino-Soviet military relationship in the late 1950's the reports that the Soviet Union assisted China in the acquisition of short-range and medium-range ballistic missiles,[11] it seems likely that the Soviet Union was interested at this time in supplying China with certain kinds of advanced weapons and equipment on condition that she accepted them *on a joint-command basis.* Apparently the Soviet Union wanted to set up a joint Sino-Soviet Pacific fleet, which would probably have meant Soviet submarine bases in eastern and perhaps even southern China, a joint air defense early warning system, the reciprocal use of airfields, and possibly even the installation of missile bases on the Chinese mainland. It seems likely, too, that in 1955 the Russians sent missions of high-ranking service advisers to China and trained Chinese officers in Soviet military academies.[12] The important point is that this represents a different conception of the Soviet Union's obligations under the Sino-Soviet defense treaty from that apparently held by Stalin. Khrushchev, it seems, was prepared to tackle the problem of commitment to the Chinese by proposing arrangements that

9 BBC Summary of World Broadcasts, Part 3, FE/1488, as reported in *China Quarterly,* No. 18 (April–June 1964), p. 238.

10 Text in William E. Griffith, *The Sino-Soviet Rift* (Cambridge: The M.I.T. Press, 1964), p. 399.

11 Alice Langley Hsieh, *Communist China's Strategy in the Nuclear Era* (Englewood Cliffs, N.J.: Prentice-Hall, 1962), pp. 164–165.

12 Ellis Joffe, "The Conflict between the Old and the New in the Chinese Army," *The China Quarterly,* No. 18 (April–June 1964), p. 122.

would have given the Chinese forces modern weapons but have left their exploitation and freedom of use strictly under Soviet control. This is, in fact, very like the Soviet arrangement with the Warsaw Pact forces, which have received, in the course of the last ten years, up-to-date military equipment — probably including tactical surface-to-surface and surface-to-air missiles — but without national control of the nuclear warheads.

Beginning with the appearance of senior Chinese leaders at the foundation ceremony of the Warsaw Pact in May 1955, the frequent visits of Chinese military delegations to Moscow, and the big Soviet naval visit to Shanghai and other ports in July 1956, the Chinese seem to have had, from 1955 onwards, high hopes of Soviet cooperation in the missile and even the atomic field. This was borne out by Marshal Yeh Chien-ying's reference in July 1955 to the need to acquire weapons abroad, and by flattering statements on the achievement of Soviet missile and nuclear technology at the time of the launching of the world's first ICBM in August 1957 and the first two Sputniks in October and November 1957. This feeling can be gauged by quotations from Chinese military leaders at this time:

> Today the Soviet Army has become a highly modernized army, and possesses the most modern combat weapons, including the inter-continental ballistic missile. . . . As indicated by Chairman Mao Tse-tung, the Chinese Army in its work of modernization, will learn from all Soviet advanced experience. (Marshal Liu Po-ch'eng, October 30, 1957.)

> . . . the Soviet armed forces . . . are the great example for the modernization of the Chinese armed forces. . . [by learning from them] the modernization of our Army may thus be accomplished with a reduction of roundabout ways. (Marshal P'eng Teh-huai, November 4, 1957.)

> The Soviet Union has consistently done its utmost to render tremendous generous assistance to its brother countries . . . . (Marshal Chu Teh, November 7, 1957.)[13]

---

[13] Quotations taken from Harold P. Ford, "Modern Weapons and the Sino-Soviet Estrangement," *The China Quarterly*, No. 18 (April–June 1964), p. 161.

By late 1957 Soviet help to the Chinese army in conventional training and to a limited extent in nuclear combat situations had made considerable progress.[14] Thus when the Chinese Minister of Defense, Marshal P'eng Teh-huai, led an imposing military delegation to Moscow in October 1957, which included Marshal Yeh Chien-ying, the Head of the Inspectorate, and Senior General Su yü, the Chief of the General Staff, all seemed set fair for Soviet acceptance of all Chinese requests. One small point of interest is that the Chinese delegation was accompanied by a Soviet Colonel-General named N. I. Trufanov, a wartime associate of Khrushchev, who was at this time associated with General Antonov, the head of Soviet military liaison with the Warsaw Pact and with other countries. It is Soviet practice that a visiting foreign military delegation is accompanied by the senior Soviet military officer serving in that country, for example, in appropriate cases the military attaché. Since the Soviet military attaché in Peking, the political Major-General Zudov, did not accompany the delegation, it is likely that General Trufanov was the senior Soviet officer in China, possibly the head of a military mission. Continued association, even in small hints of this kind, between Soviet liaison with China and officers associated with the Warsaw Pact alliance strengthens the case for the belief that Khrushchev's mind was working on the lines of a military alliance with China, which would improve its deterrent value vis-à-vis the United States and keep the control of China's use of her armed forces firmly in Soviet hands.

Subsequent Chinese statements have claimed that the Soviet Union signed an agreement with China "on new technology for national defense" in October 1957. According to the Chinese, provision was made at some stage for China to be given "a sample of an atomic bomb and technical data concerning its manufacture."[15] Allowance should be made for the fact that to the Russians the phrase "new technology" means missiles and electronic means of warfare as well as atomic weapons and also for the reluctance of the Soviet government to deny

[14] See Hsieh, op. cit.
[15] Text taken from Griffith, op. cit., p. 399.

this claim directly (they have said only that the Chinese statement "presented the facts in a distorted light").[16] It seems likely that, whatever the Russians *did* promise in October 1957, the Chinese military delegation may have accepted that the Soviet Union was offering China advanced weapons systems but it probably realized, when it left Moscow, that these weapons might not be under purely Chinese national control and that their use might be dependent on a Soviet veto. Harold P. Ford has pointed out in his article in the *China Quarterly*, already quoted, that the new Chinese army training program, published in January 1958, spoke of incorporating Soviet advanced experience and of training troops in conditions of atomic bombs, chemical warfare, and guided missiles.[17] But this was the last time that Soviet experience and, by implication, help was referred to in Chinese military commentaries, and this training program was quietly shelved. As early as January 1958, the Chinese Defense Minister, Marshal P'eng Teh-huai, referred to China's need to acquire her own advanced weapons. In May 1958, the Commander of the Chinese Air Force, General Liu Ya-lou, was already speaking of China's determination to make her own atomic weapons,[18] and during the summer of 1958, marshals Chu Teh, Ch'en Yi, Ho Lung, and Nieh Jung-chen rejected Soviet experience and the need to obtain weapons from abroad. On August 1, Marshal Ho Lung wrote an article that dealt with an earlier period but certainly was meant to refer to the present:

> We tried to solve our problem purely from the military point of view, and hoped for outside aid, instead of relying on mobilization of the masses.

And Marshal Nieh Jung-chen wrote on the following day:

> We should and absolutely can master, in not too long a time, the newest technology concerning atomic energy in all fields. . . . There are people who think that as long as we receive help from

[16] Statement of the Soviet government, in *Pravda*, August 21, 1963, pp. 1–3.

[17] Harold P. Ford, "Modern Weapons and the Sino-Soviet Estrangement," *The China Quarterly*, No. 18 (April–June 1964), p. 162.

[18] *Liberation Daily*, Peking, May 23, 1958, as quoted in Donald Zagoria, *The Sino-Soviet Conflict, 1956–1961* (Princeton, N.J.: Princeton University Press, 1962), p. 192.

the Soviet Union and other fraternal countries, there is no need for us to carry out more complicated research ourselves. This way of thinking is wrong.

By the end of August the Chinese army paper, *Liberation Daily*, was saying flatly that Soviet experience was of little use for China.

What caused this complete reversal in the Chinese attitude to Soviet military help and advice so soon after a lengthy and important military conference between the two countries? There is, unfortunately, no direct evidence, but the reasons probably led to the convening of the two-month-long conference of the Military Committee of the Chinese Party's Central Committee on May 27, 1958, which was addressed by Mao Tse-tung and all ten Chinese marshals. The conference was held at a time when the Party was preparing its "Great Leap Forward" on the internal front, and when a Chinese observer at the Warsaw Pact meeting in May 1958 was already warning the Soviet Union and its European allies against overestimating the strength of the United States. As Donald Zagoria pointed out in his discussion of the Military Committee's conference, a great deal of time was taken up with a debate between those who put the emphasis on weapons, modernization, and the slackening of Party control, and those to whom old ways of waging war, the use of manpower in the mass, close-range fighting, and political leadership in command were of prime importance.[19] But the swing away from new weapons, foreign aid and advice, and military professionalism almost certainly owed part of its origin to a collapse of the Chinese hopes of 1955–1957 and bitter disappointment with the Soviet Union.

On a largely speculative basis, what probably happened was something like this: at the October 1957 conference in Moscow, the Russians, in order to prepare the Chinese for Khrushchev's concept of a joint defense command for the Pacific on Warsaw Pact lines, promised the Chinese modern weapons, including missiles and naval vessels and increased help for the Chinese armaments and aircraft industries. Atomic bombs and warheads may also have been discussed,

---

[19] Zagoria, *op. cit.*, pp. 189–194.

for it is possible that the foundations of China's own military atomic program may have been laid shortly afterwards.[20] The Russians probably hinted to the Chinese that the delivery of these advanced weapons and their warheads would depend on acceptance of Soviet proposals for joint commands that could ensure ultimate Soviet control over their use — as in the case, for example, of the Soviet custodianship of nuclear warheads for the tactical surface-to-surface missiles probably provided by the Russians to some of the Warsaw Pact armies — though they may not have made these conditions absolutely clear. Marshal P'eng Teh-huai's January 1958 reference to China's need to stand on her own feet in weapon development may have been the first public recognition that the Soviet Union was attaching "strings" to its aid program. If the Chinese spokesman in Tokyo in February 1964 was correct when he gave April 1958 as the date of the Soviet proposal for joint command of a Sino-Soviet fleet, it seems likely that the Russians were by then pressing hard for Chinese acceptance of these "strings"; and when the Chinese finally realized that the Russians were not prepared to give them atomic or nuclear weapons unconditionally, they took the decision to build their own. This decision did not, of course, prevent the Chinese from accepting all other Soviet military aid, some of which may have been connected with the construction of the gaseous diffusion plant in north China. Military aid included armaments, aircraft, naval construction, early warning equipment, and probably missile technology, for Khrushchev told Averell Harriman on June 23, 1959, that actual missiles had been given to China.[21] For their part, the

---

[20] The whole question of Soviet aid to China's military atomic program is very obscure, and little reliable information on it is available. Basically the questions to be asked are: Did the Chinese receive practical Soviet aid in building up their military atomic capability from 1957 onwards, and if so, why did the Soviet government deliberately set about helping its gigantic neighbor to become an atomic power, especially since in 1957–1958 the Soviet Union was putting forward at Geneva nonproliferation and nuclear test ban proposals? There are, at the present, no satisfactory answers to these two questions, which remain the most puzzling aspect of the whole range of Sino-Soviet relations.

[21] *Life,* July 13, 1959, p. 36. China has its own missile research program under Dr. Chien Hsueh-shen, who worked on American missile develop-

Soviet leaders continued the military aid program to China and probably persisted in their attempts to use what influence they had in Peking, possibly in army circles, to attract Chinese leaders to their proposition.[22] If the Chinese are correct, the Russians did not "tear up" the October 1957 agreement on new technology until June 20, 1959, that is, until Khrushchev was preparing for his meeting with President Eisenhower and the Camp David talks.[23] The important point, however, is that the Chinese considered the difference of opinion with the Russians in the early months of 1958 sufficiently basic to warrant a swing away from reliance on Soviet help and advice. And the Russians probably realized that the Chinese opposition to their terms was strong enough to make them reconsider the feasibility of bringing China into any sort of Warsaw Pact-type alliance in the Far East. The importance of Soviet and Chinese reactions to this study lies in the fact that they precede by a few weeks the Taiwan Straits crisis of the autumn of 1958. Both Russia and China then had to assess the value and risks of their defense treaty during a Chinese-American military confrontation in the light of their inability to agree on bilateral military cooperation.

The 1958 crisis over the Taiwan Straits followed quickly on the heels of the Middle Eastern crisis, which began with the revolution in Iraq, on July 13, and the landing of British and American troops in Jordan and Lebanon. The first Soviet reaction to these military moves apparently involved the assumption that they were a prelude to the invasion of Iraq, and Khrushchev, characteristically, acted precipitately to bring the leaders of the Western powers to a summit meeting, if necessary within the framework of the U.N. Security Council.

ment before returning to China in 1955. See Morton H. Halperin, *China and the Bomb* (New York: Praeger, 1965).

22 It is tempting to speculate that Marshal P'eng Teh-huai may have been a target of Soviet persuasion on this point, and that this may have played a part in his downfall. See David A. Charles, "The Dismissal of P'eng Teh-huai," *The China Quarterly*, No. 8 (1961).

23 The Soviet Union has specifically stated that the Chinese asked for an atomic bomb and that the Soviet government flatly refused to give them one. No date was mentioned but it is possible that June 20, 1959, was the date of the request and the Soviet refusal, for other military aid apparently continued until June 1960.

Chinese reaction was more closely geared to the use of force to uphold the new Iraqi regime. Although Khrushchev changed his tactics several times in the two weeks after the Iraqi coup, he probably realized by July 28 that the Western powers had no intention of invading Iraq; the immediate crisis was over, and he could turn his attention to other matters. One of these was undoubtedly the disturbing suggestion of impending Chinese action in the Taiwan Straits. The Chinese press opened a campaign for the recovery of Taiwan on July 23, 1958, after the meeting of the Central Committee's Military Committee and after Khrushchev had shown his hand on the Middle Eastern crisis.[24] Five days later, on July 28, Khrushchev and his Defense Minister, Marshal Malinovski, who had commanded Soviet forces in the Far East from 1945 to 1956, arrived in Peking to the accompaniment of a barrage of Chinese press and radio accounts of rallies calling for the "liberation" of Taiwan and the offshore islands, Quemoy and Matsu. The Soviet visitors conferred with the Chinese leaders for just under a week and then returned to Moscow, after issuing a communiqué that was interesting only for its failure to mention Taiwan at all. This may have been a sign that the two sides had stated their views but had not reached any agreement on a joint policy.[25]

With some local variations, the Chinese press throughout the first part of August carried vigorous comment on the theme "peace must be fought for — it cannot be begged," until on August 23 the shelling of Quemoy and naval harassment of both Quemoy and Matsu began. On September 4, the Chinese government claimed a twelve-mile limit for its territorial waters, and shortly after this, on September 7, American warships began to escort Nationalist supply ships to the offshore island inside this limit, a high point in the

---

[24] Zagoria, op. cit., p. 201.

[25] Shortly after this meeting, correspondents in Warsaw reported "leaks" of information that claimed the Soviet Union had agreed to step up its military and economic assistance to China, including missiles and possibly nuclear warheads (see Garthoff, op. cit., p. 89). In view of the probability that the Soviet government was interested in keeping U.S. reaction to the coming Chinese actions down to a minimum, it is possible that the purpose of these "leaks" was to play a part in deterring the U.S. from extending the conflict.

rising danger of a direct Sino-American clash. Meanwhile, on September 4, the American Secretary of State, John Foster Dulles, indicated in an interview that Quemoy was "increasingly related to the defense of Taiwan," and that the United States might bomb the Chinese mainland if the Communists attacked Quemoy. Significantly enough, on the following day the Chinese offered to renew ambassadorial talks with the United States in Warsaw, which represented a lessening of tension on the Chinese side. During September a big American military build-up in the straits area took place, which included the dispatch of U.S. jet fighters to escort Nationalist planes dropping supplies to Quemoy, the completion of missile sites on Taiwan, the raising of the Seventh Fleet to six aircraft carriers, three cruisers, and forty destroyers, and the supply of Sidewinder air-to-air missiles to the Nationalist air force. Tension remained at a fairly high level for another three weeks, but on October 6 the Chinese proclaimed what was in effect a cease-fire; on October 8 the Americans ended their escort service for the Nationalist ships on the Quemoy run, and the crisis came to an end.

Soviet behavior during the Taiwan Straits crisis seems to have been uncoordinated with Chinese actions, and Soviet propaganda differed in emphasis from that of the Chinese. After the Mao Tse-tung–Khrushchev meeting of July 28, Soviet press comment emphasized the need to keep tension at a low level, and until August 21, when *Pravda* criticized the United States, only the Soviet army paper, *Red Star,* mentioned American "aggressiveness."[26] On the day after the shelling of Quemoy began, a speech by Khrushchev was reported in the Soviet press that contained the following phrase: "at the present time there is no cloud from which thunder could roll."[27] The actual shelling was mentioned twice in the Soviet press: on August 25, in a quotation from New China News Agency, and on August 27, when it was treated casually in a dispatch from London. It is true that "Observer" in *Pravda,* on August 31, declared that "he who threatenes China must not forget that he is threatening the Soviet Union

---

[26] *Red Star,* August 7, 1958, and *Pravda,* August 21, 1958.
[27] *Pravda,* August 24, 1958, as quoted in Zagoria, *op. cit.,* p. 211.

also," and that the latter would provide the necessary moral and material help in China's just struggle, but this was the only article of its kind during the first phase of the crisis. When the crisis reached its first peak on September 4–5, the Soviet comment was frankly two-faced in its attempt to placate both sides: one article stated that the Soviet Union could not remain inactive in the face of a threat to its brave ally and would not quietly watch U.S. military preparations in the Pacific; yet it preceded this declaration by qualifying it as follows: "the Chinese people have sufficient strength to counter the aggressors fully."

After the Chinese had suggested a resumption of the ambassadorial talks, Khrushchev wrote to President Eisenhower on September 6 warning him that "an attack on China is an attack on the Soviet Union," and that the Soviet Union would do everything to defend the security of both countries. On September 19, when the likelihood of an American extension of the conflict was becoming increasingly improbable simply because existing U.S. measures for the supply of the beleaguered islands were proving successful, Khrushchev wrote to Eisenhower again, saying: "If China is attacked with atomic weapons the aggressor will at once get a rebuff by the same means . . . let no one doubt that we shall honor our commitments." After the first use of the Sidewinder air-to-air missiles the Soviet army paper (but no other) discussed the possibility of Soviet volunteers going to the aid of China. This was on September 25; ten days later the Chinese put an end to the crisis, and Khrushchev crowned his contributions by a second statement containing two views of Russia's commitment. He said, first, that Russia would come to the help of China if she were attacked by the United States; second, that Russia would not intervene in China's civil war against the Nationalists and that the Chinese effort to take Taiwan, Quemoy, Matsu, and the Pescadores was "an internal affair of the Chinese people."[28]

Two points that are relevant to this study stand out about the Taiwan crisis. First, China probably decided to launch the crisis at the meeting of the Military Committee, and Chi-

[28] *Pravda,* October 6, 1958, p. 1.

nese intentions became known to the Soviet government *at a time when, the available evidence suggests, China had rejected Soviet plans for joint commands in the Far East* and, possibly, for some kind of Warsaw Pact-type of alliance. The Russians would therefore be more than usually sensitive about their ability or inability to control China's actions, and this was probably one reason for the Khrushchev-Malinovski visit to Peking. Second, after the military crisis began on August 23, Soviet reaction was cautious until Chinese Premier Chou En-lai had initiated a small relaxation of tension, when Khrushchev announced his determination to fulfill his treaty obligations if mainland China was attacked. And as the American measures to assist the Nationalists became increasingly successful, and the need for escalation more remote, Soviet commitments to China became more specific, and included retaliation with atomic weapons. At the same time Moscow absolved itself of any obligations to help China seize the off-shore island or Taiwan.

The conclusion suggested, therefore, is that while disassociating itself from the Chinese decision to make an attempt on the offshore islands, the Soviet government used the public media at its disposal to convince the United States that the Sino-Soviet defense treaty would be honored by the Soviet Union in the event of an attack on mainland China. The Soviet campaign to this end, however, seems to have been motivated by Soviet national interests rather than by coordination with Chinese policy, and may have been designed partly to display the vigor of the Soviet Union's leadership of the Communist revolutionary movement. In any case, Soviet intentions would have been related to Soviet military capability in the Far East at the time, which was not in a position to embark on war against the United States. In the strategic field, only a small part of the Soviet Union's long-range air force could have reached North America, and neither the United States nor Russia had operational ICBM's. The Soviet bomber force in the Far East was capable of attacking targets in Japan, Okinawa, the Philippines, and Taiwan, though losses would have been extremely heavy. The Soviet Pacific fleet could have defended the northern Pacific coastline and made hit-and-run submarine and air attacks on U.S. naval and merchant shipping but would have been overawed by the Seventh Fleet's carrier task forces. On land, Soviet armies could have released Chinese forces in the northeast, including Manchuria, for operations in East or South China, but since American plans probably never envisaged land operations on the mainland anyway, there would be little requirement for this kind of Soviet aid to the Chinese. On the purely military front, therefore, it is probable that Soviet military advice to the Soviet government would have been of two kinds: one, if the Chinese reversed their position and granted the Russians unrestricted use of all their airfields and ports, the Soviet Union could offer an air defense of some Chinese cities and military targets together with a possible naval defense of the North China coastline; or, two, if they refused these rights, the Soviet Union should wash its hands of this commitment. This advice would have been considered by the Presidium, and in the prevailing circumstances even the first course might have been rejected by Khrushchev as too dangerous or doomed to failure. That this might have been the Soviet position, particularly in relation to the use of atomic weapons, is suggested by the following Chinese comment on the Taiwan crisis in September 1963:

> In August and September of 1958, the situation in the Taiwan Straits was indeed very tense as a result of the aggression and provocations of the U.S. imperialists. The Soviet leaders expressed their support for China on September 7 and 19, respectively. Although at that time the situation in the Taiwan Straits was tense, there was no possibility that a nuclear war would break out and no need for the Soviet Union to support China with its nuclear weapons. It was only when they were clear that this was the situation that the Soviet leaders expressed their support for China.[29]

This evidence strongly suggests the Soviet government had told the Chinese that the Sino-Soviet defense treaty was limited in Soviet eyes to a direct and unprovoked attack on mainland China. Even then, it seems likely that the Soviet Union reserved the right to plan its counteraction, including the de-

[29] *Peking Review*, September 6, 1963 (text quoted from Morton H. Halperin, *op. cit.*, p. 58).

cision whether or not to use atomic weapons, on its own, without acceding to Chinese requests, and with Soviet security as the prime factor in the decision-making process. Moreover, the fact that Khrushchev chose to write directly to the President of the United States, presumably over the heads of the Chinese leaders, probably aroused suspicions in Peking that in any future crisis — even one involving China — the Russians might strike a bargain with the United States designed to avoid a military clash between American and Soviet forces. In these circumstances, could the Chinese feel assured, as a result of the Taiwan crisis, that they enjoyed the unreserved protection by the Soviet Union that they hoped for under the defense treaty of 1950? It seems quite likely that the Chinese concluded that while the treaty, in Khrushchev's hands, had some deterrent effect on the United States it was not fulfilling their main requirements.

The importance of the Taiwan Straits crisis lies in the fact that until the present phase of the Vietnamese war, it was the only confrontation between China and the United States in which the Sino-Soviet defense treaty might have been invoked. After 1958, Sino-Soviet political relations deteriorated to a point from which no return seems possible now without radical changes of leadership in Moscow or Peking (or in both), changes certainly far more radical than occurred in the Soviet Union in October 1964. According to the Chinese, the Soviet government "tore up" its agreement of October 15, 1957, to supply China with "new defense technology" on June 20, 1959, and also refused to give her a sample atomic bomb. In July 1960, Khrushchev ordered the withdrawal of the two or three thousand military and scientific advisers working in China following a bitter clash between the two Party leaderships at the conference in Bucharest that had been held to resolve Sino-Soviet differences.[30]

Since 1960 the Soviet Union has treated China more like an unfriendly power than an ally. Although she has continued to send limited supplies of petroleum to China, Russia has

---

[30] See p. 200, and footnote 3. It was at this conference that Khrushchev claimed China had virtually sabotaged Soviet efforts to obtain a joint defense in the Far East.

not resumed military aid on any scale, and aircraft like the piston-engined TU-4 bomber, the MIG-17 and MIG-19 jet fighters, and IL-28 light bombers remain the backbone of China's airpower.[31] Both sides have complained of frontier incidents provoked by the other.[32] According to Victor Zorza in *The Guardian*, on October 9, 1964, Soviet forces in the Far East participated in an exercise that assumed a Chinese invasion of the Soviet Maritime Province from Manchuria. Soviet state security border guard districts covering the Chinese frontier were reallocated in 1963 to allow for closer supervision of the border: three border districts instead of two now exist between Soviet Central Asia and the Pacific coast.

In July 1963 a head-on clash occurred between the Chinese and Soviet governments over the decision of the latter to sign the partial nuclear test ban treaty with the Western powers. In the welter of Chinese attacks against Soviet readiness to halt nuclear tests in the atmosphere, the most relevant criticism was that the treaty was designed "to prevent all the threatened peace-loving countries, including China, from increasing their defense capability."[33] The Chinese followed this up by releasing their version of the agreements on defense and new technology concluded in 1957 between the Soviet Union and China, and the Russians retorted that the Chinese had made public classified documents and information "relating to the defenses of the socialist community. . . ."[34]

If, as seems likely, the Chinese began to regard the Sino-Soviet defense treaty as of doubtful value after the Taiwan Straits crisis, Soviet statements from mid-1960 onwards suggest that the Russians decided to make public that they had come to the same conclusion at about the time of the withdrawal

31 Garthoff, *op. cit.*, p. 91. *The New York Herald Tribune*, April 22, 1965, adds ten TU-16 jet bombers to this inventory of Chinese aircraft; and *The New York Times* has reported the existence in China of a few MIG-21's. Indonesia, Cuba, and Egypt now have more up-to-date Soviet aircraft and missiles than China possesses.

32 For the Chinese complaint, see Griffith, *op. cit.*, p. 172; for the Soviet version, see *Pravda*, September 21 and 22, 1963, and *Kazakhstanskaya Pravda*, September 29, 1963 (an article by a former Chinese general who defected to Russia).

33 *People's Daily*, July 31, 1963, as quoted in Griffith, *op. cit.*, p. 162.

34 *Soviet News*, No. 4885 (August 21, 1963).

of the Soviet technicians from China. In August 1960 an article published in several Soviet provincial papers contained the highly significant words:

> Is it possible to imagine the successful construction of socialism. . . even in such a great country as, let us say, China, if that country were in an isolated position, not depending on the cooperation and mutual aid of all other socialist countries? While being subjected to an economic blockade on the part of the capitalist countries, such a country would be simultaneously subjected to military blows from without. It would experience the very greatest difficulties even in the event that it withstood the furious onslaught of the enemy.[35]

In January 1962 Marshal Malinovski warned that the armed might of the Soviet Union was available to help "members of the Socialist camp who are friendly to us."[36]

Since 1960, in fact, almost the only context in which the Soviet government repeated its commitment to go to China's defense — such as Suslov's speech on February 14, 1964 — was in support of the argument that China did not need a national nuclear capability because she was protected by the Soviet armed forces and the Sino-Soviet defense treaty.[37] But on October 16, 1964, the Chinese exploded their first atomic device — a uranium one, for which China, it is thought, must possess a gaseous diffusion plant for the production of weapons-grade uranium 235.[38] The second Chinese nuclear explosion occurred on May 14, 1965. It seems probable that the Chinese produced their nuclear devices partly on the basis of the nonmilitary assistance given by the Soviet Union to the Chinese atomic energy program. This included the supply of an experimental atomic reactor, which went into operation in September 1958, and the training of Chinese physicists at

[35] S. Titarenko, "Lenin's Teachings on the Victory of Socialism and the Present Day," published simultaneously on August 16 in the Baku Daily, *Bakinskii rabotchii,* and in *Sovetskaya latvia* (quoted in Zagoria, *op. cit.,* p. 335).

[36] TASS, January 24, 1962.

[37] See also *Pravda,* September 21, 1963, and *Red Star,* September 24, 1963.

[38] Morton H. Halperin, "Chinese Nuclear Strategy: The Early Post-Detonation Period," *Adelphi Paper,* No. 18 (London: Institute for Strategic Studies, May 1965), p. 3.

the Soviet Nuclear Research Institute at Dubna.[39] There is
still no firm evidence that more direct Soviet help was given
to China in the weapons field, although the method by which
the Chinese provided themselves with a gaseous diffusion
plant is not at all clear at this stage.

Soviet comment on the first Chinese atomic explosion was
restrained.[40] One probable reason for this was the change of
leadership in the Soviet Union that had occurred two days
earlier, and the uncertainty in Moscow about the future
course of Sino-Soviet relations now that the man whom the
Chinese regarded as their main enemy, Khrushchev, had been
deposed. At the time of Khrushchev's downfall it seemed likely
that, in his headlong fashion, the Soviet leader had decided
upon a full-scale clash with China, possibly involving an attempt to win a majority in the Communist movement for
China's expulsion from the bloc at the projected meeting of
Communist parties on December 15, 1964.

There is some evidence that both the new Soviet and the
Chinese leaders were interested in sounding out each others'
intentions after the fall of Khrushchev, and the dispute for
a time received little publicity in Moscow and Peking. Chou
En-lai, the Chinese Premier, attended the Revolution anniversary celebrations in Moscow in November 1964, and the
Russians announced the postponement of the December 15
meeting of Communist parties. It appears, however, that this
meeting with Chou En-lai was a failure. Chou had undoubtedly gone to Moscow expecting Soviet capitulation on Chinese
terms. The Russians did, apparently, offer to resume some aid
to China and to halt ideological polemics.[41] But they were
not prepared to reverse Khrushchev's policies on the points
at issue between the two countries, and this was unacceptable
to the Chinese. On the very day that Chou left Moscow the
World Marxist Review printed articles critical of Chinese
policies, including her territorial ambitions.

Perhaps more significant to the Chinese were the signs

---

[39] Halperin, "China and the Bomb," *op. cit.,* p. 74.

[40] TASS merely repeated the official Chinese announcement, and the
only criticism within the bloc came from East Germany.

[41] R. Lowenthal, *The New York Times Magazine,* April 4, 1965.

quite soon after the meeting in November that the Russians were considering a reversal of Khrushchev's decision not to get further involved in the situation in Southeast Asia.[42] On November 26, 1964, TASS released a Soviet declaration of readiness to help North Vietnam in its confrontation with the United States, and in December Moscow agreed to the opening of a permanent office in the Soviet capital by the Viet Cong authorities, the National front for the liberation of South Vietnam.[43] Kosygin's suggestion of a visit to Hanoi seems to have been a further step in a policy of increasing Soviet involvement in Vietnam that was decided upon after the November meeting with Chou En-lai but before the resumption of American air attacks on military objectives in North Vietnam on February 6, 1965. This policy shift was probably intended to attract Asian Communist parties away from China and toward the Soviet view in the Sino-Soviet dispute. The Russians probably hoped to use for their purposes offers of increased military aid — a field in which the Soviet Union can almost always outbid the Chinese. But there may also have been a more general feeling in Moscow that, properly handled, greater risks could be taken to effect a Soviet military presence in countries with Chinese-oriented Communist parties in control, a trend that may have something in common with new, but still tentative, Soviet military thinking on the future feasibility of longer-range political action and crisis-control operations.[44]

When Kosygin arrived in Hanoi he brought with him the commander-in-chief of the Soviet air force, Marshal Vershinin, and the general in charge of military aid to foreign countries, G. S. Sidorovich — evidence that a further Soviet aid commitment to North Vietnam was at least intended by the Russian Premier. While the Soviet Premier was in Hanoi, the

[42] TASS, July 26, 1964. Russia withdrew as cochairman with Britain of the Geneva conference on Laos, and by implication considered the same step on Indochina as a whole.

[43] At the same time the new Soviet regime was showing renewed interest in North Korea, to whose defense Russia was already committed by treaty.

[44] For example, the re-establishment of a marine corps under naval command in 1964 and renewed interest in Western "Special Operations" in the Soviet military press.

Viet Cong, in attacking the U.S. base at Pleiku in the South, triggered off the present phase of American air bombardment of military targets in North Vietnam, an event that may have taken the Russians by surprise. Kosygin left North Vietnam for Peking and North Korea with at least one failure behind him: the North Vietnamese Communist Party declined to attend the March 1 meeting of Communist parties in Moscow; but subsequent evidence of Soviet military aid to North Vietnam indicated that this refusal did not deter the Soviet leader from continuing his policy of keeping a military presence in the country. This interpretation of Soviet policy was further strengthened by the Soviet reception given to the North Vietnamese delegation that visited Moscow in July 1965 and signed an agreement on Soviet aid to Hanoi.[45]

The hard facts on exactly how much new military aid from the Soviet Union has appeared in North Vietnam are difficult to come by. There are believed to be 6 to 8 IL-28 Soviet bombers at airfields near Hanoi. *U.S. News & World Report* has stated that as many as 150 jet fighters may have been moved into North Vietnam, and MIG-17's and MIG-21's were in action against U.S. aircraft in April 1966. Steady progress on the construction of surface-to-air missile sites near Hanoi has also been reported; by October 1965 the number of sites was stated to be between 20 and 30, and in mid-1966 about 100 were believed to be in various stages of deployment. Enough information is available to show that whatever the Chinese are doing, the Soviet Union did send operational war material to North Vietnam, that some surface-to-air missile sites were being manned by North Vietnamese crews, and that some missiles had been fired against U.S. aircraft, possibly from mobile sites. China, while shouting the loudest about "American aggression," had, according to press reports, partially obstructed or slowed down Soviet military aid to Hanoi.[46] China has also said that her forces would be sent to Vietnam only "when needed" and has, unrealistically enough, offered aid directly to the Viet Cong.

[45] *The Guardian*, July 13, 1965.
[46] *The Guardian*, May 18, 1965; and *The New York Herald Tribune*, April 23–24, 1966, p. 1.

Against this background of military aid, what commitments and specific threats have been made by the major powers in Southeast Asia relevant to the Sino-Soviet defense problem? China has specifically declared that she will not intervene in the Vietnam war unless China's territory is directly threatened,[47] though the exact interpretation of this phrase remains open. The United States has told China that if it sends troops into South Vietnam, the war will be carried into China itself.[48] The Soviet Union has sent military aid to North Vietnam but is not committed to the defense of the country. Soviet policy in the Vietnam crisis is clearly aimed at the avoidance of a major military confrontation with the United States. But it is also designed to register an effective military presence in North Vietnam, to set up a ring of fixed SAM sites round Hanoi while using others on a mobile basis in order to force U.S. aircraft to decrease height and fly within the range of conventional antiaircraft guns. Ultimately the Russians hope to acquire the power to decide whether to escalate the conflict or to bring the North Vietnamese, if not the Chinese, to the conference table. A significant part of the Soviet Union's policy in North Vietnam is, therefore, directly related to its struggle against China within the world Communist movement.

It seems clear that the Vietnamese war has not, as some critics feared, brought China and the Soviet Union closer together but has hardened the differences between them. In these circumstances, it is probable that the right question to be asked about the Soviet commitment to defend China is: What action would the Soviet government take in its own interests if the Chinese became involved in a major war against the United States, as a result of which the existence of the Communist regime was seriously threatened? In other words, would the Soviet Union go to the help of an ally, fighting alongside him, and striking back at his enemy's home territory, or would it concentrate on laying plans for action in

[47] Edgar Snow, "Interview With Mao," *New Republic*, Vol. 152 (February 27, 1965).

[48] *U.S. News & World Report*, June 28, 1965, p. 39.

the event of the ally's defeat, even if verbal and limited material support were given during the military conflict?

The evidence suggests that the Soviet government began seriously to consider the second course of action after 1958, and that American military action against North Vietnam has not altered the Soviet attitude. In the first place, the realities of the nuclear-missile world have made it inconceivable that the Soviet Union would engage in nuclear conflict with the United States on behalf of Chinese foreign policy, a course that could only lead to the devastation of the Soviet Union. This was virtually admitted by Khrushchev as long ago as December 1962, when he said that the Chinese hoped to provoke a U.S.-Soviet nuclear war while they themselves sat it out.[49] This argument would apply with equal force to the launching of Soviet missiles against North America and against U.S. bases in the Western Pacific, even though attacks on the latter might limit American retaliation to the Soviet Far East. Second, in the event of a conventional American strike against limited objectives in South China connected with ground operations in Vietnam or neighboring countries, followed by a plea for Soviet help from China, it is possible if the Chinese approved, which would by no means be certain, that the Soviets might send aircraft and air defense equipment to defend major Chinese targets and centers of population in North or Central China, thus releasing Chinese planes for action in the South. The Russians might also replace Chinese aircraft lost in action against the Americans. But such Soviet regional defense activity would probably be more in the nature of a deterrent to the United States against an extension of military operations northwards toward the Soviet borders and might take the form of an experimental build-up of Soviet air defense facilities, including both fixed and mobile SAM sites, comparable to that in the Hanoi area in the summer of 1965. It is probably true to say that the Soviets discount the possibility of an all-out American nuclear attack

49 Khrushchev's speech to the Supreme Soviet on the Cuban crisis, *Pravda*, December 13, 1962. See also *Kommunist*, No. 14 (September 1963), pp. 19, 22.

on China, and regard as even less likely an American-Chinese Nationalist attempt to wage a land campaign on the Chinese mainland. But the Russians probably consider that in the last resort there could be options open to the Americans that could bring the Chinese central government close to breakdown, and it is to cope with this kind of situation that Soviet planning may well be going on.

First and foremost, Soviet planners would be bound to consider the safety of the Soviet borders. If organized administration began to disintegrate in north or northeast China, with loss of control by Peking and the threat of chaos along the Soviet or Mongolian frontiers, then it is possible that the Soviet government might consider the use of troops in a preventive occupation of Manchuria, initially in the name of preserving Chinese communism as well as protecting the Soviet frontier. The Soviet planners would probably assume that in such a situation the United States would not wish to extend a threat of war to the Soviet Union in order to prevent Soviet occupation of northeast China. As very much a secondary aim, the Soviets might exploit their occupation to rally Chinese Communist groups or individuals to their area of occupation or influence so that the Party could at least rule part of China — though under strict Soviet tutelage as well as Soviet protection. All that can be said of this very hypothetical situation is that in the event of a major U.S.-China war that resulted in catastrophic defeats for the Chinese central Communist government, some form of temporary "partition" of China on ideological as well as geographical lines might appeal to the Soviet Union, first, in order to protect the Soviet frontier from chaos, and second, as a means of salvaging some element of communism from the ruins of a country in the throes of modern war.

To conclude, therefore: much of the argument in this paper is bound to be speculative, but it seems likely that from the date of the signature of the Sino-Soviet defense treaty in February 1950 to the death of Stalin in 1953 the Soviet government used the treaty in part as a deterrent against attack on China, although it was extremely cautious both in detailing its commitment and in giving aid to build up China's own armed forces. In the event of war, Stalin's armies were well deployed for a possible military occupation of Manchuria. From 1954 to 1958, the Soviet leadership may have attempted to strike a bargain with the Chinese: modern Soviet arms (possibly including nuclear weapons under direct Soviet control) in exchange for a Soviet-dominated command and control system modeled on the Warsaw Pact. This the Chinese rejected. From 1958 onwards, with the additional lesson of Soviet behavior during the Taiwan Straits crisis, the Chinese probably assumed that the Sino-Soviet defense treaty was largely inoperative. The rapid worsening of the Sino-Soviet dispute in 1960, the withdrawal of Soviet technicians, and clashes on the Sino-Soviet frontier led to an "unfriendly nation" relationship between China and Russia in which a genuine defense treaty had little relevance — except in the general field of deterrence, or as a last-minute Soviet attempt to prevent the Chinese from acquiring their own atomic weapons. Deterrence is probably the main reason why the treaty has not been, and probably will not be, denounced by the Russians. Should deterrence fail, and China become involved in war with the United States, it would probably be in the Soviet Union's interest to carry out limited intervention by assuming responsibility for the air defense of areas of China that might not be involved in limited hostilities conducted in the south or the central parts of the country. In the event of escalation of a Sino-American war to a full-scale conflict, Soviet policy would probably be directed toward the protection of the Soviet frontier and the possibilities of salvaging something politically pro-Soviet from the wreckage. In short, the Sino-Soviet defense treaty is on paper a marginally credible deterrent; but if the Soviet Union takes action in a Sino-American war, it would be exclusively in the Soviet national interest and not in defense of a nominal ally who is in fact more hostile to the Soviet Union than many countries of the non-Communist world.

9

The American Attitude

GEORGE H. QUESTER

Introduction

An attempt will be made here to trace the evolution of the Sino-Soviet military alliance as seen by the American government. What will be sought are apparent Russian military commitments to the Communist Chinese (and commitments in reverse), the reasons assumed for such commitments, and the perceived implications for Western military policy.

What are thus of direct concern to us here are not the realities of the Communist bloc but the images of the bloc found credible in Washington. Such American images can be expected to derive logically from assessments of the military capabilities and vulnerabilities of the major Communist powers and of the political values and ideologies involved. As the views of the U.S. government on these basic questions have changed over the twenty years since 1945, analyses of the Sino-Soviet military relationship have gone through a definite evolution.

The Truman Administration

Military Assumptions, 1945–1952

In the over-all military analysis of the Truman administration, from 1945 to 1953, atomic weapons did not yet seem to ensure defeat of the Communist bloc if war were to come.

Western Europe was the prize most worth keeping; but once the Russians had recovered from their own World War II damage, they might well have to be held east of the Elbe by essentially conventional means, since atomic weapons would neither stop a Soviet army nor induce it to leave once it was ensconced in European cities.

In this military capabilities analysis of the pre-1952 period, the Chinese mainland was seen to be a trap. China seemed to have very little military potential to export, but for reasons partially geographical it could not easily be disarmed on its own ground. Any invader would therefore find the Asian mainland a military morass, for he would have to commit more of his own ground forces than he could hope to incapacitate on the other side. Naval and air forces would similarly be tied up if committed in support of such an action against the Chinese, so much so that the United States on a more global basis would find itself short of all the significant arms. While China seemed to be so minor a power, while the areas it could threaten seemed of such relative unimportance, it would thus not be worth engaging as an enemy or wooing as a satellite.

Even when the Nationalists were still making forward progress in 1946, U.S. policy was constrained by a basic aversion to becoming involved in the conflict. While China had been seen at some earlier times as a major power and potentially as the "policeman of the Far East," by 1946 it seemed a negligible military asset. The option of holding on to and militarily salvaging a part of China was also rejected, in effect until the defense of Formosa began in 1950, since the moral rectitude of not partitioning China took precedence over more tactical considerations. When a peaceful solution to the civil war became unlikely, American troops had to be withdrawn. Such estimates of the military value of China, and of the costs of penetrating the Asian mainland, would persist in the administration through the Korean War up till 1953.

Political Assumptions, 1945–1952

The Truman administration's picture of Communist goals generally assumed that the Chinese regime would prove less (or at the worst no more) aggressive than the Soviet Union.

Somewhere between the images of "agrarian reformer" and "obedient servant of Moscow" the truth apparently had to lie. If the Chinese were completely subservient to the Russians, they would of course have to serve Russian world-wide ambitions, but any amount of national independence was likely to involve a step toward domestic and international moderation. The apparent enormity of China's internal problems would preoccupy any Chinese regime for a long time, and China after all had not been able to demonstrate many imperialist tendencies in recent decades. Americans, moreover, tended to expect a grateful friendship from China, an expectation that may have illustrated an enormous self-delusion; yet in the early stages of the Chinese civil war, even the Communists had accepted the United States as a mediating agent apparently with the best interests of China at heart. After 1948 the example of Tito seemed, moreover, to offer a promising example of the behavior of independent Communist regimes.

While it was true from 1946 to 1949 that the Chinese and not the Russians were engaged in military activity, this of course reflected the basic aim of gaining power in their own country and not that they shared the ambitious plans of the less immediately violent but more universally active Russians. American observers, up to 1953 did not give up hope for Chinese Communist independence, an independence that would break up any "bloc," as indicated in a speech by Consul John Cabot in Shanghai in 1949:

> In June of 1948 the Cominform published a communiqué denouncing Tito and other leaders of the Yugoslav Government. You will say Yugoslavia is far off and ask what it has to do with China. In that communiqué the Cominform made it very clear that Tito's crime had been to refuse to follow blindly orders from the Politburo in Moscow. . . .
>
> Now my question is: Does the Chinese Communist Party blindly follow orders from Moscow or does it not? They surely cannot take it amiss if we infer from their endorsement of this communiqué (and much of the evidence) that they do. The United States does not believe that the Chinese people want to be ruled by orders from any foreign capital and in accordance with its traditional friendship, the United States has furnished aid to them to prevent this.[1]

[1] Address of January 26, 1949, in *U.S. Department of State Bulletin,* February 13, 1949, p. 183. Hereafter cited as *DOSB.*

Even if the two Communist powers did prove equal in ideological fervor, it still seemed inevitable that their outlooks on concrete issues would diverge. The establishment of communism in China would probably be more important for Chinese Communists than for Russians, while the reverse would presumably hold true for a defense of communism in Russia. Crasser issues, moreover, were thought likely to emerge; as late as January 1950, in the very speech to the Washington Press Club that seemed to exclude South Korea from the American defense perimeter, Secretary of State Dean Acheson suggested that a border issue was arising between the Soviet Union and Communist China, not, as now, involving Chinese claims on Russia but rather Russian designs on Manchuria, Sinkiang, and Inner and Outer Mongolia.

> Armed with these new powers, what is happening in China is that the Soviet Union is detaching the northern provinces (areas) of China from China and is attaching them to the Soviet Union. This process is complete in outer Mongolia. It is nearly complete in Manchuria, and I am sure that in inner Mongolia and in Sinkiang there are very happy reports coming from Soviet agents to Moscow. This is what is going on. It is the detachment of these whole areas, vast areas — populated by Chinese — the detachment of these areas from China and their attachment in the Soviet Union. . . .
>
> The only thing that can obscure it is the folly of ill-conceived adventures on our part which easily could do so, and I urge all who are thinking about these foolish adventures to remember that we must not seize the unenviable position which the Russians have carved out for themselves. We must not undertake to deflect from the Russians to ourselves the righteous anger, and the wrath, and the hatred of the Chinese people which must develop.[2]

Since this also illustrated Soviet expansionism, in contrast to a supposed Chinese predilection to tend one's own garden, the evidence seemed to jibe again with the notion that Russia was the more aggressive, trying to drag Red China along, even if at China's expense.

The Perceived Russian Commitment, 1945–1952.

From such considerations of intent and capability, a sizable Soviet military commitment to the Chinese had come to be

[2] Address of January 12, 1950, in *DOSB*, January 23, 1950, p. 115.

expected by the United States; the arguments accounting for such intervention in the event of a Sino-American crisis or war were several.

A Russian military response could not include any atomic weapons at all until 1949, and even until 1953 it depended on very rudimentary delivery systems. American fears of a Soviet-launched "world war" thus referred to a largely conventional war, exacting from the West great costs that could not be avoided by any reliance on nuclear weapons. Perhaps most important, an intervention on the Chinese mainland might tie up enough American ground forces (and air and naval forces) to leave Europe unprotected, thus spurring a Soviet attack on Europe: the Soviet Union might let China go while exploiting the confusion to seize a much more valuable prize. Or American intervention might lead to deployments on the mainland so vulnerable and exposed that the Soviets would want to reap the force-attrition benefits of a limited commitment of troops to China. Similarly it might look as though American attacks could be repulsed by a small Soviet contribution, a contribution well worth making if it ensured the maintenance of a Communist regime.

American intervention might also damage items in China that were of value to the Russians (Port Arthur, the Manchurian railways, and so on), and thus induce the Soviet Union to retaliate. This possibility was augmented in 1950 by the Treaty of Alliance between Red China and the Soviet Union, directed at Japan and any "ally," which in effect placed Russia's honor on the line.

Since the Soviet Union was more aggressive than China, American intervention might foolishly arouse Chinese resentment that even the Russians could not mobilize by themselves, thus again allowing the Russians to undertake a generally more ambitious program. American intervention might also supply a legal and moral precedent lowering the prestige costs of intervention for the Russians, shifting neutral sentiment toward their position and against the West, allowing the Russians to come in as liberators.

The prospect of American entanglement with China, and of a Russian response to it, arose essentially twice during the

Truman administration, first, during the Chinese civil war extending from 1945 to 1949, and second, after Chinese intervention in the Korean War late in 1950. In the earlier stages of the post-1945 settlement, a Chinese Communist victory had not seemed likely and the Soviet position had been slightly equivocal, showing signs of diplomatic support to the Nationalists but allowing Japanese arms to fall into the hands of the Communists. Yet even here the Russians were expected to possess some decided military advantages if they intervened. In the words of John McCloy in 1945:

> The Kuomintang must have our support to be able to cope with the situation. If the Russians, however, decide to give active support to the Chinese Communists, then we are in a real mess.[3]

or General Marshall in 1946:

> Marshall reminded the Generalissimo that, if Russian aid were given to the Communists, their supply line would be much shorter than his own and much more immune from attack.[4]

When, by 1947, the Chinese Communist position had proved to be more viable and promising, American observers not unnaturally came to expect a continuance of Soviet material aid, which might well have been stepped up into a more violent Russian participation if the United States had intervened militarily in China or if the Chinese Communists had really needed outside assistance. At the least, the Russians would exploit any American participation in the Chinese civil war to embarrass the West diplomatically. Again in Marshall's view:

> We must clear our hands out here as quickly as possible in order to avoid the inevitable Russian recriminations similar to those today regarding the British troops in Greece.[5]

Arguments about this Sino-Soviet relationship show up with General Douglas MacArthur's demands for stronger attacks

---

[3] Memorandum of meeting between Byrnes, Patterson, Forestal, Mc-Cloy, Matthews, and Gates, November 6, 1945, quoted in Herbert Feis, *The China Tangle* (Princeton, N.J.: Princeton University Press, 1953), p. 389.

[4] Harry S Truman, *Years of Trial and Hope* (Garden City, N.Y.: Doubleday, 1956), p. 88.

[5] *Ibid.*, p. 77.

on the Chinese after their intervention in the Korean War. The Truman administration held to its interpretation of China as a military morass that had to be avoided if Soviet relative strength in some more crucial areas was not to be increased. In General Bradley's testimony:

> The strategic alternative, enlargement of the war in Korea to include Red China, would probably delight the Kremlin more than anything else we could do. It would necessarily tie down additional forces, especially our sea power and our air power, while the Soviet Union would not be obliged to put a single man into the conflict.[6]

> *Senator Bridges:*. . . You are consistent whether it is China, Indochina, India, or Siam or what not, you have a basic thought for considering all factors that we should not be involved with our own troops on the mainland of Asia.

> *General Bradley:* It of course depends on the circumstances at the time, but right now I feel as I said in my statement here, I think we would be fighting a wrong war at the wrong place and against a wrong enemy.[7]

While the war in Korea had to be fought because of the threat to Japan, and on the principle of resistance to aggression, the *status quo* would have to be vindicated within the over-all boundaries of Korea, or perhaps only within Southern Korea, since China itself was neither important enough nor vulnerable enough to justify a preventive escalation to larger campaigns.

MacArthur in contradiction assumed that air and naval power could be used to weaken the Chinese without great costs to the United States and thus achieve the beneficial result of decisively repulsing aggression in Korea and of reducing future Chinese military potential for other aggressions. Yet MacArthur also saw China as a minor military power of little value to the Soviet Union, and here his argument was really only a variant of the administration's; China was militarily so unimportant to the Russians that nothing the United States could do seemed likely to affect the basic Soviet stra-

6 U.S. Senate Committee on Armed Services and Committee on Foreign Relations, Hearings on the *Military Situation in the Far East* (82nd Congress, 1st session, 1951), p. 731.

7 *Ibid.*, p. 753.

tegic plan, a plan already determined, presumably, by much weightier considerations.

> He [the Russian] knows, just as well as you and I know, that we are not going to attack him.
>
> If he has determined that he is not going to attack, that he is doing well enough in the present atmosphere, that he is acquiring and expanding as rapidly as he can digest it; and that he is not going to attack, and that is his basic policy — I do not believe that anything that happens in Korea, or Asia, for that matter, would affect his basic decision.
>
> If he has determined that he is going to use force, sooner or later, what occurs in Korea, or in Asia, might affect his timetable.
>
> I believe that he will make his decisions on a higher basis than the incidents that are occurring in Asia at the present time.[8]

If China were in fact to acquire military strength and importance, the Soviet leadership, in MacArthur's view, would not be happy about it and at this early stage might not do very much to protect Chinese military development against preventive moves by the United States.

> *General MacArthur*: There is another point that might be brought up. It is just what would be the Soviet attitude, just what would be beneficial to the Soviet from their own point of view, in the increasing strength of this new Frankenstein that is being gradually congealed and coalesced in China?
>
> Would the Soviet desire to have China become so powerful that it might even challenge the Soviet? Would it be the desire, would it be possible for the Soviet to retain a maximum degree of control if China became too powerful?
>
> The general relationship between China and the Soviet has never been clearly defined. Nobody knows it except those that are intimately connected therewith, either from China or the Soviet.
>
> But by the logic of general strategy of the general international philosophy of the forces of the world, there is a point that might well be reached where the interests of Red China and the interests of the Red Soviet did not run parallel, that they started to traverse and become antagonistic.
>
> That is a factor which I am sure would be taken into consideration by both of those countries in an endeavor to apply for

8 *Ibid.*, p. 9.

their own benefit any of these very elastic provisions that are written into this so-called treaty of alliance between them.[9]

American expertise would change the attrition exchange rates of the Chinese battlefield for MacArthur, while the relative military insignificance of that country for the United States could thus be assumed to hold for the Soviet Union too.

Unlike MacArthur, the Truman administration did not, however, expect blockades and bombings of China to be so effective, and feared that use of sizable ground forces would still be required. The possibility of Russian intervention in such a case was held to be high, especially since the bombings, to be effective, would probably also have to be extended into the Soviet Union.

> I have never been able to make myself believe that MacArthur, seasoned soldier that he was, did not realize that the "introduction of Chinese Nationalist forces into South China" would be an act of war; or that he, who had had a front-row seat at world events for thirty-five years, did not realize that the Chinese people would react to the bombings of their cities in exactly the same manner as the people of the United States reacted to the bombing of Pearl Harbor; or that, with his knowledge of the East, he could have overlooked the fact that after he had bombed the cities of China there would still be vast flows of materials from Russia so that, if he wanted to be consistent, his next step would have to be the bombardment of Vladivostok and the Trans-Siberian Railroad! But because I was sure that MacArthur could not possibly have overlooked these considerations, I was left with just one simple conclusion: General MacArthur was ready to risk general war. I was not.[10]

Implicit in the administration's arguments was the assumption that air attacks on the Chinese would arouse their hostility to the West, precluding any movement toward a more moderate independence of Moscow. MacArthur, while acknowledging the possibility and desirability of such a Sino-Soviet rift, disclaimed any American ability to affect it in one direction or another by concessions to the Chinese.

> *Senator Morse:* One of the arguments you hear in this country is that we should play for just such a split between Russia and

---

9 *Ibid.,* p. 251.
10 Truman, *op. cit.,* pp. 415–416.

China as is implied, I think, in your last few comments, and not follow a course of action within China that might cause a cementing of Red China and Red Russia together and that, therefore, we should try to avoid bombing in Manchuria which might bring in Russia. . . .

General MacArthur: To answer the first part of your query, Senator, I don't think there is any question that our own interest would be enhanced by splitting the relationship as wide as possible between China and the Soviet. The great question is the mechanics of it, how to bring it about.

I think that everyone will agree when a man and his wife have a quarrel, if you attempt to interfere, the results are quite doubtful.

I do not see how our interference with it would do more than complicate it and might actually react upon ourselves. The great factors involved are quite beyond our control, I think, along that line.[11]

In summation, the atomic bomb had not yet seemed to outweigh conventional forces in significance, prior to 1952, and Russia seemed more deeply committed than China to the spread of international communism; a credible commitment thus existed of Soviet action, in the event of a Sino-American war, either to bolster the Chinese or to exploit the ensuing confusion elsewhere. The Russians were in fact expected to welcome an American attack on China, since their real concern was thought to be China's unreliable commitment to the Soviet Union.

In reverse, up until 1952 any Chinese contribution of military strength to the Soviet Union seemed limited to a few theaters of Asia, quite minor in significance when compared to Western Europe; yet on China's own territory this strength did not seem vulnerable to attrition since the higher casualties would in fact be imposed on any American invaders who could be lured onto the mainland. The Chinese Communists, moreover, by preference seemed less willing to embark on overseas expeditions and projects either for the encouragement of revolution per se, or to further the increase of Soviet national power; for the United States to invade the mainland

[11] Senate Hearings on the *Military Situation in the Far East, op. cit.*, pp. 251–252.

would have again raised the basic issue for China and have aroused the more moderate Chinese in a way that the Russian Communists could not have done themselves. Even MacArthur disclaimed any intention to invade the mainland, and no such American step was really in prospect during either the Chinese civil war or the Korean War. Politically, any rift between the Chinese and the Russian Communists would be received as good news in Washington, since it would mean a further softening of the Chinese position and a further denial of support to the ever threatening Russians. Perhaps then the Russians might even be diverted by disputes with China and less able to keep their forces concentrated in Eastern Europe. Perhaps the entanglement involved in foreign dealings with China would thus tie up Russian energies rather than those of the United States.

The Eisenhower Administration

Military Assumptions, 1953–1960

In terms of over-all military analysis, the Eisenhower administration from 1953 to 1960 proclaimed that it was making substantial departures from the assumptions of the Truman period. Through most of this time, nuclear weapons in new configurations were to be relied upon to replace sizable ground and naval forces. While such weapons were expected both to facilitate more effective *defense* of territory and to *deter* war by making it more painful and costly regardless of who won on the battlefield, it was clear that the emphasis had shifted toward the latter. In the words of Secretary of State Dulles:

> Local defense will always be important. But there is no local defense which alone will contain the mighty landpower of the Communist world. Local defenses must be reinforced by the further deterrent of massive retaliatory power. A potential aggressor, who is glutted with manpower, might be tempted to attack in confidence that resistance would be confined to manpower. He might be tempted to attack in places where his superiority was decisive.
> The way to deter aggression is for the free community to be

willing and able to respond vigorously at places and with means of its own choosing.[12]

Specific details on American military strategy would not be disseminated, since the important thing was to keep the image of general war sufficiently horrible. The hydrogen bomb promised to be a frightening deterrent even if a Hiroshima-sized A-bomb was not, while tactical nuclear weapons might be effective on the battlefield as well as frightening triggers for escalation. The doctrine could be applied as long as the United States still held a preponderant advantage in strategic delivery systems and tactical nuclear weapons, or perhaps, instead, for as long as American leaders seemed prepared to honor commitments regardless of the consequences.

The "new look" promised to deter a Russian attack on Europe or to repulse such an attack. It might also suffice to deter attacks elsewhere in the world, as in Asia, or perhaps cheaply and effectively to repulse them. This "revolution" in theory perhaps should not be exaggerated; it was one logical evolution of the Truman administration's policies if one accepted the reality of certain breakthroughs in nuclear technology. Yet it was certainly less openly logical than Truman and Acheson would have made it. Any revolution in practical results also should not be exaggerated, for especially in the Far East the new doctrine did not fully solve the West's strategic problems.

On the specific military problems of China and the Far East, the Eisenhower administration seemed at first to share the assumptions of its predecessor that ground campaigns on the Asian mainland would impose higher casualties on the United States; but air forces, perhaps using tactical nuclear weapons, might, as MacArthur had suggested, facilitate instead some considerable attrition of Chinese military strength.

The Chinese Communist military threat to American interests still seemed very limited. Yet since the Soviet danger in Europe had become less immediate, while the Communists presumably had consolidated their new Chinese base, the prevention of further Communist expansion in Asia would nonetheless seem somewhat more important than it had before

[12] Address of January 12, 1954, in *DOSB*, January 25, 1954, p. 108.

(both objectively so and because the Republicans had traditionally been more Asia-orientated and less Europe-orientated than the Democrats). Korea still had to be defended, on principle and perhaps to shield Japan. Taiwan could be made reasonably secure by naval forces, if Chiang would only keep his army out of Quemoy and Matsu, out of harm's way; but the "rice bowl" of Southeast Asia was a resource worth having that was not inherently so safe from conventional attack. It was to the solution of these problems that the new strategy was to some extent addressed.

Political Assumptions, 1953–1960

The aftermath of the Korean War left a certain American bitterness toward China, perhaps inevitable where violent conflict replaces less destructive forms of confrontation. Moreover, the desire to retain a hold on Taiwan, a part of "China," precluded American diplomatic recognition or the opening of trade relations. Yet the "blame" for Chinese behavior still had to be laid at the door of the Russians. At the start of the Republican administration, American conflict with the Chinese still seemed to derive from a Chinese subservience to the Soviet Union, and even President Eisenhower himself felt that this subservience might be reduced to the advantage of the West, since China and "Chinese" communism were not naturally antagonistic to the United States.

The President was not convinced that the vital interests of the United States were best served by prolonged nonrecognition of China. He had serious doubts as to whether Russia and China were natural allies. He speculated on whether Soviet interests lay primarily in Europe and the Middle East rather than in the Orient. Therefore, he asked, would it not be the best policy in the long run for the United States to try to pull China away from Russia rather than drive the Chinese ever deeper into an unnatural alliance unfriendly to the United States?[13]

Yet, as hostile Chinese activities continued after the Korean armistice, some hints began to appear in American official reasoning that the Chinese might at points have become more

[13] Robert J. Donovan, *Eisenhower, The Inside Story* (New York: Harper, 1956), p. 132.

rash than the Soviets. There was nothing very profound or ideological in this but rather a simple difference in operational experience that left the Chinese foolishly somewhat more sure of themselves than the more experienced Russians. In the words of Secretary of State John Foster Dulles during the Quemoy crisis early in 1955:

> Indeed, I came back from this trip to the Far East with a sense of deep concern. What I learned there about the attitude of the Chinese Communists made me appreciate that they constitute an acute and an imminent threat.
> They seem to be dizzy with success. They entertain a very exaggerated sense of their own power, and they gravely underestimate the power and resolution of the non-Communist world. . . .
> Both the Chinese and the Soviet Communists have, of course, the same ideological motivation, but the manifestations are different.
> So far, the expansion of the Soviet Union has been accomplished by coldly calculated and deliberate steps. . . .
> The temperament of the Chinese Communists is different, and while, in the long run, the Soviet method may prove more formidable, yet, in the short run, the Chinese Communist method may prove more dangerous and provocative of war.
> The picture I have to draw is a somber one, but it is by no means a hopeless one. I believe that there is still time to bring the Chinese Communists to a more sober mood.[14]

Any alertness of the United States toward a relatively greater militance in China tended, however, to fall off again after the Bandung Conference of 1955, which among other things signaled the end of the Quemoy crisis. China now seemed "ideologically" to be committing itself to peaceful coexistence. The confrontation with China had been prolonged, from Korea to Indochina to Quemoy, but not enough to shift the American analysis of China from the "proxy-of-Russia" image; when the *détente* with the Soviet Union was launched in 1955 at Geneva, it seemed also to have brought in the Chinese, as American diplomatic contacts with the Chinese were now established.

It is thus not strange that an independent and more hostile Chinese attitude was only clearly identified almost at the end

14 Address of March 21, 1955, in *DOSB*, April 4, 1955, pp. 551–552.

of the second term of the Eisenhower administration. When the thaw of 1955 ended in 1956, with Russian action in Hungary and with missile threats against Britain and France, it was still not Chinese action that had caused it to end. In Eastern Europe, it was in fact Chinese intervention that was reported to have dissuaded Khrushchev from intervening massively in Poland (but also to have urged firmness in Hungary).[15] Thus it could not easily be concluded that China was now the more militant or more fervent Communist power.

In 1957 there were Sputnik and Western concerns over Russian strategic missile power, which in fact spurred the Chinese to demand more aggressive action by the Communist bloc but which in the West focused attention still more directly on Russia itself. The Quemoy shellings of 1958 were preceded by the Middle East crisis, presumably instigated from Moscow, and were followed by Khrushchev's ultimatum over Berlin. As long as Europe and North America were more important than Asia to the United States, any detection of a new Chinese aggressiveness would thus be difficult. "Lesser Soviet hostility" effective against more sensitive American interests would have to be compared subjectively with "greater Chinese hostility" effective against a less sensitive area, and the ideological reversal could not yet be so clear. In the 1958 Quemoy crisis, moreover, much was made of Khrushchev's visit to Peking before the beginning of the shellings and of his assurance of Soviet commitment to the defense of China. Eisenhower made a statement on September 11, 1958:

> It is as certain as can be that the shooting which the Chinese Communists started on August 23d had as its purpose not just the taking of the island of Quemoy. It is part of what is indeed an ambitious plan of armed conquest.
> This plan would liquidate all of the free-world positions in the Western Pacific area and bring them under captive governments which would be hostile to the United States and the free world. Thus the Chinese and Russian Communists would come to dominate at least the western half of the now friendly Pacific Ocean.
> So aggression by ruthless despots again imposes a clear danger to the United States and to the free world.

15 *The New York Times,* January 11, 1957, p. 1.

In this effort the Chinese Communists and the Soviet Union appear to be working hand in hand. Last Monday I received a long letter on this subject from Prime Minister Khrushchev.[16]

The solution of the 1958 crisis, with its bizarre innovation of alternate-day shelling, produced some Western statements on the immorality and inhumanity of such Chinese tactics but no real assumption yet that these had been adopted independently of outside control.[17] Only with the emergence of the "spirit of Camp David" in 1959 did the U.S. government clearly begin to recognize an independent Chinese militance. In part this was traceable also to the suppression of the Tibetan insurrection (and to Chinese border skirmishes with India from which Russia disassociated herself), but Chinese hostility toward the Western powers per se was made most apparent in the Peking reaction to Khrushchev's return from the United States. Secretary of State Christian Herter stated:

> With respect to Mr. Khrushchev's handling of himself in Peiping, there were things of very real interest. There was no question but that he talked quite eloquently with respect to the solution of international problems by peaceful means. He indicated that it was the attitude of the Soviet Government — and he referred in that particular case to his own Government — to try to work out international problems along these lines. He clearly was not speaking for the Communist Chinese at that point.
> Perhaps equally interesting was the fact that Mr. Mao [Tse-tung] never made any statement at all, either on Mr. Khrushchev's arrival or on his departure, at the time that Mr. Khrushchev made some statements at the airport, nor at any time during the conference. These matters, naturally, are difficult to evaluate, but they would seem to indicate that perhaps Mr. Khrushchev and the Soviet Government of Russia are taking a rather different line from the point of view of the solution of international problems from that of the Communist Chinese.[18]

Yet, as open Chinese objections to the improvement of relations with the West became more frequent in 1959, there was still no military activity in the Far East that could upset the general feeling of *détente*; China might in the abstract

16 Note of September 11, 1958, in *DOSB*, September 29, 1958, p. 482.
17 *The New York Times*, October 29, 1958, p. 18.
18 News conference of October 6, 1959, in *DOSB*, October 26, 1959, p. 577.

desire more injury to the United States, but it still seemed to be behind the Soviet Union in its ability to produce any such injury at costs acceptable to itself. Again Secretary Herter expressed his opinion:

> *Question:* Is Communist China a greater menace to our national security than the U.S.S.R.?
>
> *Herter:* There again it's very hard to make any comparison. The attitude that Communist China is today adopting toward the United States is, of course, a great deal tougher one publicly than that adopted by the Soviet Union. Even in comparable meetings where they are together, it's the Chinese who say the nastiest words about us. This may be a calculated thing at a time when the Russians are trying to increase the spirit of what they call Camp David. This question obviously would have to be divided into two parts, and that is present and future. At the present I would say the answer is definitely "No." For the future everything depends on the rapidity of Chinese development both from a military and an economic point of view.[19]

It could be contended, moreover, that China would still feel compelled to coordinate with the Russians, and that the Soviet Union was therefore obligated to impose the new *détente* on its more bellicose satellite. If a rift was emerging as a result of the new Russian respect for the *status quo,* it was up to the Russians to heal it. In the words of Assistant Secretary for Public Affairs Andrew H. Berding:

> Aside from ideological ties and objectives, Communist China is dependent on Soviet economic and military aid. And there are also the values to the Soviet Union and to international communism of having the partnership of the world's most populous nation. Thus it would be foolish to infer from these possible examples of differences that a serious rift is an imminent prospect.
> There is an important corollary to the fact of this senior-junior type of bond. Recently this has been described as "the doctrine of partial responsibility," meaning that, since the Soviet Union assumes the leadership of the Communist bloc, it must assume a degree of responsibility for actions of bloc members. There is nothing really new about this. We have long spoken of the close senior-junior aspect of the Sino-Soviet relationship, and a good measure of Soviet responsibility for Chinese Communist conduct has all along been implicit. The recent Soviet

19 News conference of February 18, 1960, in *DOSB,* March 7, 1960, pp. 360–361.

interest in a *detente* with the West, concomitant with a multiplicity of trouble spots in the East, has merely highlighted the implications of this major Communist partnership. We believe that, if the Soviet Union is sincere in wanting to safeguard the peace, it has the leverage, through the oft-claimed monolithic nature of the Communist camp, to insure a measure of responsibility on the part of the Chinese Communists. In pointing out this obvious fact we are not engaged in any mischiefmaking. The issues at stake are too serious for that.[20]

The shock of the U-2 incident in 1960 thus forced a deeper re-evaluation of the Chinese in the outgoing Republican administration; they were seen as perhaps the real instigators of the breakoff of the Paris summit conference, as themselves having an intrabloc influence sufficient to force such truculence on the Soviet Union. In the words of Secretary of State Herter:

> It would seem a logical deduction that some of the opposition to his conduct of foreign relations which was openly voiced by the Chinese Communists found a sympathetic response among some of his associates, and very probably among the Soviet military.[21]

Vice President Richard M. Nixon, seeking election to the Presidency in 1960 on the claim that the U.S. strategic house was in order, also hinted that the Chinese might be responsible for the U-2 uproar, but he saw no real Russian militance aroused in the process.

> As we look to the future of southeast Asia it is interesting to note the reaction of the Chinese Communist government to the developments in Paris. Peiping, almost unique among the capitals of the world, has received the news of Mr. Khrushchev's sabotage at Paris with undisguised satisfaction. . . .
> The Chinese Communists have seized upon the failure of the conference as an opportunity for renewed emphasis on the "orthodox" Communist philosophy of the need for force as an essential ingredient in world Communist tactics. In the world in which we live today this emphasis is as dangerous as it is anachronistic. Fortunately, there are good indications even since the Paris conference that this view is not shared by Mr. Khrushchev.[22]

---

[20] Address of October 16, 1959, in *DOSB*, November 2, 1959, p. 630.
[21] News conference of May 27, 1960, in *DOSB*, June 13, 1960, p. 953.
[22] Address of May 31, 1960, in *DOSB*, June 20, 1960, p. 984.

The Perceived Russian Commmitment, 1953–1960

A Russian commitment to military assistance for China after 1953 could be derived of course from some of the same arguments that had applied before. Russian assistance to China in the event of American attack would still bc logical, to exploit the advantages of the defense and perhaps to preserve the Communist regime. The onus of American aggression might allow the Soviets to intervene at lower cost, and damage to China might bruise the Russians enough to drive them to reprisals. A commitment of American conventional ground, naval, or air forces to a war with China might still tie up such forces, to the benefit of Russia, perhaps allowing the latter to launch aggressions elsewhere.

> Moreover, it seemed probable that the Soviet Union would do all it could to get the United States bogged down in a debilitating war with Communist China. Indeed, early the following month Bulganin in his inaugural speech to the Supreme Soviet assailed the United States and pledged Russian support to the Chinese Communists in the event of war.[23]

Yet much of the argument had begun to diverge. Since the potentials of air and naval action were more highly rated by the Republican administration, certain types of incursions into China no longer seemed to invite a Russian invasion of Europe. American forces would not necessarily be tied up to their disadvantage, particularly if atomic weapons in various configurations could be used to supply the firepower. But, conversely, the Russian ability to retaliate by long-range air attack would now be somewhat greater, especially after the acquisition of hydrogen bombs and missiles, while the damage in any American use of nuclear weapons against China would perhaps be harder to constrict to avoid touching Russian material interests.

If the "massive retaliation" doctrine was based on a detailed and rational assessment of immediate American strategic weapons strength and of Russian weakness, this would cast doubt on Soviet military support for the Chinese Communist regime.

[23] Dwight D. Eisenhower, *Mandate for Change* (Garden City, N.Y.: Doubleday, 1963), p. 469.

If the doctrine was based instead on a refusal to examine the options of less than total war, on a refusal to admit the possibility of America declining to undertake all-out war in support of its allies, then the credibility of the Soviet commitment to China would be enhanced. But since the rational American argument for massive retaliation threatened to diminish over time, the less rational (if more honorable) one had to be set in motion from the start, and hence Soviet commitments to Communist China were to be less subject to skeptical scrutiny.

If the intrabloc commitment required for "massive" retaliation or support was to be credible on one side of the line, it would tend to be more credible on the other too, and some Soviet behavior over the period served to confirm this symmetry; in 1956 the Soviets intervened seriously in Hungary and even hinted at rocket attacks against Britain and France on behalf of Egypt.[24] The effect of "new look" thinking in American military strategy was to strengthen somewhat the American assumption of Russian intervention on behalf of the Chinese, while also perhaps increasing the incentive to test that assumption.

In any event, what was Communist in this period was largely thought to be Russia's, and Russia still seemed likely to defend all of it with some vigor. When the Chinese or North Koreans were themselves aggressive, the assumptions on ideology just cited indicated that this would be on Russian orders, and, while not as likely perhaps to receive nuclear support, such operations would either get whatever conventional support they needed or be called back. Russia would generate whatever military aid and activity seemed tailored to the tactical situation; until 1959 or 1960 it would always seem obliged to encourage the Communist side, for Russia would probably have given the orders. The United States thus saw little possibility of a Chinese move to seize or retain territory without the approval of Moscow which would invoke a reproachful withholding of aid.

Applying the strategy of deterrence by threat of massive retaliation, the United States warned that it might extend it's actions to an air attack on China with atomic weapons to

24 *The New York Times,* November 6, 1956, p. 1.

hasten the end of the Korean War;[25] in the event, the Korean armistice was signed, for whatever reason, fairly soon after the Republican administration had come to power in the United States. The Indochina War, however, more clearly raised the problem of how one massively retaliates when deterrence has been only ambiguously successful, when the major party of the other side may also have the ability and inclination to retaliate.

Warnings had also been issued of escalation to air attacks if the Chinese intervened in Indochina with their army or air force,[26] but the Vietminh had now gained successes relying mainly on massive Chinese material assistance. The inability of the United States to intervene effectively with conventional forces was made clear to President Eisenhower by General Ridgway, while projects for air strikes with nuclear weapons (either more tactically around Dien Bien Phu, or less so on the border provinces of China) also proved unacceptable, due to problems of coordination with the allies, to objections voiced in Congress, and to the reluctance of Eisenhower himself to go quite as far as his Secretary of State in risking general war.[27] In the event of such an air attack on Chinese territory, a possibility of Russian intervention and world war was reportedly cited by the French Foreign Minister Bidault,[28] and the Soviet Union had by now tested its first hydrogen device.

Secretary of State Dulles, who was never prone to spell out the implications of his military policies too explicitly, was thus almost from the beginning induced to qualify his stress on the pure punishment aspects of massive retaliation. In fact, massive retaliation on closer examination turned out to be a mixture of reponsive defense measures and punishment.

To deter aggression, it is important to have the flexibility and the facilities which make various responses available. In many cases, any open assault by Communist forces would only result

25 John Robinson Beal, *John Foster Dulles: A Biography* (New York: Harper, 1957), pp. 181–182.

26 *DOSB*, September 14, 1953, p. 342.

27 Chalmer M. Roberts, "The Day We Didn't Go to War," *The Reporter*, September 14, 1954, pp. 30–35.

28 Roscoe Drummond and Gaston Coblentz, *Duel at the Brink* (Garden City, N.Y.: Doubleday, 1960), pp. 121–122.

in starting a general war. But the free world must have the means for responding effectively on a selective basis when it chooses. It must not put itself in the position where the only response open to it is general war.[29]

When specifically applying this stance to the Chinese case, Dulles thus avoided any clear threat to bomb Moscow, *or Peking*, in response to new aggression.

> That does not mean turning every local war into a world war. It does not mean that, if there is a Communist attack somewhere in Asia, atom or hydrogen bombs will necessarily be dropped on the great industrial centers of China or Russia. It does mean that the free world must maintain the collective means and be willing to use them in the way which most effectively makes aggression too risky and expensive to be tempting.[30]

American incursions into China by air or on land were thus generally deterred as much after 1952 as before. For a short time, however, the possibility of a Chinese Nationalist re-invasion and liberation of the mainland was not publicly foreclosed: the Republican administration had after all won an election in part on hints of a "roll back" of communism and liberation of the "satellites." The Nationalist retention of some offshore islands, essentially overlooked by the Truman administration, was thus not really discouraged at first by Eisenhower and Dulles, and American military aid to the Nationalists was stepped up. Yet when such a Nationalist forward strategy threatened to draw the United States into war, either because the Communists legitimately feared invasion or because they wished to embarrass the Nationalists, any American interest in continued retention of the islands rapidly diminished. In the 1954–1955 Chinese Communist shelling of Quemoy, proposals to encourage and assist Chinese Nationalist air attacks on the mainland or to add U.S. air attacks in the event of a Communist invasion attempt were vetoed by President Eisenhower.

> He [Admiral Radford], Admiral Carney, and General Twining therefore urged that the United States commit itself to defend the islands and help the Chinese Nationalists bomb the mainland.

[29] John Foster Dulles, "Policy for Security and Peace," *Foreign Affairs* (April 1954), p. 358.
[30] *Ibid.*, p. 359.

With this conclusion I disagreed. Such a course, I said, we could not confine to Quemoy Island. "We're not talking now about a limited, brush-fire war. We're talking about going to the threshold of World War III. If we attack China, we're not going to impose limits on our military actions, as in Korea.

"Moreover," I reminded them, "if we get into a general war, the logical enemy will be Russia, not China, and we'll have to strike there."[31]

Warnings were issued that the United States would feel driven to defend the offshore islands if this proved necessary to the defense of Taiwan, and that tactical, "battlefield" atomic weapons would be put to use in such a case[32] but no American air attacks were in fact to be launched, in part because this was thought likely to bring in the Russians at costs too high to the United States for the mere protection of the offshore islands.

The strategic concepts enunciated by Eisenhower and Dulles had thus produced some ambiguities. For a ponderous Communist attack, in Asia as in Europe, American massive retaliation was indeed credible against barracks, Peking, or Moscow, and no serious Communist aggressions involving Russian or Chinese troops occurred. Possibly the attacks on barracks, and more possibly the attack on Peking, would bring the same "massive" Soviet response as would an attack on Moscow, although this could never be certain since nothing would presumably be worth quite as much to the Moscow leadership as Moscow itself; at least until 1959, moreover, such a Soviet retaliatory response could not be so awesome as to stalemate the U.S. strategic force completely. Yet American "massive retaliations" for smaller or more obscure Chinese provocations were not likely to be so "massive," precisely because the other side's retaliation might also in turn be maximal. A problem thus remained of how the United States would react in situations that were either artificially ambiguous, as in the Nationalist Chinese decision to couple the fate of Taiwan to that of the offshore islands by stationing a large part of their army there, or naturally ambiguous, as in Chinese and Russian support for the Pathet Lao already legitimately within Laos.

The Chinese Communist shelling of Quemoy in 1958 raised

31 Eisenhower, *Mandate for Change, op. cit.*, p. 464.
32 *Ibid.*, p. 477.

more serious issues for the United States, however, because the Communist artillery was generally more efficient than it had been in 1954 (threatening to prevent delivery of supplies to, or evacuation from, the island), and because the Nationalists had in the interim moved about one third of their army, the presumed defenders of Taiwan, on to Quemoy.[33] Whatever practical arguments had applied in 1954 for Nationalist or American air strikes against the mainland (against artillery positions, air bases, or troop concentrations) were thus much more valid in 1958 even if no Communist amphibious assault on the island were to be launched. The 1958 crisis also brought Soviet statements of support that had not been forthcoming in 1954: that an attack on China would be seen as an attack on the Soviet Union and that nuclear attacks would be "rebuffed" by similar weapons.[34] Such statements seemed once more to commit the Russians publicly and thus to make their support for the Chinese again more plausible. As the crisis continued, American eight-inch howitzers capable of firing atomic shells were moved to Quemoy[35] amid open discussion of conventional or nuclear air strikes against China (but also with a public statement that nuclear weapons could not be used without the expressed approval of the President).[36]

In the event, no American air attacks had to be launched, as even the Chinese Nationalists were required this time to withhold their bomber forces;[37] a way was found instead to throw the initiative back once more to the Chinese Communists, as American naval escort was extended to within three miles of the offshore islands. Rather than attack U.S. naval vessels the Communists did not press their continuous shellings, and the crisis subsided.

Soviet support for the Chinese had seemed plausible throughout the crisis. American contingency plans for strikes

33 *The New York Times*, August 28, 1958, p. 1.

34 *The New York Times*, August 31, 1958, p. 1, and September 9, 1958, p. 1.

35 Hanson W. Baldwin, "Limited War," *The Atlantic Monthly* (May 1959), p. 41.

36 *The New York Times*, September 5, 1958, p. 1.

37 *The New York Times*, August 15, 1958, p. 2, and September 23, 1958, p. 3.

at Chinese air bases (with low-yield nuclear weapons) were carefully drawn to avoid civilian centers,[38] but the United States was apparently willing to risk a war with the entire Soviet bloc if no way other than air attack could be found to protect Quemoy. As it happened, another way was found.

In summation, the stress on American massive retaliation in the Eisenhower years had made a Soviet commitment to China's defense seem still quite plausible, if for reasons slightly different from those that had applied in 1949 or 1951. Only by 1960 had the Chinese desire for "world conquest" at last come to be seen as rivaling or perhaps surpassing that of the Russians, but not yet clearly enough to raise any serious doubts in the outgoing administration about Soviet commitment to China.

While China's ability (as opposed to desire) to export military strength still seemed small, it appeared to be growing. Yet, because of the reciprocity of its own assumptions of massive retaliation, the United States had resigned itself to wait for Chinese attacks, which would have had to be quite overt to draw a massive response. No such clearly unacceptable attack occurred.

Chinese ideological independence was seen now for the first time as a danger, with the discovery that China might choose to attack even where Russia would not; since China's inability to mount serious offensives was now not so likely to last, the suspicion of an intention to launch such offensives added to the concerns of the incoming Kennedy administration.

The Kennedy-Johnson Administration

Military Assumptions, 1961–

The third phase of American analysis under review extends from the advent of the Kennedy administration in 1961 through the Chinese nuclear detonation and Soviet deposition of Khrushchev in 1964.

The new administration began with a well-publicized revi-

---

[38] Dwight D. Eisenhower, *Waging Peace* (Garden City, N.Y.: Doubleday, 1965), p. 295.

sion of emphasis in military strategy, showing more concern about the damage the United States might suffer from Soviet air attack in a general war and placing greater reliance, therefore, on graduated deterrents and locally adequate defenses to hold back Communist forces throughout the world. Limited wars, in forms favorable (or perhaps unfavorable) to the Communist bloc, now seemed more likely, as the administration foresaw fewer possibilities of escalations that would offer an easy way out for the West. Yet the impact of this new strategic stalemate was not yet to be felt equally around the world.

Some more valuable portions of Asia, specifically Japan and Taiwan, seemed reasonably secure behind a screen of air and naval forces alone, and Kennedy in 1960 had even advocated a withdrawal from Quemoy and Matsu;[39] the threat to other areas, specifically the remains of Indochina, was not yet as serious as it was soon to become. At any rate, the U.S. government in the summer of 1962 was still willing to assure the Chinese Communist regime that it did not contemplate and would not allow any hostile incursions into mainland China[40] (while warning the Communists that it would defend Taiwan *and* the offshore islands, a warning that brought a new pledge of Russian support for the mainland regime).[41]

It was in Europe, therefore, that a real problem of nuclear stalemate and limited war now seemed to arise. Fears were expressed on both sides of the Atlantic that Soviet missile strength might soon preclude any American nuclear first strike in response to a Russian crossing of the Elbe or seizure of Berlin; the U.S. government itself, for most or all of this period, urged its European allies to establish larger conventional forces, to defend themselves against potential Soviet ground force aggressions without recourse to nuclear attacks on Russia. The Soviet threat was thus seen, and had to be portrayed, as inadequately balanced at the time but as containable by an increased European effort.

News of any Sino-Soviet rift threatened, however, to be interpreted in Europe to mean that Russian military attack

39 *The New York Times,* October 8, 1960, p. 1.
40 *The New York Times,* June 27, 1962, p. 1.
41 *The New York Times,* June 28, 1962, p. 1, and July 3, 1962, p. 1.

was less likely and that European conventional force augmentation was less required. The split might either have encouraged Russia to identify racially and culturally with the Europeans ("Europe extending from the Atlantic to the Urals") or it might have facilitated a new alignment of Europe and China against Russia (the "second intermediate zone," the "small nuclear powers," the "threat at Russia's back," and so on). As long as the European problem was more crucial than any in Asia, there seemed to be little political comfort to be derived in the United States from news of the Sino-Soviet rift. As long as the conversation with allies in Europe seemed more crucial than that with the enemy in Asia, no great stress could be placed on any expected termination of Soviet commitments to Communist China.

Yet after 1962 American perceptions of relative Communist military power had at last begun to change, serving to increase the apparent vulnerability and importance of areas outside of Europe and stimulating a less constrained American examination of the Sino-Soviet "split" and its military ramifications. The relative insignificance (and invulnerability) of Chinese military and political power had been an accepted fact of life in the early 1950's, and it still seemed to be an argument for playing down the intrabloc dispute immediately after 1960. This interpretation now began (perhaps prematurely) to be seriously amended: in the specific area of limited conventional war, and in other areas too, it now seemed that Chinese power might be more exportable than before, and perhaps more worthy of engagement or attack.

A portion of this new Chinese power seemed to derive directly from the ideological split with the Russians, the Chinese apparently capable of capturing the allegiance of Communist parties in Asia, Africa, and Latin America by whipping them into greater revolutionary activity. More immediately, Chinese-supported *military* action now began to seem more significant. The Laos crisis of 1961–1962, for which China may not have been so directly responsible, was partly screened by the American involvement in the Bay of Pigs invasion of Cuba, and by the Soviet erection of the Berlin Wall, accompanied by the resumption of nuclear testing. The invasion of India in late 1962 was also fortuitously coupled with the Cuban missile crisis. Yet the war in South Vietnam thereafter began to reach a critical stage, and this was sufficiently noticeable to make the consideration of China as an independent source of aggression rather more pressing.

The greatest Western concern of all, however, derived perhaps from Chinese progress toward the development of a nuclear weapon and the possibilities of its use or proliferation. If nothing else occurred to make China's military strength more relevant throughout the world, this seemed to be enough.

Political Assumptions, 1961–

The advent of the Kennedy administration had been accompanied by considerable intellectual excitement over the steadily more open Sino-Soviet disagreements, with fairly general acceptance of the view (perhaps oversimplified or exaggerated) that China's ideal of a bloc confrontation with the West involved somewhat more hostility than the Russians approved.

In the American government, however, this was not necessarily seen as a promising development: if the Russians had been holding back the Chinese until then, they might no longer be able to do so. This would mean new trouble for the United States, outside of Europe and throughout the world, rather than any slowdown of Communist activity — trouble into which the Russians might yet be drawn involuntarily. The United States would now have to monitor more than one Communist power center, especially if any one could drag the others along in an offensive; what was militarily enough to deter Moscow, moreover, might not be enough to deter Peking, and an augmentation of Western theater and strategic military capacities might thus be required. In the words of Secretary of State Rusk:

> Well, for example, if Peiping is determined to pursue a more militant and aggressive policy through the use of force than perhaps, say, the Soviet Union would be willing to or want to in a particular situation, and if Peiping succeeds in imposing its policy in a particular situation, where the Soviet Union itself is com-

pelled eventually to back up Peiping, then this can be an adverse development as far as we are concerned.[42]

And Assistant Secretary of State Robert Manning made the statement:

> First, the West cannot be certain that a complete rift, unharnessing a hate-propelled, unrelenting Communist China from the comparative restraints of Soviet Russia, will be a good thing for the West. Second, it should be kept in mind that this is still chiefly an ideological quarrel, not over *whether* communism will bury us but *how* communism will bury us. The desire to perform the burial ceremony still exists as strongly in Moscow as in Peiping.[43]

The Sino-Soviet dispute, in such a view, might stem largely from a disagreement over which means to use in attacking the West or which zone deserved priority as an object of conquest. The split in this case might simply be compromised in a decision to satisfy both sides by combining the projected assaults into one grand offensive. President Kennedy, however, indicated some optimism for the longer run:

> Third, what comfort can we take from the increasing strains and tensions within the Communist bloc? Here hope must be tempered with caution. For the Soviet-Chinese disagreement is over means, not ends. A dispute over how to bury the West is no grounds for Western rejoicing.
>
> Nevertheless, while a strain is not a fracture it is clear that the forces of diversity are at work inside the Communist camp, despite all the iron disciplines of regimentation and all the iron dogmatisms of ideology. Marx is proven wrong once again: for it is the closed Communist societies, not the free and open societies, which carry within themselves the seeds of internal disintegration.[44]

And Secretary of State Rusk expressed the following view:

> The principal arguments within the bloc have to do with how best to get on with their revolution. In Peiping, for example, they appear to want to take a more aggressive, more military, approach to these questions — to go back to some of the — shall I say the more primitive aspects of Leninism. In Moscow they're more subtle and sophisticiated. They talk about peaceful coex-

---

[42] *Ibid.*, p. 205.
[43] Address of January 11, 1963, in *DOSB*, January 28, 1963, p. 143.
[44] State of the Union Address, 1963.

istence. They are using such instruments as economic assistance and things of that sort. This is chiefly an argument of technique. I don't think that we ought to jump too quickly to the conclusion that these differences mean that we have any room for complacency or relaxation of effort, because they both are committed to their kind of world system.[45]

American interpretations of the Sino-Soviet political dispute thus attached perhaps too much concern to the level of Communist national hostilities to the United States; the ideal in such interpretations would not be a split at all but rather a complete agreement that the West was to be left alone and that violence was not to be applied in attempts to alter the *status quo.* A split on this was thus not ideal; such a split would, however, be preferable for the Americans to any complete Sino-Soviet agreement on a very aggressive policy. Whether a split was desirable or not, therefore, depended mainly on the alternative and on the value of the theaters immediately vulnerable to the various Communist states. As long as Russian hostility in Europe had not diminished appreciably, there was on balance much harm, militarily, in the rift.

Yet even in such terms, the aftermath of the Cuban missile crisis seemed to bring some better tidings. As a new *détente* emerged between Russia and the West, epitomized most concretely perhaps in a general lessening of pressures on West Berlin, the "split" no longer seemed to hinge entirely on increased Chinese hostility to the West but also on lessened Russian hostility.

Moreover, gain for the American position could in any event be derived from a split, even if the hostility of both the Soviet Union and China toward the West did not diminish substantially. Although China seemed more aggressive against the free world and less averse to war, it had also perhaps become much more particular as to what constituted a real Communist regime; if the Russian version of communism was no longer good enough, the Chinese would at least be somewhat inhibited from engaging the United States where such an

45 News conference on November 28, 1962, in *DOSB,* December 17, 1962, p. 915.

engagement seemed to increase Russian or other revisionist territorial influence.

A greater American optimism about the Sino-Soviet rift would also stem from some of the crasser issues that American observers had hoped would separate China from the Soviet Union as early as 1949. If the United States was more or less indifferent to the pecking order of Communist parties in bloc decision making or to the location of the Sino-Soviet border, it could welcome a maximum of disagreement over these issues; such disagreements could obstruct the bloc from implementing any aggressive foreign policies, agreed or otherwise, to which the United States was not so indifferent. It is, after all, only a traditional maxim of balance-of-power reasoning that it is to a state's advantage to maintain conflict and disorder among its rival states. A Western observer might even hope that Chinese and Soviet military forces would be tied up watching each other along their borders. Perhaps less desirable would be actual combat between them. Chester Bowles had touched optimistically on these possibilities as early as 1961.

> Although it represents a serious challenge to the food surplus nations of southeast Asia, it presents a particularly difficult problem for the Soviet Union. It is the Soviets, after all, who have a vast expanse of fertile underpopulated land adjacent to China. And there are some times when relatives can be more troublesome than enemies.
> A horde of 650 million hungry ideological relatives is struggling for a bare existence along the Soviet's 4,500-mile border. If I were a member of the Politburo, I would have somebody up nights checking that back door. Or else I would be prepared to wake up one morning and find that my ideological relatives had moved in to stay.[46]

The progress of the Chinese nuclear program after 1962 had itself revealed an obvious dispute with the Soviet Union, one that required less ideological embellishment and was therefore more easily understood in the West (being after all somewhat analogous with the contemporary dispute between the United States and France). Since the Soviet Union had voiced its objections to proliferation in clear terms, the issue seemed to facilitate a greater probing of Soviet intentions in U.S. public

---

46 Address of October 27, 1961, in *DOSB*, November 20, 1961, p. 859.

and semipublic statements. The ban on atomic testing was itself a major Soviet diplomatic pronouncement against the interests of the Chinese Communists, designed in part to encourage identification with the Soviet Union among nations confronting the Chinese. It is reported that in the test ban negotiations direct inquiries were even addressed to the Soviet delegation on Russian willingness to allow U.S. interference with Chinese nuclear development; these inquiries apparently did not, however, receive any clearly encouraging response.[47]

At a less military level, internecine political struggles now emerged between Russian and Chinese factions of various Communist parties around the world. At the least, such a disunity made coordination, communication, and joint planning among the Communist states seem more difficult.

The Perceived Russian Commitment, 1961–

Reports of any weakening of Russian support for China were thus seen in a strategic context that at first greatly reduced their relevance to the American government. Optimism might well be expressed about the long-run political consequences of the Sino-Soviet arguments, as the rift in the bloc belied and undermined some of the claims of Marxist ideology. Yet when the protection of the Atlantic Community was in any doubt, the major commitments of American forces and attention would remain there, and the strength and disposition of Communist forces in *that* theater would be crucial. The split was really of lesser value to the United States so long as the Russians, the more "moderate" Communist faction, were still in the position of causing the most trouble. And to stress the split might have engendered a premature optimism, for it was not yet clear in what way the Soviets would now be more "alone" in Berlin, or in Cuba if they tried to keep their missiles there. It seemed that the Chinese would give whatever support they could, as long as Moscow did not relent.

If the Chinese were indeed now the more aggressive, American official statements tended at first to belittle the extent of the difference and to stress instead that any major reverse

47 *The New York Times*, October 2, 1964, p. 3.

suffered by the Chinese in an independent venture would most likely restore Sino-Soviet unity, as the Chinese retreat endangered Russian interests enough to force an intervention for traditional reasons. Western initiatives designed really to exploit or to widen the split might thus raise the importance of the issue at hand sufficiently to heal the split. In the testimony of Secretary of Defense Robert McNamara:

> *Senator Russell:* In the event of any threatened hostilities between this country and either China or the Soviet Union, do you think these countries would get together rather rapidly?
>
> *Secretary McNamara:* I think we must assume that would be the case and be prepared for it.[48]

If the Soviet Union would like to see the Chinese learn a lesson, this, in the view of General Wheeler, could not go very far:

> . . . Mr. Khrushchev would enjoy seeing the Chinese Communists get a bloody nose. I am not so sure he would like to see them get their heads knocked off. And to illustrate what I mean — I think that if Chiang Kai-shek were mixed up in some aggression against the Red Chinese, that the Soviets might reverse their present policy rather drastically in favor of the Red Chinese.[49]

As Chinese power seemed to grow, however, U.S. strategic planners had to decide how much of their skepticism about the military significance of the split was in fact objectively justified. Hopefully, Chinese dissatisfaction with the Russians might become a factor dampening Chinese hostility to the West, as the Chinese had to choose whom to engage; hence it might not always be true that the split occasioned an increased Chinese aggressiveness. Yet if there was any validity to the more pessimistic view, the Soviet commitment to the Chinese could also be re-examined. Russian dissatisfaction with the Chinese might then become a factor allowing the United States more easily to repulse the Chinese where their hostility had not yet been dampened.

48 U.S. Senate, Committee on Foreign Relations, *Hearings on the Nuclear Test Ban Treaty* (88th Congress, 1st Session, 1963), p. 112.

49 U.S. Senate, Preparedness Investigating Subcommittee of the Committee on Armed Services, *Hearings on the Military Aspects and Implications of Test Ban Proposals* (88th Congress, 1st Session, 1963), Vol. 2, p. 677.

Seen as perhaps *capable* of generating more difficulty for the West, China after late 1962 became more logically a target for disabling or "counterforce" operations by the United States. Seen also as independently *desirous* of producing some difficulties for the West, China also became logically more prone to motivational or "countervalue" operations. Yet, while China thus offered more invitation to American military action, the ability of the Soviet Union to retaliate, since 1957, had also grown (even if it had not grown nearly as much as was expected in 1957). The issue of Soviet commitment to the Chinese had thus become doubly more urgent for the United States than in the past, and some decoupling of Soviet support from Chinese aggressiveness was to be searched for.

The mode of communications of course was important. To warn the mainland regime that the United States did not expect it to receive Russian help might cast doubt on the Chinese resolve in a crisis. By assuring the Soviets that it did not expect their involvement, the United States perhaps allowed them in turn more easily to opt out of a Chinese adventure, since they need not be drawn in by a fear that Americans would blindly and indifferently respond against all Communist countries. And by assuring the Russians that it would leave them out of a war with China, it might be threatening the Chinese Communists more meaningfully. Thus we have a quite different statement by Secretary of Defense McNamara early in 1964, suggesting that Soviet support, at least in some situations, would no longer be available.

> Moreover, as a result of the Sino-Soviet split, the Chinese must certainly feel considerably less confident of Soviet support in the event of a military clash with some other major power. Already in the economic field, the Chinese are attempting to reorient their trade away from the Soviet block to Japan and Western Europe.[50]

And early in 1965, suggesting that Communist China will indeed be inhibited by this lack of support, as long as the United States is willing to engage China militarily, he stated:

[50] U.S. Senate, Committee on Armed Services and Subcommittee on Department of Defense of Committee on Appropriations, *(Joint) Hearings on Military Procurement Authorization Fiscal Year 1965* (88th Congress, 2nd Session, 1964), p. 13.

Unless there is a change in Soviet policy, it still appears doubtful that the Chinese Communists will deliberately initiate any major overt aggression against their neighbors. Although they have long been the more militant of the two major Communist rivals, they have shown great caution when confronted with a determined display of military power.[51]

The incipient debate in 1965 and 1966, on the advisability of seeking an ABM system, also communicated the new doubts about the Russian commitment to China, as some advocates of ABM proposed a smaller system effective only against a Chinese missile force, thus signaling again that the Soviets might not join a Chinese attack on the United States.

Yet the communications so delivered might have to be structured so as not to embarrass the Soviets into restoring their commitments and not to focus the attention of the Communist and underdeveloped worlds on the Russian option of reneging. Doubt may remain, moreover, on how far a wedge can credibly be driven into what was once apparently a serious military alliance. Earlier assumptions of Russia's commitment had hinged on her "natural" identification with Communist regimes per se (the Soviet Union being rated perhaps in the early days with a Messianic fervor second to none), on its hope that war with China would weaken the West, and (in the Dulles era) on the inevitability of Russia bringing her nuclear weapons to bear in the event of war. There might now be more situations in which a Soviet military response to American air attack on China was unlikely and in which the United States might seem to have something to gain. But the exact degree to which Soviet responses have been so decoupled may still not be easy to determine.

A series of possibilities can revolve around Chinese first use of nuclear weapons (which the Chinese in fact have forsworn), a first use to which Russia would be very likely to object. An American nuclear attack in response to such use seems quite possible, while an automatic Russian counter-response to American action may appear less likely. Massive

[51] U.S. Senate, Committee on Armed Services and Subcommittee on Department of Defense of Committee on Appropriations, *(Joint) Hearings on Military Procurement Authorization, Fiscal Year 1966* (89th Congress, 1st Session, 1965), p. 15.

Soviet intervention in the event of an all-out city-busting attack on China may still be very plausible, but if the American
response were limited to the destruction of Chinese nuclear
facilities or military installations, lesser Soviet response might
be forthcoming.

Even in the absence of Chinese use of nuclear weapons,
there might still be a U.S. interest in excising and destroying
the Chinese nuclear capability, at least for an interim period,
while China still has no stockpile, no H-bombs, and no real
delivery system. A special situation arises where Communist
China might be tempted to give weapons to other states (to
the United Arab Republic, for example), another step to
which the Soviet Union might be opposed. Here in particular
a crisis might ensue in which the United States would feel
tempted or forced to try to eliminate China as a nuclear
power or to launch a more limited military or blockade
venture.

Using its own nuclear weapons as an umbrella, Communist
China might instead launch a major conventional attack
against India or Taiwan, which again could well bring a
tactical nuclear response from the West. Or else it might commit its air force to the war in Vietnam, perhaps leading to
U.S. air attacks against air bases in South China.

A Soviet nuclear response to other than the more blatant
Western attacks on China would generally be less credible, in
part because the attacks are likely to come in the context of
Chinese aggressive gestures of which the Soviet leadership
specifically disapproves, and in part because the Sino-Soviet
conflict over specific issues lessens the personal identification
of Russia with China on all issues. The Chinese decision to
push for an independent nuclear force and the open polemics
about Soviet reluctance to deliver or pledge nuclear weapons
serve additionally to cast doubt on the Soviet commitment.
By giving the West a Chinese bomb to focus on, the Chinese
Communists divert attention from the Russian bomb and
thus subconsciously impart an impression that there is no
question of Russian bombs being used. In part an American
perception of reduced Russian commitment also follows psychologically from the changes in American over-all strategy.
Since massive retaliation has become questionable for the

American defense of Europe, it has likewise become questionable for the Soviet defense of China.

Similarly, more "conventional" forms of Soviet aid, such
as trained manpower or special forms of weaponry or equipment, could be less forthcoming than in the past. Yet here
the Chinese venture requiring assistance would probably be
of longer duration, less likely to go so clearly against Soviet
interests, and more likely therefore (perhaps as in Vietnam
since 1964) to draw the Soviets in where the impassioned
pleas of world communism, or the opportunity of wearing
down the West, suggest it. The classic "ground war on the
mainland" still seems likely to take this form, for the issue
of Chinese ideological dogmatism might become irrelevant to
the Russians if American ground forces crossed into China
itself in an attempt to topple the Communist regime. Simple
balance-of-power reasoning suggests that the Soviet Union
cannot really want to see Communist China extinguished as
a power or to see itself rigidly aligned with the United States
against China. Ideology has, moreover, still not been canceled
out. The differences in the Chinese and Russian views of an
ideal society may yet be so small as not to eliminate the possibility of joint commitment on some challenge to the free
world. If the issue is important enough, and world attention
is focused on it, the Russians may appear to have too much
at stake to be able to remain aloof.

In summation, the advent of Chinese nuclear independence has clearly made it more plausible that there might be
wars or crises in which China would be left without a major
ally. Also, because of changes in the military strategy of the
United States itself, the Russian commitment to the Chinese
Communists has seemed less credible to the American government ever since 1961 or 1963, and probably will now remain so, while the American practical interest in testing and
questioning such commitment has somewhat increased. Knowledge of a rift may bolster the United States in crises, and the
fact that it is known may appear to undermine the Chinese.
As before, the West will cite various causes of the rift and
even hope in some situations to widen it, but for a time at
least the stress will now be on luring the Russians away from
China rather than the reverse.

10

The 1958 Quemoy Crisis[1]

MORTON H. HALPERIN AND TANG TSOU

This chapter explores Sino-Soviet relations during the 1958 Taiwan Straits crisis and concludes from the available evidence that there may not have been any major Sino-Soviet disagreement about strategy during the crisis. Specifically, (1) the Soviets did not object to the Chinese probe; (2) the Chinese did not seek a larger Soviet role; (3) neither country emerged from the crisis feeling that the other had let it down; (4) the 1958 crisis itself does not seem to have been a factor aggravating disputes over nuclear control or sharing arrangements. While Peking did charge in 1963 that Moscow had withheld its deterrent threats until the peak of the crisis had passed, the evidence suggests that this was at best a *post hoc* evaluation stimulated by other events. Moreover there is no evidence to suggest that Chinese behavior during the crisis led the Soviets to cut off aid to the Chinese nuclear program or that Soviet behavior affected the Chinese perception of important differences between Peking and Moscow.

[1] Tang Tsou wishes to acknowledge the support provided by the Rockefeller Foundation, the Committee on Far Eastern Civilization, and the Social Sciences Divisional Research Committee of the University of Chicago. Morton Halperin wishes to acknowledge the support provided by the Center for International Affairs and the East Asian Research Center, Harvard University.

Sino-Soviet Relations: 1957–1958[2]

In November 1957, Mao Tse-tung journeyed to Moscow for a meeting of the ruling Communist parties. The conference produced the 1957 Moscow Declaration, which represents the last effort at a genuine compromise of differences within the international Communist movement. The nature of Sino-Soviet relations at the time of the conference and in the months following will be examined by considering the conference itself and then, in turn, trade relations, military relations, policy toward Yugoslavia, attitudes toward the strategic military balance, and finally the Middle East crises of July 1958.

It will be argued that a clear pattern of Sino-Soviet relations seems to have emerged. In this pattern, the Chinese express their dissenting views over some strategic and tactical issues, try to persuade the Soviet leaders to accept their ideas, but politically uphold Soviet leadership of the international Communist movement. On his part, Khrushchev proved willing to move toward some of the Chinese positions. Both Mao and Khrushchev were anxious to preserve the unity of the bloc following the events of 1956.

Even in retrospect both Russia and China date their disagreement about the United States from 1959. According to a speech by Peng Chen:

> *Since 1959*, we have repeatedly advised the Khrushchov revisionists not to regard enemies as friends and vice versa. They categorically refused to listen.[3]

And in a polemic with the Russians attacking Soviet-American cooperation the Chinese asked:

> *Since 1959* Khrushchov has become obsessed with summit meetings between the Soviet Union and the United States. He has had many fond dreams and spread many illusions about them.[4]

2 See Richard Lowenthal, *World Communism: The Disintegration of a Secular Faith* (New York: Oxford University Press, 1964), pp. 139–164.

3 Peng Chen, *Speech at the Aliarcham Academy of Social Sciences in Indonesia*, May 25, 1965 (Peking: Foreign Languages Press, 1965), p. 21. Italics added.

4 "Peaceful Coexistence — Two Dramatically Opposed Policies," December 12, 1963, in *The Polemic on the General Line of the International Communist Movement* (Peking: Foreign Languages Press, 1965), p. 297. Italics added.

According to a Soviet charge in 1963:

> . . . the view concerning the supposed benefits which the cold war situation offered to the interests of the revolution was apparently only taking shape in Peking [in 1958]. . . .[5]

The 1957 Moscow Conference[6]

The 1957 Conference clearly marked a major turning point in Sino-Soviet relations, although not necessarily heralding a Sino-Soviet dispute. Because of the relatively weak position of Khrushchev at home, Soviet mishandling of the Polish and Hungarian situations, the success of Chinese intervention in Eastern Europe, and the growing prestige of Mao, the Soviet Union was forced to accept China as something close to an equal in making decisions at the conference. While there was a sharp debate at the conference over the question of peaceful transition, and there was probably some disagreement on the nature of the strategic balance and the question of how to treat Yugoslavia (both to be considered later), substantial agreement between the two countries was reached on all questions but peaceful transition. The Chinese, much to the surprise and regret of the East Europeans, pressed strongly for a tightly organized bloc headed by the Soviet Union. This move was apparently made at least in part to make a Soviet-Yugoslav *rapprochement* less likely.

The working of the conference and the declaration, in short, suggest a desire on the part of both China and the Soviet Union to avoid anything resembling an open split and to compromise on issues. It appears that neither Mao nor Khrushchev was fully aware of the *extent* of latent differences in their own attitudes.

[5] William E. Griffith, *The Sino-Soviet Rift* (Cambridge: The M.I.T. Press, 1964), p. 446.

[6] See Donald Zagoria, *The Sino-Soviet Conflict: 1956–1961* (Princeton, N.J.: Princeton University Press, 1962), pp. 145–171; Edward Crankshaw, *The New Cold War: Moscow v. Peking* (Baltimore, Md.: Penguin Books, 1963), pp. 62–73. The text of the declaration is in G. F. Hudson *et al.*, *The Sino-Soviet Dispute* (New York: Praeger, 1961), pp. 46–56. The Chinese have described the events of the conference reasonably accurately in "The Origin and Development of the Differences Between the Leadership of the CPSU and Ourselves," September 6, 1963 (cited in Griffith, *op. cit.*, pp. 396–398).

Khrushchev may well have come away from the conference with the feeling that he had "bought off" Mao by concessions in the wording of the document and by projected Soviet policy in the field of military assistance and trade. Mao may have come away with the feeling that the Russians, if pressed hard, would take the correct line on issues confronting the international Communist movement and that, therefore, a tightly organized movement headed by the Soviet party was desirable since it would in fact be guided by Chinese interpretations of Marxist-Leninism.

Trade.[7]

Sino-Soviet trade, after hitting a low point in 1957, expanded rapidly in 1958 and 1959. The large upswing in trade was caused by the urgent Chinese need for imports associated with the "Great Leap Forward." The Soviets appear to have gone out of their way to satisfy the requests and to deliver on schedule significant quantities of equipment and raw materials. The pattern of trade suggests a willingness on the part of the Soviets, in late 1958 and 1959, to alter their own economic plans in order to assist the Chinese economy, whatever misgivings there may have been on an ideological level about the Great Leap and, particularly, the communes. As Hoeffding has put it:

> The resurgence of machinery and equipment imports from the U.S.S.R. must have brought home to the Chinese authorities the dependence on Soviet support of any effort to accelerate China's rate of industrialization, but also perhaps the value of the U.S.S.R. as a *supplier willing, in this instance, to provide such support at short notice, and probably at considerable inconvenience to its planners and industrial managers.*[8]

Prior to the launching of the Great Leap Forward, the Soviets had made an effort to put Chinese-Russian trade on a more regular basis. This attempt had led to a Sino-Soviet treaty of commerce and navigation signed in April and ratified in July

---

[7] See Oleg Hoeffding, "Sino-Soviet Economic Relations in Recent Years," in Kurt London, ed., *Unity and Contradiction: Major Aspects of Sino-Soviet Relations* (New York: Praeger, 1962), pp. 295–312.

[8] Hoeffding, *op. cit.*, p. 309. Italics added.

1958. The treaty called for long-term agreements "to assure expansion of trade in accordance with the requirements of the national economies of both countries."[9] However, trade in both 1958 and 1959 was on the basis of yearly protocols, and a number of supplementary protocols and an agreement for the delivery of equipment for forty-seven plants to be built in China were signed by the Soviet Union, on August 8, 1958, after the Khrushchev-Mao meeting.[10]

It should be noted however that beginning in 1956 the net balance of trade did swing in favor of the Soviet Union, reaching a peak in 1958 and then declining again in 1959. This appears to be attributable in part to the exhaustion of Soviet credits extended in 1950 and 1954 and to reflect also the adverse Chinese balance in the service account as well as Soviet military assistance to China.

Military Aid[11]

In mid-1957 the Chinese apparently demanded from the Russians substantially increased aid to their nuclear weapons production program, and Khrushchev appears to have decided to commit himself to greatly increased aid to the Chinese nuclear program. There seems little reason to doubt the Chinese assertion that the Soviet Union entered into an agreement on modern technology with China on October 15, 1957.[12] It appears, judging from the development of the Chinese nuclear program, that the Soviet Union almost immediately began to provide extensive assistance to it, which has enabled the Chinese to build a gaseous diffusion plant for the production of weapons-grade uranium. Soviet aid was also given to other aspects of the Chinese weapons program including the development of medium-range missiles.[13]

9 As quoted in Hoeffding, *op. cit.*, p. 299.

10 *Izvestia*, August 12, 1958, p. 4, in *Current Digest of the Soviet Press* (*CDSP*), Vol. X, p. 14.

11 Morton H. Halperin, Chapter 5.

12 "Statement by the Spokesman of the Chinese Government — A Comment on the Soviet Government's Statement of August 3," *Peking Review* (August 15, 1963), p. 14. See also, "Statement of the Soviet Government, August 21, 1963," *Peking Review* (September 6, 1963), p. 21.

13 For a discussion of Soviet aid to the Chinese nuclear program that

At the same time that he agreed to aid the Chinese weapons development program, as part of an effort to bring China more clearly under Soviet control while at the same time strengthening the capability of the alliance for action against the West, Khrushchev proposed various Sino-Soviet military arrangements including the stationing of Soviet nuclear weapons on Chinese territory under joint control. The Chinese, after considerable debate between the army and the Party, rejected the proposals for joint arrangements. In retrospect the Chinese described some of Khrushchev's proposals as "unreasonable demands designed to bring China under Soviet military control,"[14] but it is not clear how they viewed them at the time.

If the Chinese felt some uneasiness about the Soviet commitment to aid their nuclear program and some unhappiness about the "unreasonable demands," the Soviets felt that a major concession had again been made to them.

Relations With Yugoslavia[15]

The Khrushchev *rapprochement* with Yugoslavia was already past its peak in October 1957, although Yugoslavia did attend the conference in Moscow. However, the Yugoslavs refused to sign the Moscow Declaration and, at the same time, appeared to be courting trouble by circulating the draft prepared by the League of Communists of Yugoslavia in April 1958.[16] Khrushchev apparently decided to respond in a rather moderate way to the Yugoslav provocations but, on May 5, the *People's Daily* launched a bitter attack on the Yugoslavs.[17]

stresses its importance, see Morton H. Halperin, *China and the Bomb* (New York: Praeger, 1965), pp. 78–82.

[14] "The Origin and Development of the Differences Between the Leadership of the CPSU and Ourselves," September 6, 1963 (in Griffith, *op. cit.,* p. 399).

[15] Zagoria, *op. cit.,* pp. 176–187; Lowenthal, *op. cit.,* pp. 70–98.

[16] Robert F. Byrnes, "Soviet and Chinese Relations with Yugoslavia," in London, ed., *op. cit.,* p. 169.

[17] "Modern Revisionism Must Be Repudiated," *People's Daily,* May 5, 1959, in *Peking Review,* No. 10 (May 6, 1958), pp. 6–8. It is not clear if the Chinese were already using attacks on Yugoslavia as a means of debating with the Soviets about the proper attitude toward the United States. However the quotes cited date the dispute about the United States to 1959,

Pravda reprinted the article on the next day,[18] and the Soviet Union then appeared to swing in line behind the Chinese attack on Yugoslavia although holding aloof from some of the more extreme Chinese statements. As Zagoria has indicated, Khrushchev probably was not at all unhappy about an attack on the Yugoslav position. However the Soviets probably were "pushed by Peking to adopt positions more extreme than they originally intended, but Moscow stopped short of the complete break desired and effected by Peking."[19]

Here again there was at least some shift toward the Chinese position: the Chinese appeared to be ready to have a major public disagreement on the proper attitude toward Yugoslavia, and the Soviet Union drew back from a clear public difference and adopted a position closer to that of the Chinese than it had originally intended. The Chinese were apparently delighted and perhaps somewhat surprised that the Soviets supported them. An article in the first issue of *Red Flag* on June 1, 1958, declared:

> The struggle of the Marxist-Leninist Parties of *all* countries against the revisionism of a leading group in Yugoslavia headed by Tito is a big event in current world affairs . . . contrary to the expectations of the Tito group, the Communist parties of *all* countries have displayed great solidarity in the struggle.[20]

The Military Balance

The launching of Sputnik and the testing of an inter-continental missile by the Soviet Union in the fall of 1957 marked a turning point in the international balance of power, heralded both by the Soviet Union and Communist China. Both the Soviets and the Chinese viewed the change as most important in giving the Soviets a credible deterrent against an American attack. The Chinese have also seen the change as

and the Soviets proved willing to join in attacks on the Yugoslavs. The Khrushchev-Mao communiqué after their meeting in the summer of 1958, for example, noted their agreement in condemning Yugoslav revisionism.

18 *Pravda*, May 6, 1958, p. 3; in *CDSP*, No. 18, pp. 13–14.

19 Zagoria, *op. cit.*, pp. 184–185.

20 *Red Flag*, June 1, 1958, New China News Agency (NCNA), May 31, 1958, and reprinted in *Survey of the China Mainland Press (SCMP)*, No. 1785, p. 6.

opening up the possibility of establishing military superiority of the Communist bloc, which would permit much more aggressive action in extending the area of Communist control and, particularly, in supporting wars of national liberation in underdeveloped areas. Even in the short run, there may have been some small difference between the two countries. However the Soviet line was not incompatible with Mao's belief stated at the Moscow meeting and then publicly that the "East Wind was now prevailing over the West Wind."[21]

As will be indicated, the Chinese probably wanted the Soviets to press harder in the Middle East than they were willing to do and may have been more confident that probes would be successful. Soviet attention continued to be focused more narrowly on Europe than the Chinese would have liked. However, it seems that the different interpretations of the opportunities that came with the change in the balance of power in 1957 did not become prominent until the Soviet failure in the Berlin crises of 1958 and 1960–1961, and in Cuba in 1962.

The Soviet public claims were more modest than those of the Chinese, no doubt in light of the Soviets' more accurate knowledge of the real state of the military balance in 1958, but the basic agreement between the two countries as to what could be gained from the new balance of power is reflected in the similarity in strategy and proximity of the Chinese probe against Quemoy and the Soviet probe against Berlin. Both countries' positions seem to be rather adequately stated in Zagoria's summary of the *Soviet* position:

> While Khrushchev was not unaware of the appreciable military gains he had made, or of the possibility of employing those gains as blackmail against the West in Berlin or elsewhere, he seemed prepared to take only minimal and controlled risks of war — minimal in the sense that there should be no Soviet initiative which could reasonably be expected to provoke either a massive Western response or a local war with the West, and controlled in

21 *People's Daily*, November 20, 1957, in *SCMP*, No. 1662, p. 2. "Two Different Lines in the Question of War and Peace," November 19, 1963, in *The Polemic on the General Line of the International Communist Movement* (Peking: Foreign Languages Press, 1965), p. 37.

the sense that there was always an avenue of retreat if the West showed signs of firm resistance. Khrushchev seemed confident that time was on his side and that such risks were unnecessary. Above all, he did not want to run the risk of engaging the West in a local military conflict, which not only might lead to defeat or stalemate, but might also spread, alienate the neutrals, unite the West, and destroy his hopes of making gains peacefully.[22]

While one can find some Chinese statements implying a belief that a more fundamental change had taken place, the behavior of the Chinese, in particular in the Taiwan Straits, suggests that their appreciation was not very different. Mao and Khrushchev both believed that it was time to probe again but in a way that would not risk a major attack by the United States.

The Middle East Crisis of 1958[23]

The disagreement between Peking and Moscow on the right reaction to the landing of American troops in Lebanon and British troops in Jordan in the summer of 1958, following the coup in Iraq, appears to have been intensive. Both countries feared that the landings might be preparatory to an allied invasion of Iraq designed to restore the pro-Western government. Khrushchev chose to react by appeals for peace and calls for great power meetings, and went so far as to accept a Western proposal for a Security Council meeting that would presumably have included Nationalist and not Communist China. The Chinese, according to Zagoria, were urging the Russians to take more vigorous military action.

Khrushchev clearly rejected the Chinese advice on this question. He was unwilling to risk a major military confrontation with the United States in the Middle East just because the Chinese wanted one. He was also prepared to risk Chinese disfavor by accepting the proposal for a Security Council meeting, although he did retreat quickly from this position, perhaps under Chinese pressure or, as Zagoria suggests, because the danger of a Western invasion of Iraq had receded quickly. The disagreements over Middle East policy were

22 Zagoria, *op. cit.*, p. 169.
23 *Ibid.*, pp. 195–199.

probably discussed by Khrushchev during his visit to Peking that began on July 31, 1958. The Russian refusal to take vigorous action here may have been one of the elements that affected the Soviet reaction to the proposed Chinese probe in the Taiwan Straits.

This analysis has suggested that on a number of key issues — military assistance, trade, relations with Yugoslavia — Khrushchev was prepared to make concessions to the Chinese position in order to avoid a public or even a serious private split with the Chinese. The Chinese were playing a major role within the international Communist movement and were coming to believe that if strong pressure were put on the Russian leadership, they would modify their position. Both sides were aware of differences between them but both were still trying to compromise their disagreements and coordinate their actions. This was the setting in which Khrushchev arrived in Peking and discussed with Mao the impending Chinese moves.

Before outlining the Soviet actions during the Quemoy crisis and then considering the nature of the Sino-Soviet relationship, it is necessary to outline briefly Chinese strategy during the 1958 Taiwan Straits crisis.

Chinese Strategy[24]

During July 1958 the Chinese Communists began to step up their level of military activity in Fukien Province opposite Taiwan. Air fields that previously had been unoccupied were activated, and there began to be some interference with Chinese Nationalist flights over the mainland. The Chinese Communist reaction to the Iraqi revolution and the landing of American troops in Lebanon started a major campaign on July 16 in the leading Chinese cities that emphasized the themes of "get out of the Middle East" and "liberate Taiwan." This campaign came to a halt in late July, and there were only a

[24] This section summarizes briefly Chinese strategy during the crisis. It is drawn from the longer work on Chinese policy toward the offshore islands, of which this chapter is also a part, being prepared by the two authors.

few scattered references to Taiwan in the Chinese press during the next several weeks.

On August 23, the Chinese Communists launched a heavy artillery barrage against the Quemoy Islands. The artillery fire and the use of Chinese Communist PT boats prevented the Nationalists from resupplying Quemoy until September 7, when U.S. naval vessels began to escort Nationalist convoys. During these first two weeks of the crisis, Chinese Communist propaganda played down the events in the Taiwan Straits. The *People's Daily* carried brief reports of the military action. These stories attributed the crisis to the attempt by Chiang Kai-shek to land reinforcements on the Quemoy Islands. There was no suggestion in Chinese Communist internal propaganda that a major international crisis was taking place; there were no domestic campaigns. In their international propaganda, the Chinese avoided any reference to the military action in the Taiwan Straits. The single exception was that they directed broadcasts at Quemoy to warn the garrison that it was isolated and calling upon it to surrender.

The Chinese probe was begun on the assumption, or at least the hope, that the United States would either remain aloof from the conflict or force the Chinese Nationalists to withdraw. With no American intervention, the Chinese Communists may well have believed that they could effectively isolate the Quemoy garrison and force it into starvation and surrender. In this case, or if the United States forced a withdrawal from Quemoy, Peking could have hoped for very serious repercussions on Taiwan, since it would have been a demonstration of American unwillingness to go to war to protect Chinese Nationalist interests. This exacerbation in U.S.-Chinese Nationalist relations, the Communists may have hoped, would lower the morale of the Kuomintang and lead to a weakening or even to a collapse of the Chiang regime.

In any case, a reduction in U.S.-Chinese Nationalist cooperation and a lowering of morale on Taiwan were clearly important steps toward the final incorporation of Taiwan into Communist China.

The Chinese Communists quickly discovered that their initial assumption was incorrect. American military and political action, beginning on August 23, soon made it clear to Peking that the United States would aid the Chinese Nationalists in breaking the blockade and would almost certainly be involved more directly if the islands were invaded.

The use of Chinese PT boats came to a halt very quickly with the presence of a large number of American ships in the Taiwan Straits, and artillery fire came to a virtual halt early in September. Chinese propaganda media continued to play down the crisis during early September, although on September 4 they did announce that they were claiming a twelve-mile limit on their territorial waters.

A major change in the Chinese propaganda line took place on September 6, after it had become clear that the United States was determined to help break the blockade but before the first escorted convoy had sailed. In a public statement Chinese Communist Premier Chou En-lai called for a reopening of the Sino-American ambassadorial talks, at the same time reaffirming Peking's determination to liberate Taiwan eventually. Chou's statement was printed prominently on the first page of the *People's Daily*.

From then on the crisis and American intervention in the Taiwan Straits were to be stressed in Chinese domestic and foreign propaganda media. At the same time, a series of "liberate Taiwan" campaigns were held in the leading Chinese cities.

On September 7, the first U.S.-escorted Chinese Nationalist convoy set out for Quemoy. The convoy reached the shore and began unloading after several hours, providing the Chinese with ample time to fire, but no firing occurred. American boats clearly remained beyond the three-mile limit and, hence, outside the range of at least some Communist artillery sited opposite Quemoy. On September 8 a second convoy sailed. Several hours after it had reached the beach, perhaps allowing time for communication back and forth to Peking, the Chinese Communists directed heavy fire at the boats, driving them off the beach. This began a period, which lasted until October 6, during which the Chinese Communists refrained from naval action but concentrated at least moderate artillery fire against Quemoy and against the convoys attempting to land on Lialo beach on Big Quemoy. This fire never was as intense as in late August, but it did succeed in preventing the landing of supplies for two additional weeks.

Chinese Communist propaganda, both domestic and foreign, continued to focus on the events in the Taiwan Straits through September and into October. In late September, the Chinese began to minimize the consequences of the failure to capture Quemoy, to emphasize the connection between Quemoy and Taiwan, and to stress the current exacerbation of U.S.-Chinese Nationalist differences.

Chinese Communist strategy during the period from late August through the end of September seems to have been ambiguous and perhaps two-pronged. Peking was forced to recognize that the United States was heavily committed to the defense of Quemoy. Therefore, the main thrust of Chinese policy was to withdraw from the crisis while disguising the failure of the effort and discouraging an American attack on the Chinese mainland. At the same time, Peking may have been somewhat reluctant to give up hope of capturing the offshore islands. During the first two weeks of convoying, the Chinese Nationalists failed to land large quantities of supplies. There may have been some hope in Peking that the United States would not step up its level of involvement and would, after all, allow the islands to fall or, perhaps more likely, force a withdrawal. However, as September wore on the level of supplies reaching Quemoy grew steadily, and by early October it was clear that the blockade was being broken without an increase of American or even Chinese Nationalist effort.

On October 6, apparently in deference to this fact, Peking announced a one-week cease-fire with the condition that there be no American escort of Nationalist convoys. This demand together with other Chinese Communist propaganda appears to have been aimed at increasing disagreements between the United States and the Chinese Nationalists. The cease-fire was put into effect on October 6 and was renewed by the Chinese Communists after one week for an additional two-week period. After a brief resumption of fire on October 20, the Chinese Communists announced that they would fire against supply areas on Quemoy only on odd days. The pattern of ood-day firing and Chinese Communist propaganda were apparently designed to exacerbate U.S.-Chinese Nationalist relations and to imply that Peking never intended to capture the offshore islands.

With this brief overview of Chinese behavior and strategy, we turn to a description of Soviet behavior during the crisis.

Soviet Behavior

There seems to be little doubt that Khrushchev and Mao discussed the impending Chinese Communist probe into the Taiwan Straits during Khrushchev's hurriedly arranged visit to Peking on July 31, 1958. Khrushchev was no doubt aware that tensions had increased in the Taiwan Straits and that the Chinese Communists might be planning a move. There had been reports of stepped-up activity in the Chinese and Western press and at least one story in the Soviet press.[25] Khrushchev thus must have come prepared to discuss the offshore islands. In a letter to Eisenhower sent during the Quemoy crisis, and to be considered later, the Soviet Premier indicated that he had discussed the situation with Mao:

> I have been to Peking lately and had a chance to exchange views with the leaders of the government of the Chinese People's Republic on all matters of interest to the Soviet Union and the Chinese People's Republic. I can tell you frankly and straightforwardly that the full unity of views of the U.S.S.R. and the Chinese People's Republic on the main thing, that is, on the necessity of continuing to struggle resolutely against all forces of aggression and of supporting the forces working for peace all over the world, was reaffirmed during our discussion in Peking.[26]

There is, however, still very little information on the meeting. We still do not know whether the meeting was arranged as a result of the planned Chinese probe or was called for other reasons.[27] The communiqué at the end of the meeting

---

25 *Pravda,* July 26, 1958, p. 4, in *CDSP,* No. 30, p. 18.

26 *The New York Times,* September 20, 1958, p. 2.

27 In the Sino-Soviet polemics the only revelation on what was discussed at the meeting is in a Soviet statement indicating that Khrushchev had expressed Soviet misgivings about the communes and the Great Leap:

implied that Taiwan had been discussed: ". . . the two parties exchanged views fully on the series of major questions confronting the two countries in Asia and Europe in the present international situation, and reached agreement on measures to be taken to oppose aggression and safeguard peace."[28] However there was no specific reference to Taiwan or the offshore islands. The Soviet press, in analyzing the Khrushchev-Mao meeting, laid stress on the need and possibilities for peace, while the Chinese press emphasized that peace would come only from opposing imperialism.[29] During the remainder of the period until firing started on August 23, the Soviet press, mirroring the Chinese press, contained only a few hints of a possible crisis in the Taiwan Straits.

In an apparently related move in early August, Polish officials in Warsaw told Western reporters that the Chinese were receiving atomic weapons from the Soviet Union. The stories appeared to have been inspired by Moscow and aimed at contributing to the deterrence of American involvement in the impending crisis.[30]

A Soviet radio broadcast on August 12 charged that the American "ruling class" was trying to make use of Chiang Kai-shek to fabricate tensions in the Far East. This was described as an effort to divert attention from American aggression in the Middle East.[31] On August 21, a *Pravda* "Observer" article declared that the friendship between the Chinese People's Republic and the Soviet Union is "as strong as steel." The editorial continued:

> The strength of the alliance between the U.S.S.R. and the People's China guarantees fresh success in the policy of peaceful coexistence, guarantees the further growth of the prestige of the socialist camp, including the Chinese People's Republic, and this means that *fresh setbacks are in store for Dulles's policy of balancing on the brink of war.*[32]

"Soviet Government Statement — Reply to Statement made by the Chinese Government, September 21, 1963" (in Griffith, *op. cit.*, p. 436).

[28] *People's Daily*, August 4, 1958, in *SCMP*, No. 1827, p. 26.

[29] Zagoria, *op. cit.*, pp. 201–206.

[30] The Polish leaks are reported in *The New York Times*, August 7, 10, and 18, 1958.

[31] Soviet Broadcast to Southeast Asia in Cantonese, August 12, 1958, 12:15 GMT.

[32] *Pravda*, August 21, 1958, p. 3. Italics added.

Two days later the shelling began. Soviet propaganda until September 6 followed the Chinese line of describing the low-level military action without suggesting that a major crisis was developing. After September 6 both the Soviet and Chinese press and radio stressed American aggression in the Straits and the Chinese determination to liberate Taiwan. On August 25, *Pravda* quoted a New China News Agency dispatch — published in the Chinese press on August 24 — stating that Chinese Communist artillery had fired on a Chinese Nationalist troopship and on Nationalist artillery positions. On the next day a Soviet radio broadcast noted that the Chinese Nationalist had on "August 24 . . . suddenly opened fire on several [Communist-held] offshore islands." The commentator charged that the United States was "trying to create a center of international tension."[33]

On August 27, *Pravda* carried two articles on events in the Taiwan Straits, one datelined Tokyo and the second datelined London. The first dispatch described Japanese reaction to the "provocative" acts of the United States and Chiang Kai-shek. The second dispatch reported criticism of American policy in the British press.[34] *Izvestia* on the same day stressed the theme that the United States was trying to provoke a crisis to create the impression that there was tension in the Far East so as to shift emphasis from the Middle East where the real aggression was taking place. The article declared that the United States seeks

> . . . to confuse world opinion and create the impression that the central problem of the international situation now threatening world peace is the fictitious threat of aggression in the Far East and not the real aggression in the Arab East committed by the United States and Britain.[35]

A day later a Soviet naval publication described the Chinese

33 *CDSP*, Vol. X (October 1, 1958), p. 37. NCNA dispatch in *SCMP*, No. 1842 (August 28, 1958), pp. 32–33.

34 Moscow Soviet South Asian Service in English, August 26, 1958, 10:45 GMT. *Pravda*, August 27, 1958, p. 5. The second of these dispatches is the one cited by Thomas and Zagoria as the first mention of the crisis in the Soviet press. See John R. Thomas, "Soviet Behavior in the Quemoy Crisis of 1958," *Orbis*, Vol. VI (Spring 1962), pp. 41–42; and Zagoria, *op. cit.*, p. 211.

35 *Izvestia*, "What is Behind the Slander?" August 27, 1958, p. 1.

shelling, in an explanation taken from the Peking press, as a punitive retaliation for attempts by the Chinese Nationalists to land supplies on Quemoy.[36] A Soviet radio broadcast on the same day drew a relationship between U.S. pressure on the Chinese Nationalists to increase tensions in the Far East and the reported decision of other NATO countries to reduce the extent of the trade embargo against Communist China.[37]

On August 31, at a time when the Nationalists had yet to breach the blockade of Quemoy, *Pravda* published an article by "Observer" on the crisis in the Taiwan Straits. The article, which appeared after growing signs that the United States would be involved in the defense of Quemoy, pledged that the Soviet Union would give Communist China "the necessary moral and material aid in its just struggle." The article noted that the liberation of Taiwan and the offshore islands was an internal affair of the Chinese people but warned that an attack on China would be repulsed by Russia as well as China. The article noted:

> Whoever presently threatens to attack the People's Republic of China must not forget that he threatens the Soviet Union, because the Soviet Union is tied to People's China with unbreakable bonds of friendship and cooperation which underlie the determination of both governments to ensure peace between nations and repulse an aggressor. The Soviet Union and CPR are united in a struggle against any and all plots of the enemies of peace. The Soviet Union will render the People's Republic of China the necessary moral and material aid in its just struggle.
>
> And let the organizers of military provocations against the CPR not be lulled (into the belief) that they will succeed in localizing events. Any U. S. aggression in the Far East will inevitably cause increased world tension and result in the spread of war to other regions with all the consequences following from that. It is necessary to remind again (of this) those who are undertaking dangerous playing with fire in the Far East.[38]

This *Pravda* article was reprinted in its entirety in the *People's Daily* on the next day.[39]

36 Soviet Fleet, August 28, 1958 (as cited in Thomas, *op. cit.*, p. 42).
37 Moscow Soviet European Service in English, August 28, 1958, 17:30 GMT.
38 *Pravda*, August 31, 1958, p. 4, translated in *CDSP*, Vol. X (October 8, 1958), p. 17. (Parentheses in *CDSP*.)
39 *People's Daily*, September 1, 1958, p. 4.

On September 5, following Dulles' statement at Newport virtually committing the United States to defend Quemoy, a second *Pravda* "Observer" article declared that the Soviet Union could not "stand idly by" if things happen "at the frontier or on the territory of its great ally." The article again distinguished between Chinese Communist operations against the offshore islands, which were declared to be an internal Chinese affair, and a possible American intervention and attack on the mainland, which would cause the Soviet Union to aid the Chinese Communists. The article declared that the Soviets would give the Chinese "all possible aid to curb the adventurous war mongers." Russia warned the United States again that it "should not calculate that a retaliatory blow will be confined to the Taiwan Straits and no less the offshore islands." It warned that the United States would "receive a crushing rebuff, which will put an end to U.S. military aggression in the Far East."[40] The *People's Daily* on the next day reported the *Pravda* article prominently on page one and reprinted the document in its entirety on an inner page.[41]

The next major Soviet diplomatic intervention came on September 7, when Soviet Premier Khrushchev addressed a letter to President Eisenhower. Much of the argument about whether or not there was Sino-Soviet disagreement during the 1958 Quemoy crisis centers about the timeliness of this letter. We shall return to this question in some detail later, but here we shall note the chronological setting in which the letter was delivered. On September 4, Dulles came close to committing the United States to the defense of Quemoy. On September 6, Premier Chou En-lai issued a statement calling for a reopening of the Sino-American ambassadorial talks,[42] and the United States publicly accepted the proposal.[43] In the Taiwan Straits there had been a virtual, if unannounced, cease-fire in artillery operation for several days; at the same time, there had been no effort by the Chinese Nationalists to

---

40 *CDSP*, Vol. X (October 15, 1958), p. 9.

41 *People's Daily*, September 6, 1958, pp. 1 and 4.

42 Text in Paul E. Zinner, ed., *Documents on American Foreign Relations* (New York: Harper, for the Council on Foreign Relations, 1959), p. 440.

43 *Ibid.*, pp. 442–443.

land supplies. The United States had announced that it was going to convoy Chinese Nationalist supply ships and the first convoy had just sailed. At this point, when the Chinese Communists had shown some political initiative but the military situation in the Straits was still uncertain, Khrushchev stated, as had the two *Pravda* articles, that the liberation of Taiwan and of the offshore islands was an internal affair of the Chinese and that the United States had no right to interfere. Going beyond the language of the "Observer" articles, Khrushchev declared:

> An attack on the Chinese People's Republic, which is a great friend, ally and neighbor of our country, is an attack on the Soviet Union. True to its duty, our country will do everything in order together with People's China to defend the security of both states, the interests of peace in the Far East, the interest of peace in the whole world.[44]

Following the dispatch of Khrushchev's letter, the Soviet press and radio devoted considerable attention to the developing crisis in the Taiwan Straits. They continued to blame American provocation for the developing conflict and to describe U.S. preparations for war. They stressed the wide support in Russia for Khrushchev's letter and repeated its main themes: that an attack on China constituted an attack on the Soviet Union and that the Soviet Union and China would stand together. The Soviet press also noted extensive opposition to American policy both in the United States and among America's allies.

On September 11 and 12, *Pravda* reported mass rallies throughout the Soviet Union to enlist popular support for the Chinese Communists, to endorse Soviet Premier Khrushchev's letter, and to condemn U.S. provocations in the Far East.[45]

In a speech to the U.N. General Assembly during the gen-

---

44 *Ibid.*, p. 449. A Moscow TASS dispatch quoted an Associated Press correspondent to suggest that Khrushchev's speech following Chou En-lai's call for reopening the ambassadorial talks was designed to encourage peace talks and to discourage the United States from carrying out an attack against China.

45 "Hands Off China," *Pravda*, September 13, 1958, p. 1, translated in *CDSP*, Vol. X (October 22, 1958), pp. 10–11.

eral debate on September 18, Soviet Foreign Minister Andrei Gromyko accused the United States of provocative action in the Taiwan Straits and declared that the United States was extending its aggression to the offshore islands. He warned that the Soviet Union would not hesitate to come to the aid of China and declared that the situation could be stabilized only by an American withdrawal from the area.[46]

On September 19, when the blockade had not yet been clearly breached, Khrushchev addressed a second letter to President Eisenhower that was so intemperate the United States rejected it. Khrushchev's note warned that a world war was now possible because of the events in the Taiwan Straits and declared that the Soviet Union would honor its commitments to China and would come to China's aid if the latter were attacked. Reflecting Chinese concern at the time, Khrushchev's letter noted the attempt of the United States to create a two-China situation and declared that this effort would be resolutely opposed. Khrushchev pointed out that if the United States were planning to attack Communist China with nuclear weapons, it should remember that the other side too has atomic and hydrogen weapons and the appropriate means to deliver them, and if the Chinese People's Republic falls victim to such an attack, the aggressor will at once suffer a rebuff by the same means. Preparations for war against the People's Republic, Khrushchev warned, mean "to doom the sons of the American people to certain death and to spark off the conflagration of a world war." He declared that unless the United States withdrew "now" from the Taiwan Straits the People's Republic would have to extend its attack.[47]

On September 21, Moscow assailed the American rejection of Khrushchev's note and declared that this was evidence of American unwillingness to listen to reason.[48]

[46] *The New York Times,* September 19, 1958, pp. 1, 5.
[47] *The New York Times,* September 20, 1958, p. 2; Gillian King, ed., *Documents on International Affairs: 1958* (London: Oxford University Press, for the Royal Institute of International Affairs, 1962), pp. 197–204.
[48] *The New York Times,* September 22, 1958, p. 1 (Text in *CDSP,* Vol. X [October 29, 1958], p. 18).

Khrushchev's second letter, according to the Soviet press and radio, received wide support in the country. The Soviet media reiterated its main themes. It was frequently pointed out that "the other side," as well as the United States, had nuclear weapons and would retaliate in the event that the United States used nuclear weapons in an attack on China: an attack on China would lead to a world conflagration. Soviet propaganda also expressed support for the intention of the Chinese people to expel the United States from Taiwan and, in addition, attacked American proposals for a cease-fire in the Taiwan Straits, echoing the Chinese claim that since there was no war between the United States and China a cease-fire was meaningless.[49]

On October 1, Moscow radio broadcast a speech by the Chinese ambassador in the Soviet Union addressing thanks to the Soviet people for Khrushchev's two letters to the American President, which he described as "strongest support to the Chinese people."[50]

In response, President Eisenhower stated that Khrushchev's letters showed clearly that the events in the Taiwan Straits constituted an international crisis and not, as the Chinese Communists claimed, an event in a civil war. Khrushchev, on October 5, sought to clarify the Soviet position along lines that echoed — rather than conflicted with — the Chinese Communist position. He declared, in answer to a question from a TASS correspondent, that the Soviet Union would remain aloof from the civil war but that "the Soviet Union will come to the aid of the Chinese People's Republic if it is attacked from without, or more concretely, if the U.S.A. attacks the Chinese People's Republic."[51] The Soviet Union supported the Chinese cease-fire declarations as well as the resumption of fire on October 20, and then the even-day cease-fire plan.

---

[49] See, for example, an "Observer" article, "Clumsy Tricks of American Aggressors," *Izvestia*, September 27, 1958, p. 3, translated in *CDSP*, Vol. X (November 5, 1958), pp. 14–15.

[50] Liu Hsiao speech, broadcast on Soviet Home Service, October 1, 1958, 20:00 GMT.

[51] *Pravda*, October 6, 1958, p. 1, translated in *CDSP*, Vol. X (November 12, 1958), p. 18.

Following the crisis, both sides stressed the importance of the other's role. Thus Soong Ching-ling in an article published in *Pravda* in November 1958 wrote:

> It was a high expression of our [Soviet-Chinese] fraternal relations as allies that when the American government was rattling its saber in the Taiwan area Comrade Khrushchev *immediately* and resolutely warned the U. S. Government that any attack on the Chinese People's Republic would be an attack on the Soviet government and the Soviet people.[52]

Soviet statements emphasized the Chinese role. For example, in alluding to the crisis in a speech to the Twenty-first Party Congress, Khrushchev declared that "only the resolute actions of the Chinese People's Republic and other peace-loving forces averted" a war.[53]

As we shall indicate, at the height of their polemics in 1963 both countries were to present retrospectively very different interpretations of their respective roles.

Soviet Strategy

Having laid out the pattern of Soviet political behavior during the 1958 Taiwan Straits crisis, we turn to an attempt to analyze the nature of Sino-Soviet relations during this period. While we shall emphasize the probability that there was no intense Sino-Soviet disagreement during the crisis, we wish to stress that the available material on which to base a judgment remains extremely limited and, to some extent, contradictory. Our interpretation does take issue with those presented by Zagoria, Hsieh, and Thomas,[54] but even more with those who, in general discussions of the Sino-Soviet dispute, have pointed to the Quemoy crisis as one of the earliest manifestations of disagreement and a cause of such later Soviet actions as the decision to discontinue assistance to China's nuclear program.

---

[52] "Socialist Camp in Contemporary International Situation," *Pravda*, November 10, 1958, pp. 3–4 (in *CDSP*, Vol. X, No. 45, p. 17). Italics added.
[53] *Pravda*, January 28, 1959, p. 7 (in *CDSP*, Vol. XI [March 4, 1959], p. 21).
[54] Thomas, *op. cit.*, pp. 38–64; Zagoria, *op. cit.*, pp. 219–221; Hsieh, *Communist China's Strategy in the Nuclear Era* (New York: Prentice-Hall, 1962), pp. 119–130.

As has been indicated, the critical discussion between Communist China and the Soviet Union prior to the crisis probably took place during the Khrushchev-Mao meeting. The key to the disagreement was the type of demand that Mao presented to Khrushchev. If, for example, Mao had asked for the immediate transfer of a large number of nuclear weapons and delivery systems coupled with a statement by the Soviet Union that it would use whatever force was necessary to liberate the offshore islands and Taiwan, there is little doubt that Khrushchev would have turned this down. At the other extreme, if Khrushchev had been asked only for Soviet neutrality, this would have posed no difficulty for the Soviet leader. However, Mao's demands were somewhere between these two extremes and the precise nature of the demands must have affected Khrushchev's response.

It is our contention that Mao asked Khrushchev approximately for what he subsequently received and that discussion between them about Chinese strategy and the Soviet role led to agreement. During the period when the Chinese Communists were hoping to capture the offshore islands by keeping the United States out of the crisis, Mao probably wanted from Khrushchev only very general statements of support designed to suggest Soviet defensive support for China but not suggesting a deep Soviet involvement in the crisis. If it became clear that there was the possibility of an American attack on the Chinese mainland, then Peking would have wanted a stronger statement of Soviet support, one designed to deter the now-to-be-feared American attack.

Alternate explanations and interpretations have suggested that Mao wanted a strong statement of support from Khrushchev as early as he could get it, including, presumably, some mention of the liberation of Taiwan in the communiqué following their talks. It is around this issue, and the later question of the timing of Khrushchev's first letter, that much of the disagreement at this time turns.

The argument that the Chinese would have wanted a strong Khrushchev statement as early as they could get it rests on the assumption that they believed such a statement would reduce the likelihood of American intervention to defend Quemoy. Attempts to analyze this possibility can proceed at two levels. First, was it in fact more likely that the United States would remain aloof if there was a strong Soviet statement expressing involvement in the crisis and, second, what were the views of the Peking leaders likely to have been?

On the first level there is little doubt that a strong Soviet statement would have increased rather than decreased the likelihood of American intervention. It would have changed the situation from a local clash in the Taiwan Straits to a Soviet-American showdown, which could be seen as a test of American will in light of Sputnik and the Soviet ICBM tests of the previous year. The importance of not backing down under Soviet pressure, if American commitments elsewhere were to be reaffirmed, would have substantially increased the possibility of American involvement. As a matter of fact, the American government, in justifying its decision to defend Quemoy, stressed the signs of Soviet support for the Chinese — including Khrushchev's visit to Peking.

To turn to the second level of analysis, Chinese behavior during late August and early September suggests that Mao was aware of this line of reasoning. As has been noted, Chinese propaganda played down the seriousness of the crisis during this period, and external propaganda was directed only at Quemoy itself, calling upon the garrison to surrender. There was little internal propaganda and no statements were directed abroad. If the failure to receive a strong Soviet statement of support was what forced the Chinese to be very cautious, they could have modified their behavior on September 8 following the arrival of Khrushchev's letter in Washington. On the contrary, the Chinese seem to have recognized that by downgrading the crisis they were most likely to succeed in gaining American aloofness. Moreover the Chinese wanted to deal with their "civil war" on their own, keeping out both the Soviet Union and the United States.

If we are correct in arguing that Mao asked Khrushchev to issue a strong statement only if and when it became clear that the United States would be involved and the Chinese Communists were in the process of disengaging, there is little reason to believe that Khrushchev would have resisted this request. As we have already argued, Khrushchev's approach during this period was to yield to Chinese Communist pressures where these did not seem to touch on vital Soviet interests and where it seemed necessary for the maintenance of a united front in the international Communist movement. In view of his unwillingness to take such risky action as the Chinese Communists were suggesting in the Middle East, Khrushchev may have looked upon the intended Chinese probe in the Taiwan Straits as a way of permitting the Chinese themselves to take the action that they were suggesting elsewhere. In agreeing to Mao's moderate request for Soviet support, Khrushchev could have been demonstrating his willingness to back up the Chinese Communists in their efforts to discover if, in fact, Quemoy could be captured. In addition, provided the crisis did not last unduly long, the action in the Taiwan Straits could give a useful indication to the Soviet leadership of the possible American response in the event of a probe against Berlin. Whether a Berlin move was already planned is not clear, but if such a move were contemplated, it may have provided an additional motive rather than a disincentive for Soviet acquiescence in the limited Chinese probe.

Khrushchev may not have had as high an expectation as the Chinese that the effort would be successful, and he may have cautioned about the danger of provoking an American nuclear attack. Nevertheless, given the rather cautious Chinese strategy and the limited demands put upon him, he may well have acquiesced with little hesitation in the Chinese move, and the proposed Russian role in it.

Soviet statements between August 1 and 23 provided a quiet background of affirmation of Sino-Soviet solidarity and of the Soviet desire for "peace." And as early as August 30, when there were already clear signs of American involvement in the defense of Quemoy, a *Pravda* "Observer" article committed the Soviet Union to the defense of China.

An even more explicit statement of Soviet support came in the Khrushchev letter of September 7 to Eisenhower. It has been argued by a number of analysts and, more recently, as will be indicated, by the Chinese Communists, that the

Khrushchev letter arrived after the danger of nuclear war in the Taiwan Straits had passed, and was sent in typical Soviet fashion, only to get credit when all was over. It is our contention that an examination of the military situation in the Taiwan Straits on September 7, in conjunction with an analysis of the political situation, does not support this assertion. We argue that no serious danger of a nuclear clash existed before September 7 and that if the Chinese Communists had intended to provoke a nuclear clash, they could have done so after that date.

As the Russians took pains to point out at the time, the letter followed the call by Premier Chou En-lai for a reopening of the Sino-American ambassadorial talks. This in turn had followed the release of a statement by Dulles that virtually committed the United States to the defense of Quemoy and announced that the Americans were going to escort Chinese Nationalist supply vessels to the island. By the time they read Dulles' statement, the Chinese must have been convinced that their original assumption about the United States had proved to be wrong. From this time on, while the Chinese continued to hope that they could secure Quemoy, their primary emphasis was on avoiding an American overreaction that might lead to an attack on the Chinese mainland while at the same time trying to exacerbate relations between the Americans and the Chinese Nationalists.

In order to help accomplish both of these latter objectives, Chou proposed a reopening of the Sino-American talks. The Chinese may have learned from their experiences in Korea and Vietnam that the United States was less likely to expand a military conflict if talks between the two sides had been proposed and appeared to be getting under way. The Soviets no doubt had learned the same lesson. Thus Chou's statement was an attempt to reduce the likelihood of an American overreaction. At the same time, the call for Sino-American talks recognized American involvement in the crisis and hence reduced the likelihood that the United States would see this as an isolated event from which it should remain aloof. This action by Chou, we argue, was the signal of a change in Chinese strategy, which meant that Khrushchev would now be asked to fulfill his commitment and issue a statement that would reduce the likelihood of an American attack on China.

Politically, then, there were signs that the Chinese were prepared to take at least some steps to reduce the likelihood of American expansion of the conflict but not necessarily to call off their effort to capture Quemoy. There is little doubt that Khrushchev waited for this signal before sending his letter. However, as we have indicated it might well be that this is precisely when the Chinese wanted the statement.

An analysis of what was actually happening in the Taiwan Straits suggests that the danger of nuclear war still existed, if it ever had existed. If the Chinese were prepared to run the risk of an American nuclear attack, they could have pressed the blockade after September 7. If they were not prepared to risk a clash with the United States, a statement from Khrushchev at an earlier date would have been just as safe. Chou En-lai had by then issued his call for a reopening of Sino-American ambassadorial talks; but on the other hand the American Secretary of State had just committed the United States more deeply than at any previous time to the defense of Quemoy. Thus if Khrushchev had any reason to believe that the Chinese Communists might push ahead with an attempt to capture Quemoy, September 7 would be a much more dangerous time to issue the statement than, say, September 1. It was only because (and if) Khrushchev was confident that the Chinese had an overriding desire to avoid a nuclear confrontation with the United States that he could have found September 7 a safe moment to issue his warning. And, to repeat, if he found that date safe, he would have found any previous date only slightly more dangerous at most.

If, diplomatically, Chou's statement suggested less of a danger of an American attack on China, and Dulles' statement somewhat more, the actions in the Taiwan Straits were to reach the point of greatest danger for a Sino-American clash in the very hours after Khrushchev's letter was sent. The United States had begun making preparations to escort a Chinese Nationalist convoy to Quemoy very early in September. Dulles had indicated on September 4 that a convoy would soon sail. In fact, on the very day that Khrushchev's letter was sent, the first American convoy set out. There was great uncertainty, at least in Washington, as to the result and whether it would lead to a Sino-American clash. It was not known just how far in to the islands the American ships would go and whether or not the Chinese Communists would fire on them. Given this military situation, given the American commitment to the defense of Quemoy and the great uncertainty as to how much American involvement this would take, Khrushchev's letter seems to have arrived at an extremely dangerous moment. Only if he had great confidence that the Chinese Communists would be willing to back down, that they would not fire on American ships, and would permit the resupply of the islands when that seemed the only alternative, could Khrushchev have issued his statement with relative impunity on September 7. It is difficult to believe that there was substantial Sino-Soviet disagreement about the strategy to be followed in the crisis and, at the same time, very high confidence on Khrushchev's part that the Chinese Communists would not change their tactics once they got Soviet public support.

If, in fact, the Chinese had been restrained in their strategy because they had not received a strong commitment from Khrushchev earlier, there was no reason inherent in either the military or political situation that could stop them from changing their tactics once he had sent his letter. The blockade of Quemoy had been complete until the time when the letter was sent. Peking had called for a reopening of the Sino-American ambassadorial talks; but it was possible to delay the opening of these talks or even to begin the talks and still apply intensive military pressure designed to capture the islands. However, the Chinese did not change their tactics, even with the Khrushchev letter to back them up. On September 8, prior to the receipt of Khrushchev's letter in Washington, they fired on the second convoy only after it had been on the beach for some time — the American ships remained beyond firing range. At no time after the sending of the first, or for that matter the second letter, did the Chinese Communists show that they were now prepared to take greater risks of nuclear war because they had Khrushchev's guarantee.

Khrushchev's letter of September 7, then, did come after

Chinese Communist strategy had entered a new phase; one in which the deterrence of the United States and exacerbation of U.S.-Chinese Nationalist relations were to be given prominence over an attempt to drive the Chinese Nationalists off the Quemoy Islands. Khrushchev's letter, following Chou En-lai's call for a reopening of Sino-American ambassadorial talks, *was part of this change in strategy* and came just at the time that the Chinese Communists needed it. The Soviets felt that the risks of being drawn into a war were reduced because they were intimately aware of and confident about the Chinese Communists' strategy, namely, that Peking would do everything to avoid a direct military clash with the United States.

If Khrushchev's letter was sent on the expectation that the military phase of the crisis was over and that Sino-American talks would soon begin and resolve the crisis, it was sent with false expectations. In fact, as contemporary and later accounts make clear, the crisis continued to grow during September. American-escorted convoys had little success in landing supplies and continued to meet with heavy Chinese Communist artillery fire. The American commitment to Quemoy increased in intensity, and the prospect of the war being carried to the Chinese mainland to prevent a blockade of the islands appeared, according to press reports, to be getting serious consideration in Washington. In these circumstances, if the Khrushchev letter had been sent simply as a token gesture after the crisis had ended, one might have expected Moscow to back away from these commitments during the course of September.

In fact, as has been indicated, Soviet propaganda gave heavy attention to the crisis and to a reiteration of the commitments to the Chinese. During September, when the possibility might have been high, in Russian eyes, of the war being carried to the Chinese mainland because of the reports and stories coming out of Washington, there was no sign that the Russians hoped to backtrack.

It was only at the end of September and in early October that the Russians issued clarifying statements which have frequently been quoted as diluting their commitment. However, by then the blockade was being breached and there was little danger of an American attack against the mainland. Khrushchev's answer to a TASS correspondent's question on October 5 reiterated the Chinese Communist position that their attempt to liberate Taiwan and the offshore islands was a purely internal affair with which no foreign power should be involved. On the other hand, Khrushchev asserted that any attack on China by the United States would involve the Soviet Union. It is difficult to believe that the Chinese Communists would have found anything objectionable or unsatisfactory in this clarification of Khrushchev's position; the statement supported their own position and it is not inconceivable that they asked for it. Moreover, Khrushchev's statement was almost certainly not the cause of the Chinese decision to initiate a cease-fire. The announcement of a cease-fire came just as a very large well-publicized convoy was about to sail to Quemoy. By stopping when they did the Chinese Communists were able to disguise the total failure of the blockade.

Sino-Soviet Polemics on the 1958 Quemoy Crisis

As has been indicated, the public polemics between the Soviet Union and Communist China have not shed much light on the nature of Sino-Soviet relations or, indeed, of Chinese strategy during the 1958 Quemoy crisis. Even now both countries view the events in the Taiwan Straits as a major victory and argue only about who is entitled to the credit. Much of the discussion of the crisis in the polemics has been within the context of a disagreement about whether the Chinese need their own nuclear weapons. The Soviets have argued that the Taiwan Straits crisis and other events indicate that the Soviet Union is prepared to put its nuclear weapons at the service of all socialist countries. The most serious challenge to this interpretation by China came in one of the polemics on the nuclear test ban treaty in 1963. At that time the Chinese disputed the Soviet claim that *all* of the credit for the success in the Taiwan Straits in 1958 should be given to Soviet nuclear power; however, they did not accuse the Russians of failing to act as the Chinese wanted them to. They attacked only the Soviet emphasis on the role of its nuclear power. In doing so, they revised their position on the timing of the Khrushchev letter and ignored the earlier *Pravda* editorials, as well as the danger of nuclear war that did exist after September 7:

> It is especially ridiculous that the Soviet statement also gives all the credit to Soviet nuclear weapons for the Chinese people's victory in smashing the armed provocations of U.S. imperialism in the Taiwan Straits. . . .
>
> What were the facts? In August and September of 1958, the situation in the Taiwan Straits was indeed very tense as a result of the agression and provocations by the U.S. imperialists. The Soviet leaders expressed their support for China on September 7 and 19 respectively. Although at the time the situation in the Taiwan Straits was tense, there was no possibility that a nuclear war would break out and no need for the Soviet Union to support China with its nuclear weapons. It was only when they were clear that this was the situation that the Soviet leaders expressed their support for China.[55]

Before assessing these later Soviet and Chinese comments on the 1958 crisis, we shall present what is, as far as we know, a complete compilation of references to the crisis in the Sino-Soviet polemics. The first public reference to the 1958 Quemoy crisis came on January 8, 1963, when the Soviet Union declared:

> *Who prevented war in the Middle East and in the Taiwan Straits in 1958?* This was done by the Soviet Union, by all the countries of the socialist camp, by the peace-loving forces. It was they and, above all, the might and vigorous actions of the U.S.S.R. that compelled the imperialist warmongers to retreat.[56]

The Chinese did not at the time respond to the Soviet remarks, and the next reference to the crisis did not come until August 6 and 7, 1963, at the World Conference Against Atomic and Hydrogen Bombs in Hiroshima. In what the Japanese News Agency, Kyodo, described as a bitter exchange,

55 "A Statement by the Spokesman of the Chinese Government — A Comment on the Soviet Government's Statement of August 21," *Peking Review* (September 6, 1963), p. 13.

56 "Strengthen the Unity of the Communist Movement for the Triumph of Peace and Socialism," *Pravda*, January 7, 1963, translated in *New Times* (Moscow), No. 2 (January 15, 1963). Italics added. This statement is reprinted from the same source in Alexander Dallin, ed., *Diversity in International Communism; A Documentary Record, 1961–1963* (New York: Columbia University Press, for the Research Institute on Communist Affairs, 1963), Document 107, p. 734.

the Soviet delegate, Zhukov, declared that to accuse the Soviet Union of betraying the people of the world was only to serve the purposes of imperialism. He asked the Chinese: "Was it not Russia that saved Communist China from the Taiwan Straits crisis?" According to Kyodo and the TASS dispatches, he remarked that he could only express surprise that some speakers had insisted upon an all-or-nothing approach:

> Pointing to the danger in such statements, the head of the Soviet delegation criticised the argument that . . . the American imperialists could create a climate of opinion that would prevent other socialist countries from possessing nuclear arms and thereby to deprive the socialist camp of the possibility of strenthening its power to resist blackmail by the U.S.A. G. Zhukov then gave examples of how the Soviet Union's nuclear strength had been completely and undividedly put at the service of the socialist camp. So it had been in September 1959 [sic], at the time of a sharp increase in tension in the region of the Taiwan Straits. . . .[57]

> Comrade Chu Tzu-chi is a responsible man who represents the C.P.R. — a socialist country, an ally bound to us by a treaty of friendship, alliance and mutual aid, a country which, as I have already said, we have more than once saved from attempts at aggression by Taiwan. We then said bluntly that we would use atomic weapons to defend China.[58]

On the following day, according to NCNA, the Chinese delegate attacked the Soviet delegate's statement as "preposterous." He declared that in the past the Chinese people had relied mainly on their own strength and that the Soviet statement on the protection of China with nuclear weapons was an insult to the Chinese people. He referred specifically to the Chinese civil war, the Korean War, and the Cuban crisis, but did not mention the Taiwan Straits incident.[59]

The first mention of the crisis in formal statements of the two governments on the nuclear test ban came in the Soviet Union's statement of August 21, 1963:

[57] Kyodo press release, August 7, 1963 (BBC, SWB, FE/1320/C2/4, August 8, 1963).

[58] TASS dispatch, August 6, 1963, in Russian (BBC, SWB, FE/1320/C2/4–5, August 8, 1963).

[59] NCNA broadcast, August 6, 1963, at 14:00 GMT, and Peking Home Service broadcast at 16:00 GMT (BBC, SWB, FE/1320/C2/3, August 8, 1963).

It cannot be effaced from the memory of the peoples that at the most critical moments, when aggressive circles brought the world to the brink of war, the Soviet Union has without hesitation applied all its international weight, its military might to stay the aggressor's hand raised over any country, whether small or big, geographically distant or close to us. This was the case at the time of the Suez crisis, this was the case during the events concerned with Syria and Iraq in 1958. This was the case during the tense period in the Taiwan Straits — and the Chinese leaders and the Chinese people certainly remember it. This was also the case during the crisis in the Caribbean Sea, when the Soviet Union protected revolutionary Cuba with its nuclear rocket might. Maybe the Chinese leaders regard all these as minutes of "tranquillity." But it can be said outright that nobody else will agree with them. These steps by the Soviet Government were also an expression of genuine proletarian internationalism, not the kind which Peking likes to talk about and which is backed by *nothing but noisy slogans and paper resolutions.*[60]

Four days later the Soviet newspaper Red Star declared:

There was a time when only the U.S.A. possessed nuclear weapons. Taking advantage of this, it tried to dictate its will to nearly the whole world, to blackmail the socialist countries. An extremely dangerous situation was created. The Soviet people were obliged to mobilize all their material and spiritual forces in order to remove the threat to peace posed by the U.S. nuclear monopoly and to create their own nuclear weapons in the shortest possible time.

And who knows what China's fate would have been had not the Soviet Union acquired nuclear weapons? After all, you don't stop an aggressor by declaring him a "paper tiger" or sending him hundreds of maledictions and highly serious "warnings."

Let us recall the summer and fall of 1958, when there were frequent provocations against the Chinese People's Republic in the Taiwan Strait. The Soviet government then reminded the President of the U.S.A. that "the security interests of People's China are inseparable from the security interest of the Soviet Union." Have they forgotten in Peking how firmly and decisively the Soviet Union acted to shield China from the aggressor? In Peking, have they not read the American newspapers, which have more than once admitted that the U.S.A. decided not to attack China because "Soviet air and atomic might have reached a level at which they could devastate the U.S.A."

The nuclear might of the Soviet Union, the very country the

60 "Statement of the Soviet Government," August 21, 1963, *Peking Review* (September 6, 1963), p. 21 (in Griffith, *op. cit.*, p. 365).

Peking slanderers now abuse, saved millions of Chinese from nuclear death and protected the sovereignty, security and independence of their country.[61]

It was in response to these claims that in September 1963 Peking issued the statement, quoted earlier, charging that Khrushchev's letters were sent only after there was no possibility of a war breaking out.[62] In replying to the Peking statement, Moscow specifically denied the Chinese interpretation of the 1958 crisis and pointed out that China's immediate postcrisis interpretation was different:

> The Soviet Union has more than once proved by deeds its loyalty to its duty as an ally in relation to fraternal countries, including China. Who does not remember, for instance, that when a dangerous situation arose in the area of the Taiwan Strait in 1958, the Soviet government warned the President of the United States that it would regard an attack on the People's Republic of China as an attack on the Soviet Union and that if the aggressor used nuclear weapons, the Soviet Union would use its own nuclear rocket weapons to defend China.
>
> During those anxious days the Chinese leadership was grateful for the effective Soviet support and duly appreciated the role of the Soviet Union in ensuring the security of the People's Republic of China. A letter from the central committee of the Communist Party of China of October 15, 1958, signed by Mao Tsetung, said:
>
> "We are deeply touched by your boundless devotion to the principles of Marxism-Leninism and internationalism.
>
> "On behalf of all the comrades who are members of the Communist Party of China, I convey heartfelt gratitude. . . ."
>
> After that, the letter continued as follows:
>
> "We are fully confident that should the events on Taiwan resolve themselves into a war between China and the United

[61] "Dogmatists at the Wall," *Red Star*, August 25, 1963, p. 3, translated in *CDSP*, Vol. XV (September 18, 1963), p. 32.

[62] Later in September the Chinese included a discussion of the offshore islands crisis when listing issues on which they asserted Tito had taken an incorrect position:

> 7. The Events in the Taiwan Straits. In the autumn of 1958, the Chinese People's Liberation Army shelled Quemoy in order to counter the U.S. imperialist provocations in the Taiwan Straits and to punish the Chiang Kai-shek gang, which is a U.S. imperialist lackey. The Tito clique maligned China's just struggle as "a danger to the whole world" and "harmful to peace."

"Is Yugoslavia a Socialist Country," *Peking Review*, Vol. VI (September 27, 1963), p. 22.

States, the Soviet Union will unfailingly render assistance to us with all its strength. Actually, in our struggle with the Americans we have already now received powerful support from the Soviet Union."

The newspaper *People's Daily* wrote in the same vein (September 11, 1958):

"The statement of the Chairman of the U.S.S.R. Council of Ministers to the effect that an attack on the People's Republic of China would be tantamount to an attack on the Soviet Union and that the U.S.S.R., together with China, would do everything to uphold the security of both states and the interests of peace in the Far East and throughout the world, constitutes effective and powerful support for the people of China in their struggle against American armed provocations. This is a serious warning to the American rulers."

Now that the critical days of the Taiwan crisis are behind us, the Chinese government is claiming the direct opposite.

"A still greater absurdity," it says, in its statement of September 1, "is the fact that the Soviet statement also credits Soviet nuclear weapons with the victory of the Chinese people in smashing the armed provocation of American imperialism in the Taiwan Strait in 1958. . . . Although the situation in the area of Taiwan Strait was tense, nevertheless the possibility of nuclear war did not arise and there was no need to render support to China with Soviet nuclear weapons. When all that became clear to the Soviet leaders, they came out in support of China."

The Chinese leaders, it seems, have short memories. They think that facts can be assessed in one way today and in another tomorrow, and in yet another way the day after tomorrow. Unfortunately, such treatment of facts has become a usual method of struggle of the leaders of the People's Republic of China against the Communist Party of the Soviet Union and the other Marxist-Leninist parties. But slander and deceit only undermine their own authority and give rise to still greater doubts about the political aims of the Chinese leadership.

Matters, however, are not confined to this. Now that the United States imperialists are well aware of the strength of the Soviet nuclear rocket shield, which is reliably guarding the security of all socialist countries, the Chinese leaders are less afraid of the possibility of American aggression against China. In this situation they believe they can permit themselves to jeer at those very measures of the Soviet Union during the Taiwan crisis for which, at that time, they themselves warmly thanked us. The Chinese leaders now say cynically in their statement of September 1: "Well, Soviet leaders, protect us with your nuclear weapons, but we shall still criticise you."

In this connection one cannot but recall the old Russian proverb: "Don't foul the well; you may need its water!"[63]

In November 1963, the Chinese mentioned the crisis when discussing the Soviet charge that China sought a U.S.-Soviet clash. They did not state that the Soviet Union had refused to intervene but that they did not want the Soviet Union to clash directly with the United States — and that they preferred to shield the former.

> The Chinese Communist Party is firmly opposed to a "head-on clash" between the Soviet Union and the United States, and not in words only. In deeds too it has worked hard to avert direct armed conflict between them. Examples of this are the Korean War against U. S. aggression in which we fought side by side with Korean comrades and *our struggle against the United States in the Taiwan Straits.* We ourselves preferred to shoulder the heavy sacrifices necessary and stood in the first line of defence of the socialist camp so that the Soviet Union might stay in the second line.[64]

Soviet analysts continued to argue that the Soviet nuclear forces had been both necessary and sufficient:

> All the peoples now realise that at the most critical moments the Soviet Union has never wavered in throwing the full weight of its international authority and military might to tip the scales and stay the aggressor's hand about to fall on any country, big or small. Such was the case during the Caribbean crisis, in the period of tension in the Taiwan Strait, during the Anglo-French-Israeli aggression, and during the 1958 events in the Middle East, when the Soviet Union used its nuclear rocket might to shield Socialist Cuba, to avert aggression against the Chinese People's Republic, and safeguard the independence and freedom of Egypt, Syria and Iraq.[65]

In 1964, in a radio broadcast from Russia, the Chinese people were told:

[63] "Soviet Government Statement — Reply to Statement made by the Chinese Government," September 21, 1963 (in Griffith, *op. cit.,* pp. 439–440).

[64] "Two Different Lines on the Question of War and Peace — Comment on the Open Letter of the Central Committee of the CPSU (V)" (in Griffith, *op. cit.,* pp. 486–487). Italics added.

[65] I. Glagolev and V. Larionov, "Soviet Defense Might and Peaceful Coexistence," *International Affairs* (Moscow), Vol. XI (November 1963), p. 29.

In the autumn of 1958, when the United States massed its troops in the Taiwan Strait and the danger of a large-scale military clash was imminent, Khrushchev, chairman of the U.S.S.R. Council of Ministers, in his letter of 10 September 1958 to U.S. President Eisenhower pointed out: "China is not alone and has faithful friends who are ready to come to its aid should China be attacked [sic] because the security of People's China is closely related with that of the U.S.S.R."

The Soviet Government warned: "Any attack on the C.P.R., the great friend, ally, and neighboring country of the U.S.S.R., will be considered as an attack on the U.S.S.R. The U.S.S.R., which is loyal to its obligation, will do its best to maintain security of the two countries and safeguard the interests of peace in the Far East and the world in close cooperation with People's China."

Ulbricht, first secretary of the SED Central Committee, said on September 9, 1958 that the G.D.R. people deeply sympathized with the Chinese people who are struggling for justice. On 8 September 1958, the American ambassador to Czechoslovakia was summoned at the Czechoslovak foreign office and was told that the presence of U.S. troops in the Taiwan Strait and U.S. intervention in China's internal affairs were termed aggressive against the C.P.R. The Czechoslovak Government emphatically pointed out that it supported the Chinese people's legitimate rights. China highly praised the Soviet support and its unfailing loyalty to proletarian internationalism and obligations to allies.[66]

The Soviets renewed their interpretation of the crisis in an article in *Kommunist* in February 1965:

> In autumn 1958, when an American military clique created an immediate threat to the CPR's safety, the Soviet Government quite resolutely declared that it would regard an attack on the CPR as an attack on the Soviet Union, and that it would do everything in order to defend, together with People's China, the safety of the two states and the interests of peace in the Far East and throughout the world. *People's Daily,* an organ of the CCP Central Committee, wrote that this declaration was an "efficient and powerful support of the Chinese people in their struggle against U.S. military provocations."[67]

This is the last reference to the crisis of which we are aware.

66 Radio broadcast in Mandarin from Moscow to China, second in a series by Professor Kapitsa, "The Chinese People Have Their Faithful Friends," 13:00 GMT, October 2, 1964.

67 O. Ivanov, "The Friendship Treaty Between the Soviet and the Chinese Peoples," *Kommunist,* No. 3A (February 1965), p. 101.

Thus the Soviets, despite Chinese protests, continue to claim that their nuclear weapons were responsible for victory in the Taiwan Straits in 1958. The Chinese dispute this claim but have not made any counterclaims and discuss the crisis only in response to Soviet references to it. On a number of other issues, including the Sino-Indian border dispute, the Chinese have accused the Russians not only of refusing to support them but of actually aiding China's opponent. No such charge has been made, however, in reference to the crisis over the off-shore islands. The dispute represents symbolically for the Chinese their ability to operate without Soviet support but not an example of Soviet betrayal. For the Russians it demonstrates China's need for, and willingness to rely on, Soviet nuclear power, but the crisis is not cited as an instance of Chinese dogmatism or adventurism.

The extent to which the crisis has become an issue in the polemics can be explained in general terms by the fact that in the heat of debate both sides have reinterpreted various events to reinforce their arguments. More specifically the 1958 crisis has become intertwined with three major issues in the Sino-Soviet dispute: the Chinese need for nuclear weapons, Soviet support for the liberation of Taiwan, and the relationship between Khrushchev and the Chinese military.

The Chinese have charged, and the Russians have confirmed, that in 1959, during his visit to Peking, Khrushchev suggested to Mao that he postpone any attempt to recover Taiwan by force.[68] In retrospect the Chinese may have come to doubt Khrushchev's sincerity a year earlier when he appeared to be willing to support an operation to recover Taiwan. Both China and Russia have accused the other of meddling in their internal affairs, and there is considerable evidence to suggest that P'eng Teh-huai, who was defense minister in 1958, later had discussions with the Soviet leadership about the line being taken by the Chinese Communist

---

[68] "The Origin and Development of the Differences Between the Leadership of the CPSU and Ourselves — Comment on the Open Letter of the Central Committee of the CPSU," September 6, 1963 (in Griffith, *op. cit.*, p. 400); "Soviet Government Statement — Reply to Statement made by the Chinese Government," September 21, 1963 (*ibid.*, p. 438).

Party.[69] If P'eng had expressed any doubts about the Quemoy probe — and there is reason to think that he may have — the Chinese, in retrospect, may associate this criticism with the Russians. These two issues have been touched on only slightly in the Sino-Soviet polemics, but the question of the Chinese need for nuclear weapons has been frequently and bitterly debated. The Russians have argued that the crisis demonstrated that China could rely on Soviet nuclear forces; the Chinese have denied this without asserting directly that Soviet nuclear support might not have been available if needed. Both sides have undoubtedly found it more comforting to discuss a past event than a hypothetical future crisis.

Even if this interpretation is correct, it does not shed much light on the Soviet role during the crisis. However, the treatment of the crisis in the polemics, in contrast to other events such as the Sino-Indian border dispute and the Cuban missile crisis, reinforces the hypothesis that neither Russia nor China construed the behavior of the other during the crisis as necessitating a split or of making one more likely.

69 See David A. Charles, "The Dismissal of Marshall P'eng Teh-huai," *The China Quarterly*, No. 8 (October–December 1961), pp. 63–76.

The Sino-Soviet Pair:
Coalition Behavior from 1921 to 1965[1]

BERNHARDT LIEBERMAN

Introduction

Much of the conduct of international affairs can be conceived of as the management of coalition structures — directing coalition formation, handling and maintaining already existing coalitions, and controlling changes in coalition structures as such changes appear likely. The conflict between the leaders of the Soviet Union and the leaders of the government of mainland China, and the attendant relations of the leaders of the U.S. government to both parties, provide probably the most obvious, if not the most significant, example of unstable coalition behavior on the contemporary international scene.

In recent years mathematicians and behavioral scientists have produced some theoretical notions and empirical results that yield insights into the general processes involved in coalition formation and change. The mathematical theory of games of strategy, and modifications of it, have analyzed in detail some of the fundamental processes involved when three persons[2] are interacting in certain coalition situations. This paper

[1] I am indebted to W. Clemens, D. Doolin, M. Halperin, G. Quester, J. Stone, and O. Young for many helpful ideas and suggestions. Additional support for the work came from the International Dimension Program of the University of Pittsburgh, with funds supplied by The Ford Foundation and the University.

[2] The term "person" is used here, as it is in game theory, to stand for a

will describe briefly what these concepts are and what this mode of reasoning is like, and *then proceed to analyze certain aspects of Sino-Soviet relations using these notions.* There will also be additional discussion of U.S.-Sino-Soviet relations indicating what further analyses must be made to obtain a description of such relations as a three-person game.

Game Theory Analysis of the Three-Person Situation

Numerous attempts have been made to comprehend the essential elements of social conflicts. U.S.-Sino-Soviet affairs are an example of such conflicts, and game theory is one such attempt; it is a mathematical construction designed to analyze social conflicts and then to prescribe a resolution of the situation that should seem reasonable to the participants. It is an intellectual construction of depth and significance that makes use of the rigor of mathematics. By a process of simplification, abstraction, and analysis, the theory provides insights into situations of pure conflict and others in which there are elements of both conflict and cooperation. U.S.-Sino-Soviet affairs, particularly in this period of changing and uncertain coalition structures, may be conceived of as a game situation.

The mathematical theory is essentially normative; it attempts to prescribe proper, reasonable, or appropriate behavior to the persons involved when they are in conflict for a quantifiable good or commodity. Upon examining the normative theory, behavioral scientists, whose primary task is descrip-

set of interests. Thus, a war between two nations and the game of bridge are two-person games. In conceiving of U.S.-Sino-Soviet relations as a three-person game we treat each party as if it were a single person, a single set of interests. Quite obviously this is an abstraction, a fiction adopted for the purposes of the present analysis. Even in the discussions of this paper the fiction proves to be not wholly adequate; it is necessary, at times, to point out the different sets of interests that exist within each group. When one analyzes any particular conflict, there are many ways to identify the number of persons involved. All such identifications are, to some extent, arbitrary; different analysts will judge different identifications as "best." The present analysis identifying three persons is justified if it yields interesting or useful results.

This paper takes a behavioral approach; when we speak of the Chinese Communist Party, the Soviet Union, or the United States we are really referring to the leaders of each group, those men who make the decisions concerning the conduct of foreign affairs, and the behavior of these men.

tive — to understand behavior rather than prescribe what appropriate behavior should be adopted — were struck by the perspicacity of the analysis of game theory. Although the problems studied were age-old, game theoretic analyses yielded results that were fascinating and exciting. As a result, behavioral scientists examined a number of two-, three-, and n-person situations to see how persons actually behave.[3] Behaviors from a variety of domains were examined, including individual behavior, political behavior, bargaining and negotiation behavior, and decision making in groups. The present study is another example of an attempt to use game theoretic analyses to shed light on a much-studied problem.

The game theoretic analysis of the three-person situation reveals some fundamental characteristics of all three-person interactions. In the two-person situation it is possible to have pure conflict, pure opposition of interests — the two-person zero-sum game.[4] However, when the number of participants is

[3] The mathematical and empirical work that has been done concerning this question is quite abstract and different from complex real-life situations with their numerous details. It is possible, however, that there are common, general principles that describe the interactions of three persons as conceived of by game theorists, and the interactions of the leaders of three nations in the conduct of international affairs. If this is true, then the theoretical and empirical behavioral work can shed some light on the conduct of international affairs. Some believe that game theory reasoning is not complex and sensitive enough to capture important aspects of the conduct of international relations, while others believe the behavioral approach will prove worth while. This attempt, and others, are being made to answer the question; the final answer will be apparent in the future, with the presence or absence of interesting results. For an example of this type of work see B. Lieberman, "i-Trust: A Notion of Trust in Three-Person Games and International Affairs," *Journal of Conflict Resolution,* Vol. VIII (September 1964), pp. 271–286.

[4] In the game theory literature a game is defined rigorously by the players involved, the permissible moves or behaviors available to them, and by the payoff function. In this paper the meaning of the term "game" has been broadened to stand for a situation of interaction in which the persons or players are in conflict but also have certain common interests. A three-person game involves three sets of interests. A zero-sum game is one in which, on each play of the game, the sum of the payments to the players equals zero. A nonzero-sum game is one that does not have this restriction. For an introduction to game theory, see J. D. Williams, *The Compleat Strategyst* (New York: McGraw-Hill, 1954); and R. D. Luce and H. Raiffa, *Games and Decisions* (New York: Wiley, 1957). For a review of behavioral studies, see A. Rapoport and C. Orwant, "Experimental Games: A Review," *Behavioral Science,* Vol. VII (January 1962), p. 1.

increased to three, this complete opposition of interests disappears. In a two-person zero-sum game, what one player wins is lost by the other, so there is always complete conflict of interests. In a three-person zero-sum game, a particular move of one player that is advantageous to him may be disadvantageous to both other persons but may also be advantageous to one and disadvantageous to the other. Three persons often experience common interests in addition to experiencing conflicts of interest. One of the purposes of game theory is to disentangle and clarify the complicated relationships that can exist among the participants of an interaction situation.

The analysis of the three-person situation focuses on coalition formation and its effects on the interaction. A fundamental distinction is made between *essential* and *inessential* games or situations. If the interaction situation is one in which a coalition provides no advantage to the players, that is, they can do just as well by not forming coalitions, by playing a "lone hand" against all others, we call the game an *inessential game;* in this situation there is no inducement to form coalitions. However, in most three-person situations there are advantages and inducements to form coalitions; such games are termed *essential.* This distinction is obviously of central importance.[5]

One three-person game that has received both theoretical and empirical study is the majority game: an essential game in which rewards accrue to the two players who form a coalition or pair against the third. It is a thesis of this paper that it is profitable to conceive of U.S.-Sino-Soviet affairs as a multiphase, three-person majority game, where advantages accrue to the members of the pair who unite against the third.

Games are described by their payoff functions: statements that indicate what the results of permissible actions will be. The following three-person game, which has actually been played by intelligent, responsive individuals, will serve to illustrate the majority game. The players in the game are denoted

---

[5] This explication follows the discussion in J. von Neumann and D. Morgenstern, *Theory of Games and Economic Behavior* (Princeton: Princeton University Press, 1944), pp. 220–237.

1, 2, 3. A single play of the game consists of each player choosing the number of one of the two other players. When two players choose each other, three possible pairs can form: (1,2), (1,3) or (2,3). The payoffs after choices are made are described by the following function:

If coalition (1,2) forms, that pair receives 10 cents from player 3.

If coalition (1,3) forms, that pair receives 8 cents from player 2.

If coalition (2,3) forms, that pair receives 6 cents from player 1.

When this particular three-person majority game was played by eight groups of intelligent, responsive individuals, an interesting notion of trust emerged from the bargaining and negotiations. The fact that the subjects developed this notion enabled them to obtain stability in an essentially unstable situation. On examination, the notion of trust that the subjects developed sheds light on the phenomenon of trust as it exists in the conduct of international affairs.[6]

By employing an analogy it is possible to conceptualize U.S.-Sino-Soviet affairs as a multiphase three-person game in which rewards accrue to the pair that forms on each play of the game.[7] A play, in the abstract game, consists of the three players making choices and forming a pair; a play of the game in international relations consists of the players — nations — uniting to effect some decision, for example, the signing of a test ban treaty.

Although it is quite obvious that there are great differences between the relatively simple play of a three-person majority game and the complex processes involved in effecting a deci-

6 For a full discussion of this particular game and the notion of trust, see Lieberman, *op. cit.*

7 In a three-person majority game, where the players are designated 1, 2, 3, it is possible to have the following three pairs: (1,2), (1,3), and (2,3). In the zero-sum game the payoff to the pair comes from the third player. It is also possible to have situations in which no coalition forms and ones in which the three players unite to maximize the payoff to a three-person coalition (1,2,3).

sion to agree or not to agree to a treaty, it seems quite possible
to construct a game, a laboratory situation, that will capture
some of the complexity of three-nation interaction. To do this
it is necessary to examine the histories of the three pairs of
players, examine the coalitions that have existed between the
United States and the Union of Soviet Socialist Republics, the
United States and the Chinese Communist Party (CCP), and
the coalition behavior of the Soviet Union and the CCP. Much
has been written about the relations between the CCP and the
Soviet Union, and so it is this history that the present paper
describes. The coalition behavior[8] of the Soviet and Chinese
Communist leaders is to be reviewed. To get a complete picture of the situation, similar analyses must be done of U.S.-
Soviet and U.S.-Chinese relations.

The History of Sino-Soviet Coalition Structure

For the purpose of this analysis, the interaction between the
Soviet Union and the Chinese Communist Party can be said
to have begun with the founding of the CCP in 1921; analysis
of their coalition behavior will be carried forward until mid-
1965. Coalitions may be analyzed along many dimensions —
the present analysis will stress which partner determines the
joint decisions that are made by the pair, how well policies
are coordinated, and what assistance the partners offer each
other. Thus, it is possible to have two-nation relations in
which one partner, exclusively, or almost exclusively, determines the decisions or actions of the second, as in the case of
the Russians and the East European nations shortly after
World War II. Or, it is possible to have a coalition or alliance
between two countries that are quite independent of each
other but see the advantage of uniting for certain purposes.
The history of Sino-Soviet coalition behavior, the relationship between the leaders of the CCP and the leaders of the
Soviet Union, is summarized in the accompanying table.

---

[8] For the present discussion, the term "coalition behavior" is not defined
precisely; the analysis of this paper exemplifies what is meant by the term.

	The Three Periods of the Sino-Soviet Coalition
One:	*The Period of Russian Direction: 1921–1933.* * From the founding of the Chinese Communist Party until the Fifth Plenum of the Central Committee of the CCP.
Two:	*The Period of CCP Independence and Deference to Russian Policies: 1933–1959.†* From the time Mao Tse-tung took control of the CCP until the Sino-Soviet conflict became acute.
Three:	*The period of Conflict, Contention, and Loose Alliance: 1959–1965.* From Khrushchev's trip to Peking in 1959 to the present.

* Scholars are agreed that the Chinese Communist Party was founded in 1921. However, it is not at all clear at what time Mao and his close associates took control of the Party. Party relations in the period 1927–1935 are extremely complicated and much scholarship has been devoted to them. I have set the date of the termination of the first period as 1933, with full awareness of the arbitrariness involved. However, for the purpose of this analysis it matters little whether one sets the date at 1931, 1933, or 1936.

† Again scholars disagree somewhat in dating the termination of the coalition between the Russians and the CCP. I have selected 1959; certainly by the early 1960's Sino-Soviet relations had reached a state quite different from that of the early and middle 1950's.

The reader should bear in mind that this type of analysis — of coalition structure — is extremely abstract, eliminating much of the detail of the relations between the two parties; the analysis concentrates on how decisions are effected and determined. For many of the first years of the history of Sino-Soviet affairs the Chinese Communist Party was, in the main, directed by Comintern representatives, agents of the Soviet Union. For the long period from 1933 to 1959, from the time Mao Tse-tung and his close associates took control of the Party, decisions about internal affairs of the party and the Soviet areas of China, and then all of mainland China itself, were made largely by this autonomous ruling group. But in the field of foreign affairs, in relations with the Kuomintang (KMT), in relations with the United States during World War II, and in other foreign relations, the CCP often (but not always) deferred to the direction of the Soviet Union, even when the leaders believed that such deference might be contrary to certain interests of the Chinese Communist movement. From the period, somewhat arbitrarily set at 1959, until the present (1965), the alliance between the mainland Chinese and the Russians has been characterized by some coordination but also by much contention and conflict. The discussion to follow will attempt to justify this characterization of Sino-Soviet coalition behavior.

The Period of Russian Direction: 1921–1933

It is an hypothesis of this paper that during the period from the founding of the Chinese Communist Party in 1921 to the Fifth Plenum of the Central Committee in 1933, when Mao Tse-tung and his close colleagues took control, the CCP was directed by the Comintern, which in turn was directed by the leaders of the Soviet Union. Not every decision made by the leaders of the CCP was directed by a Comintern agent; however, in major policy decisions, if the leaders of the CCP and the Comintern disagreed, and if the latter wished to exercise their influence and power, they could determine the decisions. Let us examine the history of Sino-Soviet affairs for confirmation of this particular hypothesis.

Prior to, and at the founding of the Party in 1921, the Chinese Communist movement was miniscule and impotent when compared to the power, wealth, and influence of the Soviet-Russian state and the Comintern apparatus. Ch'en indicates that there were 57 founding members of the CCP and 12 representatives to its first Congress.[9] It is not unreasonable to assume that such a group, no matter how autonomous, would look to the Soviet Union for support and direction. Indeed the entire tone of Benjamin Schwartz's description of the founding of the CCP indicates that not only was the Comintern agent, Voitinsky, instrumental in the founding of the Party but he felt it necessary to shape it into a genuine Bolshevik Party from its Chinese-Marxist origins.[10]

[9] J. Ch'en, *Mao and the Chinese Revolution* (London: Oxford University Press, 1965), p. 361.

[10] B. Schwartz, *Chinese Communism and the Rise of Mao* (Cambridge: Harvard University Press, 1958), p. 33.

By 1922, at the First Congress of Toilers of the Far East, there is evidence of Comintern influence upon, if not direction of, the CCP. Zinoviev complained that Comintern policy makers had insufficient information about South China; and Maring, a Comintern spokesman, advised the Chinese Communists to enter trade union work in China to shift the whole Communist movement to the left.[11] However, it would not be correct to say that the Soviet Union spoke about Chinese affairs with a single voice in the period 1921–1924. At least three Russian agencies were commenting on, and attempting to influence, the CCP; they were the Comintern, the Foreign Ministry, and the Red International of Trade Unions.[12] In the early part of the period 1921–1924, CCP-Soviet relations were complicated by the very complex situations within both countries. The Russians wanted recognition from the Chinese government in Peking, they were attempting to establish good relations with Sun Yat-sen and the KMT, and they wanted to encourage the revolutionary program of the CCP. The conflicts concerning a united front between the CCP and the KMT, and the relative weight given to organizing the urban proletariat as against organizing the rural peasants — issues that were still to be in contention many years later — were already obvious.[13] However, it seems clear that in these early years the CCP leaders deferred to the power, resources, and experience of their more senior partners, the Russians.

In the period 1924–1927, the direction of the CCP by the Soviet Union is certainly clear. The CCP engaged in policies that were contrary to its interests, and this was recognized by many members of the Party. Comintern agents Borodin, Voitinsky, and others could use the force of "Party discipline" to persuade the CCP leaders to follow their direction.[14]

In this period there was much disagreement between those who wished to separate the CCP from the KMT, and the

11 A. Whiting, *Soviet Policies in China* (New York: Columbia University Press, 1954), pp. 87–88.
12 *Ibid.*, pp. 121–130.
13 *Ibid.*
14 C. Brandt, *Stalin's Failure in China: 1921–1927* (Cambridge: Harvard University Press, 1958).

Russians who insisted on the "bloc within."[15] Stalin's directives to maintain the alliance resulted in part from his own struggle for power within Russia; in addition the Russians were attempting to influence the KMT to adopt policies congenial to the Russians.[16] The CCP at this time was still not a very powerful force, and the Russians did not hesitate to direct it to take actions contrary to its own interests.[17] In March 1926, Chiang Kai-shek committed a series of acts that were clearly detrimental to the CCP. He arrested the commissars attached to the KMT troops, most of whom were Communist; he confined his Soviet advisers to their quarters; and he disarmed the strike committee that had halted foreign business in South China. In effect, he removed the Chinese Communists from all influence in the Canton branch of the KMT.[18] Shortly afterward, the CCP took the official stand that it should work outside of the KMT, but the Russians insisted on maintaining the coalition within.[19] After the massacre of a large number of Chinese Communists in Shanghai in April 1927, the Russians broke with Chiang, labeling him a "bourgeois traitor," but the break with the KMT was not complete. Stalin allied himself with some leftist elements of the KMT ruling at Wuhan.[20] At this time (1927) Mao Tsetung and others left the cities and moved to the rural areas, seeking their strength, power, and support from a peasant, rural base.[21] The Russians did finally call for a break with the KMT;[22] but it is important, for this analysis, to realize that for many years the leaders of the CCP had taken direction from the Russians when they believed this direction to be contrary to their interests, and had done so until the Chinese Party was almost destroyed.

Russian direction of the CCP continued after 1927: the Sixth Congress of the CCP was held in Moscow during the

15 *Ibid.*, p. 74.
16 *Ibid.*, p. 78.
17 *Ibid.*, p. 78.
18 *Ibid.*, pp. 71–72.
19 *Ibid.*, p. 78.
20 *Ibid.*, pp. 114–119.
21 *Ibid.*, p. 165.
22 *Ibid.*, p. 166.

summer of 1928.[23] Mao did not attend this congress; he was leading his group in the countryside.[24] For the period 1931–1934 Mao operated in Kiangsi with a full-fledged Communist government, with himself as one of the most prominent if not the principal leader.[25]

Some time in the period 1933–1935 Mao obtained the leadership of the CCP. Schwartz believes it was at the Tsunyi Conference in 1935.[26] But it does not matter for the purposes of this analysis whether the date is 1932 or 1936, or a year or two earlier or later; for scholars are agreed that once Mao took control of the CCP it had new autonomy and independence from Moscow. This autonomy was based on the Red Army and the organizations of the Soviet areas that Mao controlled. Once Mao took control, the nature of the alliance between the CCP and the Russians changed. Though it was clear that Mao was still weaker than the more powerful Russians, and often deferred to them and followed their lead, the CCP no longer was directed in its decisions.

The Period of CCP Independence and Deference to Russian Policies: 1933–1959

In the years from 1933 to 1959 the Chinese Communists and the Russians were allied in a number of common endeavors. In this period, which extends over a total of twenty-six years, the status of the CCP changed drastically from that of a small, revolutionary minority to that of the ruling group of mainland China. However, in all that period, despite the drastic changes, there were certain similarities in the relations of the CCP to the Soviet Union. From the time Mao Tse-tung became the leader of the CCP in the 1930's until Sino-Soviet relations were characterized by contention and conflict in the late 1950's, the CCP had a particular kind of relationship to the Russians. It maintained an independence of the Russians based upon an independent revolutionary plan and an inde-

---

23 *Ibid.*, pp. 168–169.
24 *Ibid.*, p. 169.
25 *Ibid.*, p. 171.
26 Schwartz, *op. cit.*, p. viii.

pendent military force. At the same time, Mao and his colleagues deferred to many Russian decisions about the conduct
of international affairs, generally supported Russian leadership of the international Communist movement, and sought
and received aid in their own revolutionary movement, but
did all these things as an independent, although weaker,
junior partner. It is clear that Mao and the other CCP leaders
did not allow their interests to be sacrificed by Russian direction as in the period prior to 1927. The period from 1933 to
1959 can be subdivided into the years from 1933 to 1940, when
the CCP was engaged in survival and the building of its
strength; the years of the Second World War, 1940–1946; the
years from 1946–1949 ending in the defeat of Chiang Kai-shek
and the successful culmination of the revolution; and the
years from 1950 to 1959, which included Sino-Soviet collaboration during and after the Korean War.

McLane states that the change in the relationship between
the Russians and the CCP took place not because there was
any change in Russian Communist international goals but
because the strength of the CCP was located in the South
China rural areas, and attempts to control it in the 1930's
would have met with severe difficulties or might have failed
completely.[27] Although the Russians largely ceased their operational activities in China they still maintained a serious
interest in the country, as witnessed by the many theoretical
articles about China that appeared in Russian publications.[28]

In the period 1930–1935 the rural Soviets led by Mao and
his followers were looked upon with favor by the Russians.
Stalin stated that the Chinese revolution was entering an
"agrarian phase" against feudal elements of the Peking regime.[29] However, the rural Soviets were seen as forerunners
of the urban Soviets that would develop, and would lead to
the revolution. There is no evidence that Mao and his group
contested this theoretical view, and although Mao probably
did not hold identical views he apparently did not disagree

---

[27] C. McLane, *Soviet Policy and the Chinese Communists: 1931–1946*
(New York: Columbia University Press, 1958), p. 12.

[28] *Ibid.*, p. 14.

[29] *Ibid.*, pp. 14–15.

overtly.[30] As long as he was receiving support and encouragement from the Russians, it was not to his advantage to exacerbate theoretical disagreements. It was not until approximately twenty-five years later that Mao felt it advisable to oppose Russian ideological leadership.

The exact positions that Mao held in the CCP are a matter of some question and dispute. He was, apparently, at the First Congress of the CCP in July 1921. He held responsible positions through the twenties, lost some of them in the late twenties and early thirties, obtained control of the party in the mid-thirties, and by 1938–1939 the Russians publicly acknowledged his leadership of the Party. McLane believes that Mao set up rural party organizations in the 1930's and assumed leadership of the total CCP in 1935.[31]

Whether there was communication between the CCP and the Comintern during the Long March is an unanswered question. McLane states:

> Lacking precise information on the ties that may have been established between Moscow and the Mao leadership following the conclusion of the Long March in the Autumn of 1935, we can, I think assume only a parallel and not closely coordinated working out of the United Front Policy in Moscow and China. By the Autumn of 1936 in any case, both the Comintern and the Communists appear fully to have accepted the idea that the Nanking government and the majority of the Kuomintang should be included in the proposed anti-Japanese alliance.[32]

By July 1937 when the Japanese attacked the Marco Polo Bridge, the United Front was accomplished, and on August 21, 1937, it was announced in statements by the CCP and the KMT.[33] In this period, 1936–1937, Russian and CCP polemics seem to have been coordinated; there is no evidence of disagreement between the two or of domination of one by the other.

Initially the United Front was successfully managed. The Russians appeared genuinely to have wanted CCP-KMT cooperation against Japan. They were willing, for the time be-

---

30 *Ibid.*, pp. 27–29.
31 *Ibid.*, p. 43.
32 *Ibid.*, p. 78.
33 *Ibid.*, pp. 99–100.

ing, to suppress CCP interests in sovietizing China in the face of the Japanese enemy; Mao and the CCP agreed. However, both Comintern statements and CCP documents published at this time agreed that the ultimate Communist objective was a successful revolution and control of China by the CCP.[34] Unlike the period 1924–1927, the CCP did not put itself into a vulnerable position in its cooperation with the KMT.

By the late 1930's, even on the question of the "theory" of the Chinese Communist revolution, the initiative was passing to the CCP. Moscow was often silent on these matters, and Mao and his associates were beginning to evolve concepts of their own.[35]

As an example of CCP deferrence to Russian leadership in international relations, we can consider CCP statements in support of the Russo-German nonaggression pact in 1939 and of the Russo-Japanese nonaggression pact in 1941; the CCP endorsed both treaties.[36] McLane believes that it is not possible to relate precisely these simultaneous developments in China and the Soviet Union, but it is likely that there was some coordination, together with a coincidence of views.[37] It is also likely that direct links existed between the CCP and Moscow during the period 1935–1941, but these links, and the agreements resulting from them, were not discussed and revealed in the open, available literature.[38] To maintain good relations with the KMT, which they wanted at this time, the Russians were motivated to maintain a "distant and somewhat noncommittal" attitude toward the CCP.[39] The picture of coordination of policies, and possible contacts, supports the view that this was a period of independence and coordination.

During World War II, despite differences between the CCP and the Russians, the evidence points to an alliance between the two, or at least no overt opposition. Early in the Russo-

34 *Ibid.*, pp. 102–114.
35 *Ibid.*, p. 117.
36 *Ibid.*, pp. 132–136.
37 *Ibid.*, p. 148.
38 *Ibid.*, p. 152.
39 *Ibid.*, p. 154.

German war the Russians were too involved with their own difficulties to devote much attention to the CCP. They did want a united front against Japan. Once the United States was in the war and the Russians were allied with them, they did not want to offend the latter by openly supporting the CCP. They said little about such matters in their publications. Their statements were complimentary to Chiang Kai-shek even when they attacked other KMT officials. Although there was conflict between the KMT and the CCP, the CCP apparently accepted Soviet support of the KMT without overt opposition.[40] Even if these policies were objectionable to Mao, he probably reasoned that deference to Soviet policies at this time would do much to assure support of CCP policies at a more critical time in the future.[41]

In the period immediately following World War II, the Russians publicly disclaimed ties to the CCP.[42] However, it is best to regard such claims as attempted deceptions in the light of Russian actions in Manchuria. By denying the Nationalist forces access to South Manchuria in October and early November of 1945, the Russians supplied the CCP with a great advantage over the Nationalists in the struggle for Manchuria.[43] The CCP took control of large parts of Manchuria, partly because of Soviet assistance: the Russians blocked KMT troops, and withdrew at appropriate times, enabling the CCP to gain control. By the time the Soviet forces quit Manchuria they left behind them a Communist regime that was solidly entrenched; McLane believes the desire to aid the CCP accounts, in part, for the Russian decision to prolong the occupation of Manchuria.[44]

In 1945–1946 some attempts were made to form a KMT-CCP coalition government in China. When these failed, the existence of the CCP-Soviet coalition became even more obvious; the Russian stake in the CCP success increased. For Russia a strong CCP could serve a number of purposes; even without controlling all of China it could serve as a military

40 *Ibid.*, pp. 156–193.
41 *Ibid.*, p. 184.
42 *Ibid.*, pp. 194–195.
43 *Ibid.*, pp. 216–217.
44 *Ibid.*, p. 231.

ally and a buffer between itself and the KMT; if the CCP completed a successful revolution it would then control all of China.[45]

McLane offers the following summary description of the state of the Sino-Soviet alliance for the period 1931–1946:

1. There is no clear evidence that the Russians made any efforts to intervene in the internal affairs of the CCP.

2. There is no good evidence that the Chinese Communists ever used their independence to evade Soviet policies they found objectionable, or to refute Russian statements about Marxism-Leninism.[46]

In the period 1947–1949, during the Chinese civil war, Beloff gives a picture of the Russian-CCP relationship that is somewhat ambiguous. The Russians opposed "American influence in China," maintained diplomatic relations with the KMT, and factually reported the successes of the Chinese Communist army. Little or no evidence of direct Russian aid to the CCP could be found, and nothing could be proved about such aid. However, the Chinese Communists did have much Japanese war material, some of which may have come from the Russians. It is likely that the Russians were playing a "waiting game"; they wanted to maintain KMT-Russian relations in the event the KMT was able to hold South China.[47]

However, with the establishment of the mainland Chinese government (Chinese People's Republic) in 1949, the Russian-CCP alliance became obvious. On April 25, *Pravda* talked of the liberation of Nanking as putting an end to the "reactionary rule of the KMT," and said that the KMT government ceased to exist. In July 1949, Mao discussed a CCP alliance with Russia. In October, the Russians withdrew recognition of the KMT and established relations with the mainland Chinese government.[48]

The period 1949–1950 gave evidence of considerable Sino-

---

45 *Ibid.*, pp. 232.
46 *Ibid.*, pp. 261–265.
47 M. Beloff, *Soviet Policy in the Far East: 1944–1951* (London: Oxford University Press), pp. 54–64.
48 *Ibid.*, pp. 65–70.

Soviet cooperation and a formalization of the alliance. In February 1950, a treaty of friendship and alliance was signed; it contained economic provisions, with the Russians extending credit totaling 300 million dollars to the Chinese. Beloff believes that there were some disagreements between the Chinese and the Russians at the time, but these were not revealed in any public statements.[49] In this period, a limited number of Russian advisers worked in China under Chinese direction; Chinese students studied in Russia; efforts were made to improve transportation facilities between the two countries; and similarities in ideological beliefs were emphasized.[50]

Whiting believes that the Korean War served to strengthen the Sino-Soviet alliance; "it forced the Chinese and Russian Communists into closer political and military collaboration than had previously existed."[51] The attack on South Korea was directed by the Russians, and while there is no evidence that the CCP participated in the planning of the attack, there is evidence that Peking knew of the invasion of North Korea well in advance of June 1950. There is little evidence to suggest that either the Russians or the Chinese expected the United States to intervene.[52] By August 1950, Chinese propaganda indicated a greater interest in the Korean War.[53] From that date, the activities of the Russians in the United Nations and the statements of the Chinese indicated coordinated policies.[54] Russia supplied the Chinese with a very important military weapon, the MIG jet aircraft; in fact, Soviet military assistance provided China with a modern, powerful jet airforce.[55] Clearly, the Korean War brought the two nations into closer cooperation, despite any adverse effects resulting from the failure of the invasion and the necessary Chinese intervention.

[49] *Ibid.*, pp. 70–75.
[50] *Ibid.*, pp. 83–90.
[51] A. Whiting, *China Crosses the Yalu* (New York: Macmillan, 1960), p. vii.
[52] *Ibid.*, p. 45.
[53] *Ibid.*, pp. 79–80.
[54] *Ibid.*, p. 91.
[55] *Ibid.*, p. 167.

The Period of Conflict, Contention, and Loose Alliance: 1959–1965

For more than twenty years, from the early 1930's until the late 1950's, relations between the Soviet Union and the CCP were marked by the coordination of policies, cordial statements of solidarity, and the image of agreement. Undoubtedly difficulties existed, perhaps serious ones, and certainly, as recent analyses show, there were serious conflicts of interest.[56] But whatever conflicts did exist were suppressed; they were not aired publicly in the various government and Party publications. Then in the late 1950's and early 1960's a very bitter dispute broke out; at first it was disguised by euphemistic phrases, but by 1963 Chinese Communist and Russian publications contained open attacks on each other. At the present time (1965) the status of the coalition is questionable. The stability of the Sino-Soviet coalition is uncertain, and a U.S.-Soviet coalition, extending to many issues, is a distinct possibility, despite the many points of contention between the Russians and ourselves. The following discussion will describe only briefly the development of the conflict: the details have been presented most thoroughly in a series of books and articles.[57]

Zagoria has reviewed the period 1956–1961, detailing the development of the dispute from its origins in public statements to the point where the split was obvious to serious students of Sino-Soviet affairs.[58] After describing the "ties that bind" the two countries, which are essentially a common ideology and an opposition to American and European political-economic systems, he describes the sources and development of the Sino-Soviet conflict. The roots of the conflict lie

[56] Dennis J. Doolin, *Territorial Claims in the Sino-Soviet Conflict: Documents and Analysis* (Stanford, Calif.: Stanford University, The Hoover Institution on War, Revolution, and Peace; Hoover Institution Studies No. 7, 1965).

[57] Descriptions of the course of the Sino-Soviet conflict can be found in D. Zagoria, *The Sino-Soviet Conflict: 1956–1961* (Princeton: Princeton University Press, 1962); W. Griffith, *The Sino-Soviet Rift* (Cambridge: The M.I.T. Press, 1964); and W. Griffith, *Sino-Soviet Relations, 1964–1965* (Cambridge: The M.I.T. Press, 1967).

[58] Zagoria, *op. cit.*, pp. 39–54.

in a difference of viewpoint over underdeveloped areas and in the history of Sino-Soviet relations. The Russians believe that in underdeveloped areas the first task is to eliminate Western influence: Communists should form alliances with nationalist leaders, even if this is at the expense of the native Communist movement. The Chinese want militant revolutionary activity. In the period 1920–1927, Stalin sacrificed CCP interests for the sake of his alliance with the KMT. The CCP believes that the current Soviet leaders are repeating the errors of the past and that they do not understand the proper course of revolutions in underdeveloped areas.[59]

Zagoria describes a number of factors behind the Sino-Soviet conflict:

1. Maoist chauvinism: Mao's claim to ideological and theoretical superiority.

2. Differences in revolutionary experiences: the Russians had a quick urban-based revolution, whereas the Chinese had a lengthy rural-based one.

3. The issue of Taiwan: the Chinese are willing to take risks to obtain a piece of territory they consider theirs, while the Russians are reluctant to support the use of force.

4. The isolation of China from the United Nations and other countries.

5. Economic differences; the Russians have a relatively wealthy country, the Chinese are relatively poor.

6. The Chinese must rely on Russian military and nuclear power.

7. Finally, differences in revolutionary interest: the Chinese want to foment revolution while the Russians are not so militant.[60]

Dissatisfaction with Khrushchev's leadership, specifically disapproval of the de-Stalinization program, and the Polish and Hungarian developments in 1956 were additional causes of conflict. Also, the failure of the Russians to exploit advantages, which the Chinese believe the Russians have as a result of the technological and weapons developments sym-

59 *Ibid.*, pp. 10–13.
60 *Ibid.*, pp. 13–20.

bolized by the 1957 Sputnik, have exacerbated the conflict. In the late 1950's the Chinese became, and still are, seriously dissatisfied with the less militant Soviet policies.[61]

Two additional issues that have served to weaken the alliance are the conflict over the communes and the proper strategy for achieving socialism in underdeveloped countries. The Russians disapproved of the communes on both practical and ideological grounds. They believed that the communes would not work and that the theory behind them, if accepted, would lead to Mao's pre-eminence as a theoretician. Related to this question was the entire strategy for achieving communism-socialism. The Chinese in the late fifties and early sixties were advocating, and still do advocate, a more radical, energetic approach. Khrushchev, and the Russians, had been advocating a less militant, conciliatory stance. The more militant Chinese position is based on a belief that the Communist countries have military equality, if not superiority, over the United States and the Western countries and that they should not fear an activist strategy, even at the risk of armed conflicts.[62]

The Chinese also opposed any *détente* with the United States and other Western countries. Cordial relations between the Soviet Union and the United States, Khrushchev's statements that economic competition rather than military conflict should be used to demonstrate the superiority of communism, all served to increase the conflict.[63]

Zagoria concludes his analysis by stressing that although the alliance has been weakened there has not been a total break.[64]

Griffith, in reviewing Sino-Soviet relations during 1962–1963, confirms the picture of a loose alliance rent by serious conflicts but states, nevertheless, that the two nations remain united by certain interests and beliefs. He stresses that the Sino-Soviet border disputes and the issue of China obtaining atomic weapons are indicative of the genuine conflicts of in-

61 *Ibid.*, pp. 20–22.
62 *Ibid.*, pp. 153–172.
63 *Ibid.*, pp. 236–237.
64 *Ibid.*, p. 384.

terests that exist. He also feels that current Soviet relations with the United States and with India produce conflict.[65]

Two quotations best summarize the state of the Sino-Soviet alliance in 1962–1963:

> The more one reviews the developments of the past eighteen months and the more one reflects on the Soviet cancellation of atomic aid to China in June 1959 and the circumstances of the removal of Marshal P'eng Teh-huai at the Lushan Plenum in August of the same year, the more one thinks that the Sino-Soviet dispute was probably already then irreparable.[66]

But Griffith cautions against predicting an end to the alliance:

> Yet even so one should still beware of predicting an inevitable, total and above all a permanent Sino-Soviet break. Marxist-Leninist ideology has already shown itself remarkably able to preserve ritualistic unity amid actual schism; and the acquisition of a Chinese atomic capacity would even more deter the Soviet Union, as Soviet atomic capacity does China, from any military sanctions to change the situation. Furthermore, in the near future both Moscow and Peking still have common and powerful enemies: the United States and its Western allies.[67]

Griffith's review of Sino-Soviet relations in 1964–1965 confirms the earlier picture. Khrushchev's fall did not change the situation substantially. And "the accelerated decline of Soviet influence in the Communist world, climaxed by the failure of the second Soviet attempt to mobilize its allies for collective actions against China," gives us a picture of the current status of the coalition. Finally, the increased American military activities in North Vietnam, together with the Russian decision not to risk a military confrontation when its own interests were not involved and when the benefit of such a confrontation would accrue to its enemies or unreliable allies in Peking and Hanoi, serve to characterize the current ambiguous and ambivalent status of the Sino-Soviet alliance.[68]

---

[65] W. Griffith, *The Sino-Soviet Rift, op. cit.*, pp. 27–29.
[66] *Ibid.*, p. 29.
[67] *Ibid.*, p. 30.
[68] W. Griffith, *Sino-Soviet Relations, 1964–1965, op. cit.*

The Test Ban Treaty as a Play of a Three-Person Majority Game

In the three-person majority game, two players select each other and receive a reward or payoff, normally at the expense of the third. On each play of the game the two who select each other can be said to have formed a pair or coalition. The limited test ban treaty signed in 1963, banning all but underground nuclear tests, can be and was seen by the Americans, Russians, and Chinese as similar to a single play of a three-person majority game (though the phrases of game theory were not applied). The United States and the Soviet Union formed an alliance on this issue, excluded the Chinese who were opposed to a test ban, and concluded a treaty that appears to be mutually advantageous. All parties involved perceived the great importance of the treaty and, as Clemens asserts, its symbolic as well as substantive importance in the decline of Sino-Soviet relations.[69] It is safe to say that on this particular play of the game the United States and the Soviet Union formed a coalition at the expense of the Chinese. It is likely that the Chinese may have opposed the test ban treaty for this reason alone. When one adds the fact that if the Chinese agreed to the treaty they probably could not develop an independent nuclear capability, the importance of the treaty to U.S.-Sino-Soviet relations is obvious. Clemens cites a photograph, which appeared in a Peking publication, of Khrushchev physically hugging Harriman after the signing of the treaty, with a caption below the picture stating, "Khrushchev Embraces Capitalism."[70]

Concluding Discussion

The argument of this paper, that it is profitable to view U.S.-Sino-Soviet relations as a three-person game, led to the present review of Sino-Soviet affairs. To complete the three-person analysis it will be necessary to do a similar analysis of U.S.-Soviet relations and one of U.S.-CCP relations. This game theoretic approach directs the analyst in a number of

69 Walter C. Clemens, Jr., Chapter 6.
70 *Ibid.*, p. 26.

ways: first, to consider all three pairs of relations separately, and over specific time periods; second, to view these processes as occurring simultaneously and to look at the interactions among the three participants; finally, to speculate about the future of the coalition structure, looking not only at probable future events but at the interests that have pervaded the history of the inter-nation relations.

The history of U.S.-Soviet relations can be reviewed relatively easily as there is a considerable body of literature on the subject. But the type of analysis done here raises a number of interesting questions about the relations between the CCP and the United States. Were there significant relations between the two early in the history of the CCP? Were there any such relations in the middle and late thirties? What was the nature of any relations that did exist?

Once these analyses are complete, it should be an interesting task to speculate on the future of the three-person relations. Even now it is obvious that in the more than forty years that these three parties have been in interaction the initial Sino-Soviet coalition has weakened and the U.S.-Soviet coalition structure has undergone a series of changes. It is possible that American officials may be able to manipulate the coalition structure to advance their aims, and the conclusion of arms control agreements may provide levers for such successful manipulations.

Participants in the Conference on Sino-Soviet Relations and Arms Control

Airlie House, Warrenton, Virginia
August 29-September 4, 1965

Participants:*

Professor A. Doak Barnett
East Asian Institute
Columbia University

Mr. Seweryn Bialer
Research Institute on Communist Affairs
Columbia University

Dr. Donald G. Brennan
Hudson Institute

Professor Zbigniew Brzezinski
Research Institute on Communist Affairs
Columbia University

Professor Walter C. Clemens, Jr.
Center for International Studies
Massachusetts Institute of Technology

Professor Jerome Cohen
The Law School
Harvard University

Dr. Herbert Dinerstein
The RAND Corporation
Santa Monica

Professor Dennis Doolin
Stanford Studies of the Communist System
Stanford University

Dr. Raymond Garthoff
Office of Politico-Military Affairs
Department of State

Dr. William E. Griffith
Center for International Studies
Massachusetts Institute of Technology

Professor Gregory Grossman
Department of Economics
University of California
Berkeley

Professor Morton H. Halperin
Center for International Affairs
Harvard University

* Affiliations as of the time of the Conference.

Dr. Abraham Halpern
Council on Foreign Relations

Dr. Harold Hinton
Institute for Defense Analyses

Mr. Thomas C. Irvin
Arms Control and Disarmament Agency

Professor Herbert Levine
Wharton School of Business and Finance
University of Pennsylvania

Professor Bernhardt Lieberman
Department of Sociology
University of Pittsburgh

Dr. John Lindbeck
East Asian Research Center
Harvard University

Professor Richard Lowenthal
Free University
Berlin

Mr. Roderick MacFarquhar
The China Quarterly
London

Mr. Malcolm Mackintosh
Institute for Strategic Studies
London

Colonel Kent Parrot
Arms Control and Disarmament Agency

Professor Dwight Perkins
East Asian Research Center
Harvard University

Professor Ralph Powell
Far Eastern Studies
American University

Dr. George H. Quester
Center for International Affairs
Harvard University

Professor Benjamin Schwartz
East Asian Research Center
Harvard University

Professor Marshall Shulman
Fletcher School of Law and Diplomacy
Tufts University

Mr. Helmut Sonnenfeldt
Bureau of Intelligence and Research
Department of State

Dr. Jeremy J. Stone
Center for International Affairs
Harvard University

Professor George Taylor
Far Eastern and Russian Institute
University of Washington

Professor Kei Wakaizumi
National Defense College
Tokyo

Dr. Allen S. Whiting
Bureau of Intelligence and Research
Department of State

Col. Thomas Wolfe
The RAND Corporation
Washington, D. C.

Professor Donald Zagoria
Research Institute on Communist Affairs
Columbia University

Rapporteurs:

Mrs. Andrea H. Chadwick
The Hoover Institution
Stanford University

Mr. Oran K. Young
Center of International Studies
Princeton University

The Contributors

WALTER C. CLEMENS, JR., is currently Associate Professor of Government at Boston University; he is also associated with Harvard University's Russian Research Center and the M.I.T. Center for International Studies. During 1965 he was executive officer to the National Citizens Commission of the Committee on Arms Control and Disarmament of the International Cooperation Year. He was editor and contributor to *World Perspectives on International Politics* (1965) and *Soviet Disarmament Policy, 1917–1963* (1965), and co-author of *Khrushchev and the Arms Race* (1966).

MORTON H. HALPERIN completed his work on this volume before assuming his current position as Special Assistant for Planning in the Office of the Assistant Secretary of Defense for International Security Affairs. He is on leave from Harvard University where he is Assistant Professor of Government and Research Associate at the Center for International Affairs. He has written books and articles on military strategy and arms control and on Chinese foreign and military policy, including *China and the Bomb* (1965) and *Limited War in the Nuclear Age* (1963).

HAROLD C. HINTON is Associate Professor of International Affairs at The George Washington University and a senior staff member of the Institute for Defense Analyses. He has also taught at Georgetown, Oxford, Harvard, Columbia, and Johns Hopkins universities. His published works include *Communist China in World Politics* (1966).

331

BERNHARDT LIEBERMAN is Associate Professor of Sociology at the University of Pittsburgh. He has held positions at Harvard University, in the Department of Social Relations and the Center for International Affairs, and was Assistant Professor of Psychology at the State University of New York at Stony Brook before joining the faculty at Pittsburgh.

MALCOLM MACKINTOSH is a consultant to the Stanford Research Institute. He spent the years 1944 to 1946 as a British liaison officer with the Soviet military command in southeastern Europe. From 1948 to 1960 he worked as a program director in the East European Service of the British Broadcasting Corporation in London, and from 1960 to 1965 with the Institute for Strategic Studies. He is the author of *Strategy and Tactics of Soviet Foreign Policy* (1963) and a forthcoming book on the history of the Soviet armed forces.

GEORGE H. QUESTER is Instructor of Government and Head Tutor in Government at Harvard University; he is also a Research Associate at Harvard's Center for International Affairs where he has done work on military and defense policy and American foreign policy. His publications include *Deterrence Before Hiroshima* (1966).

HELMUT SONNENFELDT is Director of the Office of Research and Analysis for the Soviet Bloc, Department of State. He is also a lecturer on Soviet affairs at the Johns Hopkins University School of Advanced International Studies and has been a research consultant of the Washington Center for Foreign Policy Research and a senior fellow at the Russian Institute, Columbia University. In the United States Government he has also served as Soviet affairs specialist in the Arms Control and Disarmament Agency.

JEREMY J. STONE is Assistant Professor of Mathematics at Pomona College in Claremont, California. For the past two years he has been a Research Associate of the Center for International Affairs, Harvard University, working on problems of arms control and nuclear proliferation. He has published articles on arms control, proliferation, and game theory; recently he has published a book entitled *Containing the Arms Race: Some Specific Proposals* (1966).

TANG TSOU is a Professor of Political Science at the University of Chicago. He is the author of *America's Failure in China: 1941 to 1950* (1963) and of a monograph on the 1958 Quemoy crisis, "The Embroilment over Quemoy: Mao, Chiang and Dulles" (1959).

ORAN R. YOUNG is a Research Associate at Princeton's Center for International Studies and Lecturer in Politics at Princeton University. His publications include *The Intermediaries: Third Parties in International Crises* (1966); he is currently preparing a study on bargaining under conditions of crisis.

Index